TOUCH THE WORLD
THROUGH PRAYER

TOUCH THE WORLD THROUGH PRAYER

Wesley L. Duewel

ZondervanPublishingHouse

Grand Rapids, Michigan

A Division of HarperCollinsPublishers

Touch the World Through Prayer
Copyright © 1986 by Wesley L. Duewel

Requests for information should be addressed to:
Zondervan Publishing House
Grand Rapids, Michigan 49530

Library of Congress Cataloging in Publication Data

Duewel, Wesley L.
Touch the world through prayer.

1. Prayer. I. Title.
BV210.2.D78   1986   284.3   86-10711
ISBN 0-310-36271-7

Edited by Anne Severance
Designed by James Ruark

Printed in the United States of America

98 99 00 / LP / 26 25 24 23 22

Dedication

To the One who loved me enough to agonize in prayer for me and for the harvest of the whole world in Gethsemane until His prayer-sweat became great clots of blood dropping upon His seamless garment.

Acknowledgments

My gratitude to my godly, praying mother, on whose grave are the words: *Ida Duewel—Intercessor*; to my wife, Betty, who permitted me to spend many extra hours working in my office on this book; and to my secretary, Hilda Johnecheck, for constant assistance in preparing this manuscript.

Contents

Foreword

Touch the World through Prayer by Dr. Wesley L. Duewel is so convincing in its many biblical references, its logic, its illustrations, and its examples that, by the time you finish reading this marvelous, inspiring book, you will no doubt agree that you can touch—yes, even help change—the world through prayer.

Dr. Duewel, a missionary to India for twenty-five years, former president of the Oriental Missionary Society (now OMS International) and former president of the Evangelical Foreign Missions Association, is a man of prayer. Out of his own long, rich, and fruitful walk with Christ, he draws many spiritual lessons and shares dramatic experiences of answers to prayer.

Dr. Duewel's life-long burden for prayer has been powerfully expressed through his many writings on prayer, the Holy Spirit, soul-winning, and spiritual awakening. He even edited for many years *Revival Magazine*, which was dedicated to calling the Body of Christ to prayer, repentance, and revival. We share that burden with Dr. Duewel.

For thirty-four years, prayer has played a major role in our personal lives and ministry with Campus Crusade for Christ. Our first act when God called us to start this world-wide ministry was to organize a twenty-four-hour chain of prayer, which continues world-wide to this day. We are convinced with Dr. Duewel that the greatest power available to the children of God is prayer: "You have not because you ask not."

This motivational book is filled with many practical suggestions and numerous faith-building experiences. It contains a number of simple suggestions to the new believer and more profound instructions for mature believers. Its principles of prayer and rationale for revival, when applied, could help to bring a spiritual awakening to our country and, indeed, to the entire world.

It could well be that you are about to enter the greatest, most satisfying adventure of your life—a ministry of intercessory prayer. Yes, you can *Touch the World through Prayer.*

Bill and Vonette Bright

1

God Calls You
to Prayer

God has a wonderful plan by which you can have world-wide influence. This plan is not just for a chosen few. It is for you. Let me tell you about it.

Through prayer you can stand beside Billy Graham as he preaches in crusades anywhere in the world. You can strengthen him, bless him, lift him up at the very moment he is bringing the Good News to thousands. Through prayer you can stand beside Luis Palau in his Latin American crusades. Through prayer you can stand beside George Beverly Shea as he sings the glorious gospel.

Through prayer you can accompany any missionary to remote reaches of the earth. Through prayer you can walk through crowded bazaars, minister in steaming jungles, feed millions of starving men, women, and children, hungry for bread for their bodies and for the Bread of Life.

Through prayer you can contribute to the ministry of any pastor or evangelist in a church or gospel hall anywhere in the world. Many a time I have felt that through prayer I was at the side of some man or woman of God.

Through prayer you can take a suffering infant in your arms. Through prayer you can touch a fevered brow in any hospital, mediating the healing love of Jesus.

God has given you a way to make your presence count, a way to be a true partner in His kingdom's work, if you really want to be.

True, there have been outstanding praying saints over

the centuries. By no means do we forget them or the tremendous history-changing role they played through prayer. Thank God for James, the half-brother of Jesus, who spent the latter years of his life praying for the churches God was raising up. When he died and his body was prepared for burial, it was found that his knees were so calloused from hours and hours of kneeling that they almost resembled the knees of a camel. He became known as "Camel-knees." Thank God for Savonarola in fifteenth-century Italy, who prayed down revival in that corrupt age. Thank God for Brainerd, missionary to the American Indians, and his life of prayer and tears. Thank God for "Praying Hyde," the missionary to India, who was perhaps the greatest prayer warrior of this century.

But God does not depend solely on a few staunch saints. He has planned for ordinary Christians like you and me to become mighty in prayer for the blessing and salvation of people and the reaping of Christ's harvest among the nations today.

There is no reason in the world why you cannot become so steadfast in your personal prayer life that Christ will count on you to help build His church and advance His kingdom in many parts of the world. Beginning with your family, your church, and your community, you can play a significant part through normal daily prayer that will make a difference, even in distant lands.

Again and again God has used persons like you and me to help Him meet special emergency prayer needs on a particular day or occasion. When He calls on someone for this special and temporary role, He usually selects one of His children who has been praying faithfully and consistently.

You don't have to spend hours each day to qualify for God's prayer army. Thank God for those who can and *do* pray like that. But He knows the limitations of your own situation, your schedule, your home and employment responsibilities. His plan is intended to add a whole new dimension to your prayer life. Whether you are a business executive or a housewife, a factory worker or a student, a layman or a minister of the gospel—God desires for you to begin a thrillingly new and more effective life of prayer.

I do not claim to have a magic formula to transform you into a spiritual giant overnight. But I do want to point out the possibilities of this simple plan as outlined in the Bible. You can have new power and effectiveness in prayer. You can play a significant part in Christ's plan. You can be the praying person God wants you to be— you can, if you will. Will you try?

God's Wonderful Plan for You

God has great expectations for you and me. He has every right. The average person has more ability to influence others today than ever before. This is especially true for Christians. Billy Graham has said he would rather be alive today than to have lived when Jesus was on earth. I fully agree. The average Christian can have a greater influence for God than the average Christian of any previous generation.

This is an exciting time in our history. More believers are living today than at any other time. Christ's church has spread into more areas of the world, praises God each week in more languages, and is witnessing to or is in contact with more people than ever before. There are more gospel workers, more local churches, more Bible training institutions, more Christian organizations, and more missionary societies.

Through the tremendous media of radio, television, and literature we have the facilities to speed up God's work beyond anything we have yet known. We can reach the farthest nations more quickly, we can present the gospel in more languages, and we have the means to recruit and guide prayer for the whole world more efficiently. We can reach our world, if we will. The greatest lack today is not people or funds. The greatest need is prayer. Without increasing the number of Christian workers or their financial support, we could see multiplied results if we would only multiply prayer.

Prayer is the greatest resource of the church. It is the

most effective means of preparing the way of the Lord available to us as Christians today. You yourself can influence more people for God and have a greater role in advancing Christ's cause by prayer than in any other way. It is not the *only* thing you must do, but it is the *greatest* thing you can do. It has often been said,

> The Devil trembles when he sees
> God's weakest child upon his knees.

If that is true, think what could happen if every Christian really took his prayer role seriously and began to pray regularly and specifically, uniting with thousands or millions of others, all praying for the same priority needs around the world. Are you willing to be a part of such a prayer army?

The Urgency of Your Prayer Now

God's timetable of the ages may be rapidly nearing the countdown toward Christ's return. God's great plan, for which He created the world and man, has been delayed and frustrated by the long reign of sin and Satan since Adam's fall. But according to the Bible, the delay of Christ's return is not so much because God is patiently waiting for the world to repent as because He is patiently waiting for us to lead them to repentance (2 Peter 3:9). This is further emphasized by the fact that, of all the conditions and signs that must precede Christ's coming, perhaps only one remains to be fulfilled: "This gospel of the kingdom will be preached in the whole world as a testimony to all nations, and then the end will come" (Matt. 24:14).

We do not know what in God's view constitutes adequate witness to the comparatively unreached nations, but by means of radio we are today able to beam the gospel message to practically every corner of the earth. Millions unreached by resident missionaries have access to the gospel through missionary radio. Virtually every province and village in China has been covered in this way. Millions of others in Russia, Albania, and the Muslim lands are known to be listening to Christian messages, broadcast in their own language or in one that may be understood in part.

It is always far more effective when people can hear the gospel in their mother tongue. Although it has been reliably estimated that 95 percent of the people of the world now have available to them some portion of the Scripture printed in a language known to them, may God speed the efforts of those giving their lives to completing the task of putting Scripture into *all* remaining dialects and languages. In addition, *Gospel Recordings* reports that Christian music has been recorded in more than 4,362 of these dialects and languages.

Delivering the gospel message to every human being is not enough, however. The crucial factor is assuring that the message will be understood and accepted. Prayer is the answer. The Holy Spirit is given as God's people ask (Luke 11:13). Undoubtedly this is not only true when we ask for ourselves, but also when we ask for others. So the effectiveness of present mission efforts depends on our prayer, enabling the Holy Spirit to work in power.

In other words, the key to world evangelization, thus clearing the way for Christ's return, may be your prayer and mine. If the main delaying factor is lack of prayer, do not be surprised if God makes special provision for prayer to be more effective today than ever before.

2

God Is Preparing
Harvest for You

Your prayer for world harvest can be more effective today because God in His sovereignty is coordinating world trends to make rapid fruitfulness available to His children. If we will put priority on prayer and obedience, this can be earth's greatest harvest time. Not every Christian is called to go. Not every Christian is able to make a substantial financial contribution to the work of Christ's kingdom. But there is no limit to what any Christian may accomplish through prayer!

Earth's Population Explosion

Statisticians of world population growth tell us that earth's population at the time of Christ was about 250 million. It took over eighteen hundred years, or until about the year 1850, for the total population to reach one billion. Eighty years later, approximately 1930, world population rose to two billion. By about 1960—only thirty years later—world population climbed to three billion. Four billion was reached about 1975. By the end of 1986 we pass the five-billion mark, and the next billion may be added in less than ten years. Earth's population has exploded so fast that the billions who must be reached for Christ almost overwhelm us. How can we catch up? Only by multiplying harvest through prayer.

Rapid Urbanization

God is moving people to the cities of the world to enable us to reach them more quickly. Throughout the world the villages are static and dying, since the first to suffer in famine are the villagers. The prospects of enough to eat, education, health services, and job opportunities available in the cities are beckoning the young and ambitious.

The exodus to the cities is a phenomenon that has accelerated in the 1980s. The greatest urban migration in the history of the world will occur during this decade and the next. It is estimated that one billion people from Third World countries will migrate to the cities during the 1980s alone. Note these examples: Mexico City is growing at a rate of 80,000 per month. Twenty percent of the population of Mexico resides in Mexico City. More than 34 percent of all Argentines live in Buenos Aires. And more than 50 percent of the inhabitants of Uruguay live in Montevideo. In addition, about half the babies of the world are now born in cities.

Cities of one million or more are called "world-class cities." There are some 273 at this printing. The average world-class city doubles every fourteen years; some, in only ten years. Because of the intense concentration of people living within a smaller radius, we can reach far more in a city than in a village, and in a shorter period of time. Paul centered his evangelistic efforts in cities, and then the city churches reached out to the villages. Should we not adopt this proven technique in our own work today?

Cities are ripe for spiritual harvest. But the ripest time ever is now. Why? In the first ten to fifteen years after new city dwellers arrive, they are more responsive than at any other time. While living in the villages under the scrutiny of family, members of the caste, friends, and village priests and religious leaders, it is difficult for individuals who hear the gospel to step out alone. Upon reaching the city, they are comparatively rootless and often restless and disillusioned in not finding the new home to be the longed-for utopia. Liberated from the surveillance of relatives and religious leaders, those individuals are vulnerable and ripe for the gospel message. It is crucial that we reach them now.

Within fifteen to twenty years the major urban migration will be complete, and people will have put down roots again. More than ever before in earth's history, now is God's hour to work and to pray. Prayer is the only adequate way to multiply our efforts fast enough to reap the harvest God desires.

Our Young World

Thank God for the comparative responsiveness of youth. The vast majority of those won to Christ in our land or in any land receive Christ in their youth.

Statisticians tell us that we are living in a time in which world population on the average is younger than ever before. Half of the populations of Latin America and Asia are now twenty years of age or below. Forty percent of the world is now under fifteen years of age. The population is exploding so fast that in the next twenty-five years more children will be born than have lived from the days of Adam until 1960. Seven percent of the entire human race from Adam till now is alive today!

While the exploding population of Third World countries makes theirs a young society, in another twenty years the Third World is expected to begin aging like the Western world. The opportune time for reaching responsive youth is during our generation. That's why the call to prayer given by the Holy Spirit to the church is stronger and more urgent today than ever before.

Our Empty-Hearted, Disillusioned World

The Western world is beginning to realize that the false god of materialism has failed. Countries of the Far East are realizing it, too, as evidenced by the rising suicide rate in Japan. And more and more in the coming days, the Third World, which is desperately grasping for material wealth as a solution to their problems, will understand that "as goods increase, so do those who consume them" (Eccl. 5:11). The upsurge of militant Islam is a testimony to the disillusionment brought about by the failure of materialism.

Communism, too, has greatly influenced much of our

world. Its seduction lies in the failure of governments and people to meet the hopes and needs of the masses. But it is a false god. It maintains its power only by force, lack of freedom, and dictatorship, and much of the communist world is already disillusioned and empty-hearted. They cry for change, for more freedom, and for something to satisfy. Years ago an ex-Marxist wrote a book entitled *The God That Failed.* For millions under communism, their god has failed them.

Undoubtedly this is one of the reasons for the tremendous spiritual harvest in China during the past decade—perhaps the greatest harvest in such a short time in the history of the world. Of course, the faithful life, witness, and suffering of believers, the volume of continuing prayer both inside and outside China, and the ministry of missionary radio have all had major roles.

Other millions have been disillusioned by the false gods of education and materialism. Reactions have come in the form of militant revivals in some of the old religions.

Yes, the people of the world are perhaps more empty-hearted and disillusioned than ever before. Their gods have failed them. We know that Jesus is the answer they have been seeking. What a time to reap earth's harvest for Him!

God Is Calling
You and Me

If ever there was an hour in history with potential for maximum world harvest, it is now. If ever there was a time when Christ's imminent return gave a sense of urgency to missions and to prayer, it is now. If ever there was a time when a Christian who cannot go to the mission field for personal service could yet have a world-wide role through prayer, it is now.

If evangelical believers supporting the various missionary societies, missionary radio, and evangelistic teams could ever block the power of Satan and prepare the way of the Lord by prayer, it is now. Let us all issue the call to prayer more clearly. Let us all join our prayers with the believing prayers of others who share the same commitment to the Lord, to world harvest now, and to Spirit-born revival now. This is the day the Lord has made, the day God has been preparing for us as His co-laborers.

This book was written with the purpose and prayer that it will help you to be the man or woman of prayer that Christ longs for you to be. It is gloriously possible. Let's believe and press forward in prayer. This hour is God's gift, His call to you and to me.

3

Your Indescribable Power

The greatest privilege God gives to you is the freedom to approach Him at any time. You are not only authorized to speak to Him; you are invited. You are not only permitted; you are expected. God waits for you to communicate with Him. You have instant, direct access to God. God loves mankind so much, and in a very special sense His children, that He has made Himself available to you at all times. There are at least seven elements to this amazing power He gives to you.

The Power to Contact
Heaven's Throne Room

As a child of God you have full authority to contact God, the Sovereign of the universe, whenever you desire. He is always enthroned in heaven; yet, through prayer, you have as much access to His presence as any angel or archangel. You need not wait for an invitation; the invitation is already yours. You need not make a prior appointment; you are already authorized to approach God instantly. God is never too busy to listen to you; He is never too involved to answer you.

Before meeting Queen Elizabeth, I was told: "You must never speak first; wait until you are spoken to. You never ask royalty anything; you answer royalty." I was told, "In your first reply, you must add the words, 'Your Majesty.'"

When you speak to the Lord of the universe, this is completely reversed. Jesus said, "When you pray, say:

'Father'" (Luke 11:2). There are no formal titles which you dare not omit lest you dishonor God, no recommended phrases to make your prayer more sacred or certain of answer, no official words you are duty-bound to use.

When Queen Elizabeth visited India, a little girl was selected to hand the queen a bouquet of flowers. For weeks the child practiced exactly how to curtsy before the queen, and how to back away from the queen (without falling over!), so as to be sure not to turn her back to her majesty. But you can be sure that the queen's own children did not have that restriction imposed on them!

In prayer, you come to God as His child. You need not wait for an angel to introduce you. You need not try to make yourself more acceptable. You need not first prepare carefully what you want to say. You come just as you are, opening your heart and telling Him how you feel and what you desire. There is no one prayer posture which is more sacred than another. You are God's child, and He is eager and willing to see you!

The Power to Cooperate with God

God has chosen to accomplish many of His sovereign purposes with our help. Paul repeatedly reminds us that God has appointed us to a sacred partnership for the purpose of gospel advance. Paul emphasizes our sacred responsibility to work with God. Every form of obedience to God is urgent, but there are many situations in which we are limited. We may not be at the place of the need. We may lack special skills or training. But we can always work with God through prayer.

Through prayer we can cooperate with Him in any place, at any time, and for any kind of need. We are created to pray. We were saved by God's grace to enter into a ministry of prayer. We have the liberty, the right, and the position of official children of God, called to work with God, chosen for this specific purpose.

Furthermore, God said in Exodus 19:5–6, "Although

22

the whole earth is mine, you will be for me a kingdom of priests." Isaiah prophesied, "You will be called priests of the Lord" (Isa. 61:6). Why did Jesus make us "priests" to serve God (Rev. 1:6)? Why are all Christians called "a holy priesthood" (1 Peter 2:5), "a royal priesthood" (v. 9)?

Obviously, part of God's purpose in designating us priests is that we are to worship and praise Him. But it includes far more than that. We are to be a *royal* priesthood." Christ today rules the world through prayer. We are to share this rule by intercession for others even as Christ constantly intercedes for them (Heb. 7:25). We have been given official access to heaven's throne room so that we may join our intercession with that of Christ!

If Christ intercedes, why is our intercession necessary? What could our puny prayers possibly add to His powerful intercession? God has been pleased to build into His eternal plan that we His children join with Christ in His intercessory role and rule today. If we are not using spare minutes in the ministry of intercession for others and for God's work, we are failing God in the special calling to which He has called us. If we will, we can turn any radio or T.V. newscast or newspaper article into a call to prayer. We can be alert to share God's heartbeat for a broken world. Prayer is the supreme way to be workers together with God.

The Power to Resist
and Defeat Satan

Satan is the archenemy of God and man. "Your enemy the devil prowls around like a roaring lion looking for someone to devour. Resist him" (1 Peter 5:8). He is the master strategist behind all the evil in the world. His kingdom consists of fallen angels, demons, and sinners. He is constantly seeking to discourage, delay, and defeat Christ's workers and Christ's work. He is determined to oppose in every way he can. One of his names is "Destroyer" (Rev. 9:11). He seeks to destroy people, homes, nations, and the plan and work of God.

Satan coordinates a host of unclean spirits called

23

demons. They seem to have power to afflict people whom they indwell. Satan at times seems able to exert some control over forces of nature, and to counterfeit the work of God by demonic "miracles" (2 Thess. 2:9–10). He has such power and evil authority that even the archangel Michael called on the Lord to rebuke Satan (Jude 9).

How could you and I possibly resist or defeat Satan? Surely only God can restrain, bring under control, and defeat such a powerful enemy. But no, the Bible clearly gives this power to ordinary Christians like you and me.

We must not yield to temptation. Jesus set an example of how to do this by using God's Word (Matt. 4:1–11). He urged Peter to be victorious by watching and praying (Matt. 26:41).

We must stand firm in faith. Scripture promises, "Resist the devil, and he will flee from you" (James 4:7). The Greek word for *resist* means "to stand against." When Christ is with us, we can resist Satan.

We must pray. This is our most powerful weapon. Prayer brings the presence of Christ into manifestation, and Satan and his demons have to fall back like the mob in the Garden (John 18:6). Prayer grasps hold of the promises of God and erects them like a wall between us and the powers of darkness. Prayer can bring God's angels rushing to our assistance (2 Kings 6:15–17; Dan. 10:13; Heb. 1:14). Prayer can overthrow the plans of Satan. Prayer can battle any combination of Satan's forces.

When Paul describes our spiritual warfare in Ephesians 6, he says, "Our struggle is not against flesh and blood, but against the rulers, against the authorities, against the powers of this dark world and against the spiritual forces of evil in the heavenly realms" (v. 12). In the previous verse Paul had spoken of our need to take our stand against the Devil's schemes. He then lists the various aspects of the spiritual armor which we must wear in the warfare with Satan. But when we are fully armed, how do we fight? Paul suggests two ways—with the sword of the Spirit, which is the Word of God, and with prayer.

Prayer is the master strategy that God gives for the defeat and rout of Satan. "Pray in the Spirit on all occasions with all kinds of prayers and requests" (Eph. 6:18). Through prayer the Holy Spirit can so empower us that Satan's hold on lives is broken, Satan's hindrances to the kingdom are removed, and Satan's work is destroyed. Christ came to destroy the work of the Devil (1 John 3:8). He did this potentially at Calvary, and Christ enforces Calvary's victory through the prayers of His bride, the church. That is why the people of God are also the army of God.

If God's people would only accept their sacred role as the army of God, if they would call one another to God's priority of prayer, if they would join one another in militant, Spirit-guided, Spirit-anointed intercession, we could see Satan defeated and revival visitations descend from God. We could see the greatest harvest of souls we have ever known.

We are called to stop Satan, to drive back Satan, to defeat Satan through prayer and fasting. But we are too prayerless, too passive, too content with spiritual mediocrity and comparative spiritual barrenness. We seem content to let the Devil gain the victory. God, wake us up! God, teach us to pray! God, lead us to such prayer warfare that we claim key people, whole families, and even entire continents for Him! To your knees, and world evangelization can be revolutionized! To your knees, and Christ's triumphs will be manifest!

The Power to Transcend
the Laws of Nature

Prayer can transcend "the laws of nature." Prayer can bring God's miracle answers to man's desperate needs. It would be useless to pray for many problem situations if this were not true. If there are limits to what God can do when we pray, then prayer is playing games with God, trifling with human need, and deceiving ourselves. No! Never! Prayer is as real as God is real. There is absolutely nothing that God cannot do if it will advance His kingdom and is in accord with His will. Prayer releases God's power.

Christ is the Creator and Preserver of the universe (John 1:3; Col. 1:16–17). He is a God of plan, regularity, and power. His normal ways of working we call "laws" of nature. He has so planned and created the universe that lower laws can be transcended by higher laws. The law of gravity, for example, can be temporarily transcended by the law of force. When we throw a ball, the law of force dictates that the ball will remain suspended in flight until the force is expended, at which time the law of gravity again takes over, and the ball falls to the ground.

Lower laws regularly serve the purpose of higher laws and harmonize with and can be transcended by these higher laws. The laws governing matter can be transcended by the laws of biology and life. These, in turn, may serve the laws of psychology. Moral laws transcend physical laws, and spiritual laws transcend all. God is Spirit, and He transcends all creation. He is absolutely free, the Creator and Sustainer and Governor of all. He is free to transcend any of His laws, for they are but the expression of His creative mind—the way in which He normally chooses to work in the world He has created. Transcending a "law" does not "break" or destroy the law, but temporarily supersedes it for a higher purpose.

When God overrides His usual way of working ("the natural law") by some special expression of His will, we call it a miracle. To God it is just another of His works. Thus Jesus referred to His miracles as "works" (Gk. *erga*; see John 9:4; 10:25, 32, 38). Prayer is possible because God is almighty, the Sovereign of all His works. He has eternal purposes and plans. He will always transcend any of His normal ways of working to accomplish His moral and spiritual purposes and His eternal plans. Thus prayer always has the possibility to cooperate with God's eternal purpose and to secure the miracle power of God. He does not guarantee miracle, but God is always open to our prayer for His will to prevail for His glory. Prayer is God's ordained way to bring His miracle power to bear in human need.

26

The Power to Obtain
Angelic Assistance

We live in an age which is skeptical of the supernatural. Many Christians seldom think of the Bible teaching concerning angels. Hebrews 1:14 assures us that all angels are "ministering spirits sent to serve" God's children. We do not know all the ways they serve, but the Bible specifically mentions these:

They protect from danger. They protected Jacob after his night of prayer (Gen. 32:1). They protected Elisha, the man of prayer (2 Kings 6:17).

They deliver God's children. Angels delivered Peter from prison (Acts 12:1–11). An angel came and assured Paul that he and all aboard ship would be delivered (Acts 27:23) and their lives would be "graciously given him by God," indicating Paul's prayer request.

They bring messages to God's children. There are many biblical examples of this. Angels brought the message to the shepherds (Luke 2:9–13), to the women at Christ's resurrection (Matt. 28:2–7), and to Cornelius in answer to his prayers (Acts 10:1–7). They can bring suggestions to you or others through thoughts.

They renew physical strength. They strengthened Christ following His ordeal in the Garden of Gethsemane (Luke 22:43).

Undoubtedly the angelic assistance of God's children is usually invisible. But it is real just the same. Christian biography lists many examples of angelic help, both visible and invisible.

While serving in India, I feel sure ministering angels helped me on many occasions, although I did not see them. In one of several examples I was made to sense danger and the need to change my direction, and later discovered I had barely missed a rioting anti-Christian mob. On another occasion I passed without fear through a mob shouting at me. Not a hand touched me, and I was unusually aware that I was surrounded by God's presence. In both cases I later discovered that one of God's children on the opposite side of earth was at that very time alerted and burdened to pray for me because I was in danger, although that person knew nothing of my circumstances at the time.

God will gladly use whatever means are needed to protect His own, if we do our part and pray as He prompts us. We have the promise of God and have every right to claim it, asking Him for angelic guard to be assigned to His servants who minister in places of special danger—such as inner city ghettos or volatile mission posts. Nor should we hesitate to ask God for special angelic protection for loved ones.

The Power to Move Mountains

In the Bible, mountains are sometimes used in a symbolic sense, typifying strength and stability. On the other hand, mountains often symbolize difficulties, problems, and hindrances. Thus, if we would prepare the way of the Lord, the crooked must be made straight and the mountains leveled. Then the glory of the Lord will be revealed (Isa. 40:3–5; Luke 3:4–6). When God's mighty Spirit works, mountains immovable in any other way are as nothing before the power of God (Zech. 4:6–7). The Holy Spirit, who alone can accomplish this, can turn the most impossible mountains into roads and highways for rapid advance (Isa. 49:11).

Jesus used this Old Testament illustration in several of His teachings. When His disciples had failed to cast out the demon from the afflicted boy, Jesus told them that if they had possessed faith even as small as a mustard seed they could speak to "this mountain" (symbolic of any insurmountable situation or problem) and "it will move. Nothing will be impossible for you" (Matt. 17:20). He immediately added that this kind of dramatic display would be the result of prayer and fasting (v. 21 KJV).

Again, when the disciples were amazed at Jesus' power to wither the fruitless fig tree, He repeated that not only could they do the same, but also could even command mountains to throw themselves into the sea, for "if you believe, you will receive whatever you ask for in prayer" (Matt. 21:21–22). Mark records the same incident and quotes Jesus as saying, "Therefore I tell you, whatever you ask for in prayer, believe that you have received it, and it will be yours" (Mark 11:24).

God expects His children to face mountains of difficulties and to move them (see chapter 15). He does not intend for us to be stopped by them, but to accept them as a challenge—either to turn them into highways for God's greater glory or else to cast them into the sea, completely removed from sight, as if they had never existed. Jesus assures us that this is fully possible when His children confront the mountains, believing, but reminds us that such mountain-moving may require prolonged prayer and fasting. The Holy Spirit will do the miracle. It will not be done by our might or power (Zech. 4:6).

Hundreds of mountains are impeding the advance of missions and Christ's church today because we are relying almost completely on our own wisdom, skill, and effort. We had rather do almost anything but really give ourselves to prayer and fasting!

Prayer has mighty power to move mountains because the Holy Spirit is ready both to encourage our praying and to remove the mountains hindering us. Prayer has the power to change mountains into highways.

The Power to Bless

The God of the Bible is a God who blesses. His Word is full of multiplied promises that He will do just that. We can be assured that, except in cases where God must discipline or punish, it is always His will to bless people, especially His obedient children.

"[Jesus] went around doing good" (Acts 10:38). Like Him, we are to go through life blessing everyone we can. We, His disciples, are to be known for our good deeds of blessing to others (Matt. 5:16; Eph. 2:10). We are to be rich in good deeds (1 Tim. 6:18). We are to be "thoroughly equipped for every good work" (2 Tim. 3:17).

The greatest way in which Christians can mediate blessing is through prayer. We have the opportunity to pray for those we can contact in no other way. From the leaders of our nation and the leaders of our church to the poor, the needy, and the suffering—we can bring blessing to all through prayer. From our family and closest friends whom we see often, to those we may meet but once or only hear about—we can be God's agents of blessing. The often-repeated request, "Pray for me," is really a plea for blessing and help.

As a Christian, you should go through life blessing others. You can bring streams of blessing, refreshment, and encouragement wherever you go just by punctuating your days with unceasing prayer for others. As time and opportunity permit, you should bless in every possible way as many as you can (Gal. 6:10). Your presence should always bring a blessing. But this will be most true if you are faithfully asking for God's blessing on all about you. You can find opportunities to fill your day with prayers of blessing if you are observant.

General Stonewall Jackson said, "I have so fixed the habit in my mind that I never raise a glass of water to my lips without asking God's blessing, never seal a letter without putting a word of prayer under the seal, never take a letter from the post without a brief sending of my thoughts heavenward, never change my classes in the lecture room without a minute's petition for the cadets who go out and for those who come in."

A beloved English physician of the 1600s, Sir Thomas Browne, was an example of constant prayers of blessing. He said, "I have resolved to pray more and pray always, to pray in all places where quietness inviteth, in the house, on the highway and on the street; and to know no street or passage in this city that may not witness that I have not forgotten God. . . . I purpose to take occasion of praying upon the sight of any church which I may pass, that God may be worshipped there in spirit, and that souls may be saved there; to pray daily for my sick patients and for the patients of other physicians; at my entrance into any home to say, 'May the peace of God abide here'; after hearing a sermon to pray for a blessing on God's truth and upon the messenger; upon the sight of a beautiful person to bless God for His creatures, to pray for the beauty of such an one's soul, that God may enrich her with inward graces and that the outward and inward may correspond; upon the sight of a deformed person to pray God to give them wholeness of soul, and by and by to give them the beauty of the resurrection."

Abraham was promised that God would bless him and make him a blessing (Gen. 12:2). This should be the experience of every Christian—the more God blesses, the more each of us should bless others. Prayer is the certain route to blessing, and prayer is the greatest means of being a blessing to others. Prayer is God's gift of power to bless others. Oh, fill every day with prayers of blessing and take hold of the tremendous power God has given you!

4

Your Amazing Authority

During the last week of Jesus' life, before His mediatorial death and resurrection, He gave His disciples some special instructions concerning prayer. These were among His deepest teachings. One of His primary emphases was that, hereafter, Jesus' disciples were to bring their petitions *in His name*. No leader has ever given such amazing authority to his followers. In order to be able to use this authority to the glory of Jesus and the advancement of His kingdom, we need to know the answer to three questions: What does the word *name* imply in Jewish thought? What does it mean to pray in Jesus' name? How can we use Jesus' name most effectively in our praying?

The Meaning of *Name* in Jewish Thought

The word *name*, as it was used in the time of Christ, implied three things:

The name is the person. To praise the name of Jesus is to praise Jesus Himself. To love the name of Jesus is to love Jesus. To dishonor the name of Jesus is to insult Jesus.

The name represents all we know of the person. When Moses hungered to draw closer to Jehovah, he asked to see His glory. God replied that a human being could not survive such a divine encounter, for His glory would be greater than the physical body could bear. But God promised to reveal Himself partially. He put Moses in

32

the cleft of a rock, covered him with His hand, and passed in front of Moses, removing His hand for a second so Moses could see the glory that lingered after God had passed by. As He did so, He proclaimed His name—a revealing two-sentence name: " 'The Lord, the Lord, the compassionate and gracious God, slow to anger, abounding in love and faithfulness, maintaining love to thousands, and forgiving wickedness, rebellion and sin. Yet he does not leave the guilty unpunished' " (Exod. 34:6–7). To know God was to know all that His name represented. To understand the name was to see God.

The name of Jesus represents all we know of Him from Scripture and personal experience. It includes His transforming power, His love, His mercy, His intolerance of hypocrisy, His desire for us to be holy as He is holy. It includes our knowledge of Him in His eternal glory, His creation of the universe, His incarnation, His atoning death, His resurrection, and His coming again.

The name is the person actively present. To the early Christians, to be gathered "in Jesus' name" (Matt. 18:20) meant for Jesus to be personally present in their midst, as He truly is today. To be sent "in Jesus' name," to do all "in the name" of Jesus (Col. 3:17), meant acting by the authority of Jesus, manifesting His character. When we act "in Jesus' name" today, we likewise believe that we are not acting alone, but with Jesus by our side, even though He is invisible to our eyes.

The Meaning of Praying
in Jesus' Name

Several important concepts must be kept in mind before you can pray in Jesus' name:

To pray in Jesus' name is possible only if you are "in Jesus." Jesus said, "I will do whatever you ask in my name, so that the Son may bring glory to the Father. You may ask me for anything in my name, and I will do it" (John 14:13–14). In that same conversation with His disciples shortly before His death, He reminded them: "If you remain in me and my words remain in you, ask whatever you wish, and it will be given you. . . . Apart

33

from me you can do nothing" (John 15:7, 5). Jesus used the phrase "in me" seven times in John 14 and 15. To be "in Jesus" means:

1. To be in spiritual unity with Jesus (15:4–7)
2. To be in the vine (15:4)
3. To be in Jesus' love (15:9–10). Love is the prevailing topic of John 13–16. Love must be mutual; if it is to be received, it must be responded to. His new command is love (13:34; 15:17). You cannot love Jesus unless you love His other children (13:34). To love Jesus is to obey Jesus (14:15, 23). If you love, you will remain in Jesus (15:10).

4–5. To have Jesus living within you (14:20; 15:4–5).
6. To be indwelled by the Holy Spirit (14:15–18).
7. To have Christ's words remaining in you (15:7).

Our ability to pray in Jesus' name depends upon this "in Christ" relationship.

To pray in Jesus' name is to be conformed to His nature. The example given in John 13 is Jesus in His servant role, washing the disciples' feet. As you know truth you must do truth (13:17). When you joyfully do His will, reflecting His Christlikeness, you may pray in Jesus' name.

To pray in Jesus' name is to pray for His sake. You must so desire what Jesus desires that your every request is in the spirit of the Lord's prayer, "Your will be done" (Matt. 6:10). This was the attitude of Jesus as He prayed in Gethsemane. You are to pray actively, aggressively that Jesus' will may prevail. To pray in His name is to insist that His total victory be made manifest in the world.

To pray in Jesus' name is to use His name as your reference. This aspect of God's truth is clear in *The Living Bible* parapharse of John 14:13–14: "You can ask for anything, using my name, and I will do it, for this will bring praise to the Father because of what I, the Son, will do for you. Yes, ask anything, using my name, and I will do it." Jesus is your reference as you approach God the Father in prayer. When Satan tries to block and oppose you, use the name of Jesus to gain total victory.

34

To pray in Jesus' name is to claim Calvary's victory for your need. Because Jesus openly defeated Satan and all his evil hosts of demons (Col. 2:15), Satan is a defeated foe. He is a usurper. He tries to frighten and bluff you, but he has already lost the last battle. In Jesus' name you claim the actualization of the victory Christ won on the cross.

To pray in Jesus' name is to acknowledge His full role as God's anointed—your Prophet, Priest, and King. As Prophet, He is your Counselor and Guide. As Priest, He is your Intercessor. As you pray He says the "Amen" to your prayer (Rev. 3:14). "For no matter how many promises God has made, they are 'Yes' in Christ. And so through him the 'Amen' is spoken by us to the glory of God" (2 Cor. 1:20). As King, He is your Sovereign Lord. As you pray in His name, you claim His prophetic guidance for your prayer, His priestly intercession for your prayer, and His kingly answers to your prayer.

To pray in Jesus' name is to pray in all His authority. He has delegated to you the authority to pray and ask God to accomplish great things in His name. You can rebuke Satan and his schemes, his demons, and all his infernal work in the name of Jesus. This is your protection; this is your might; this is your victory.

How to Use the Name of Jesus in Prayer

Oh, holy privilege! You need no other recommendation to God, no other introduction. Come instantly, directly to God's throne. Lift up your heart and look to your Father. Don't be embarrassed to come. God has been expecting you, waiting for you to come in prayer. As a child of God your sin and guilt have been forgiven. You are no longer a servant. You are Jesus' friend; you are His official prayer partner. You come to the throne of grace, not in your own name, but in Jesus' name, representing His interests, by His authority. You are officially appointed to intercede. How shall you use that wonderful, almighty name?

35

Remember what His name represents. The name of Jesus represents His person, His purposes, His honor, His authority—all that He is.

Rejoice in the preciousness of His name. The name of Jesus signifies all His beauty and loveliness. Recall all His graciousness, especially His lovingkindness to you. His name represents His constant, personal love for you, and for the ones for whom you pray. Use His precious name in praise and song as you pray (Ps. 135:3).

Express your love by use of His name. Those you love are thrilled to hear you speak their name. Jesus loves you more than any other, and no matter how many thousands call His name, He thrills to hear you say it again. No matter how many times you have spoken it before, He constantly rejoices to hear it spoken in love. Confessing His name is a true sacrifice of praise. "Through Jesus, therefore, let us continually offer to God a sacrifice of praise—the fruit of lips that confess his name" (Heb. 13:15).

Believe in His name. As you pray, Jesus wants you to exercise your faith through belief in His name (1 John 3:23). His name creates expectancy, gives firmness to your confidence, and fills you with joy (Rom. 15:13; 1 Peter 1:8). Faith in His name brings miracle answers (Acts 3:16).

Make your prayer requests in His name (see John 14:13–15; 15:6–7; 16:26–27). Be sure you are in unity with Him. Pray for what pleases Him, what will glorify Him. Claim your inheritance in His name. Ask, for His name's sake.

Use the authority of His name. The name of Jesus expresses His sovereign authority, recalls the victory He has already won at Calvary, and suggests the availability of the angelic host who are subject to Him. His name endorses His plan and program; it guarantees Satan's failure and defeat. His name has been given to you to use in prayer. Be firm in claiming its authority to resist Satan and promote Christ's will to prevail.

Sanctify your prayer in His name. There is a sanctifying influence as you use the name of Jesus in prayer: (a)

His name guards the nature and motive of your request. You cannot pray selfishly or carnally in His name. (b) His name demands that He be given the glory. (c) His name expects your integrity and obedience. (d) His name calls for your perseverance in prayer. You only pray in His name for that which is truly important.

Involve His partnership through His name. Christ is your great High Priest, interceding at the right hand of the Father (1 Peter 3:22; Rom. 8:34; Eph. 1:20–23). You can join in His intercession and involve His prayer partnership by praying in His name. That which the Holy Spirit prays through you on this earth as you pray in the Spirit is prayed by Christ as He sits enthroned at the right hand of the Father in heaven. Using His name in the full biblical sense makes you prayer partners.

Give honor to His name. God wants you to glorify the name of Jesus. Your prayer in Jesus' name enables Him to bring glory to the Father (John 14:13–14). God has exalted Jesus to the highest place and given Him the name which is above every name (Phil. 2:9). You give glory to the name of Jesus by praying in His name.

Rebuke Satan in His name. Even the angels rebuke Satan and his demonic hosts in the name of Jesus. Remind Satan who Jesus is. Remind Satan of Jesus' victory on the cross and of His resurrection, and remind Satan that he is already defeated. Remind Satan of your identity with Jesus and the authority you have been given through His name.

Use the name of Jesus as your refuge. "The name of the Lord is a strong tower; the righteous run to it and are safe" (Prov. 18:10). Rejoice in your privilege to bear and use the name of Jesus. Claim the ministry and protection of God's holy angels for yourself and for others for whom you pray, especially missionaries serving in dangerous places. Angels are on constant assignment to help you and all God's children (Heb. 1:14). All are subject to Jesus and follow His command. You are safe in the refuge of His name.

Do all in the name of Jesus. Colossians 3:17 is all-inclusive: "Whatever you do, whether in word or deed, do it all in the name of the Lord Jesus." Live for the glory of Jesus' name. Pray in His name. Serve in His name. Trust in His name. Glory in His name. Take the name of Jesus with you and thus be triumphant wherever you go. Rejoice in all that the name of Jesus adds to your prayer.

You have amazing privilege and authority in the name of Jesus. Using His name brings the dimension of the supernatural to your praying. It clears the way before you. It pushes back the darkness from you. It is the key to heaven's resources. Rejoice in His name! Clothe yourself with His name! Learn to pray in the full authority of the name of Jesus!

5

Your Enthroned
Prayer Partner

Prayer brings you into a sacred partnership with Jesus
Christ, the enthroned Son of God. If God had not
revealed this to you in His Word, it would have been
blasphemous to suggest that you could share such
partnership. "The Lord worked with them" is a succinct
history of the early church (Mark 16:20). Further, Scripture calls all Christians "God's fellow workers" (1 Cor.
3:9; 2 Cor. 6:1).

There are many ways to "work" with God—through
obedience, through service to others, and through sharing His love. But He wants to have even more intimate
contact with you. He wants to bring you into His inner
circle where you can hear His great heart beating for a
lost world. He has created you with the ability to speak to
Him and fellowship with Him. Above all else, as His
"fellow worker," you were created to pray—as He prays.

Why Does Jesus Pray?

We are told repeatedly in Scripture that Jesus prayed
and that He continues to pray today. But why is prayer
necessary for Jesus who spoke worlds into existence
(John 1:3) and sustains all things (Heb. 1:3)? Why must
He pray? Why not merely command? No demon from
hell or combination of demonic forces could stand
against His powerful word. Why does Jesus not just
rebuke them, stop them, or consume them by His word?

One day He will (2 Thess. 2:8). One day He will rule
with an iron scepter (Rev. 12:5), and so will we (Rev.

2:27). But today Christ has chosen to rule the world by prayer. This is the day of grace, not the day of His power and glory. Christ is already enthroned at the right hand of the Father. What is He doing? He is reigning. But how is He reigning? Not by His scepter, but by prayer! Even before His death and resurrection, when He forewarned Peter that Satan had asked permission to sift the disciples as wheat (Luke 22:31–32), Christ did not say, "I will stop Satan." Instead, He said, "I have prayed for you."

Jesus Reigns by Interceding

Today Jesus Christ is seated at the Father's "right hand in the heavenly realms, far above all rule and authority, power and dominion, and every title that can be given, not only in the present age but also in the one to come. And God has placed all things under his feet" (Eph. 1:20–22). Christ is already seated on His throne. And what does Christ do there? Grant interviews to the angels or departed saints? The only picture Scripture gives is that He is "at the right hand of God . . . interceding for us" (Rom. 8:34). Jesus lives forever, has a permanent priesthood, and always lives to intercede (Heb. 7:24–25).

Does Jesus not live to reign? Yes, but He also lives to intercede. He reigns by interceding. He is the Sovereign over all, but He is also the great High Priest praying for all. Prayer secures results; prayer conveys blessing. He blesses as He prays. He is the royal Intercessor and Giver of blessing.

Your Priestly Prayer Role

And that is exactly the role He has chosen for you. He loves you so much that He desires you to intercede with Him as He intercedes with the Father, and to bless the world as He does. He mediates blessing through prayer. You and I are to do the same.

Thus we read in 1 Peter 2:9, "You are . . . a royal priesthood." John writes us that Jesus loves us, has freed us from our sins by His blood, has made us into a kingdom, and has made us priests to serve His God and Father (Rev. 1:5–6).

Jesus is God's High Priest (Heb. 2:17). He has made us priests to God also (Rev. 1:6). This is how we are to serve God (v. 6). The greatest service you will ever do for God will not be your external ministering, witnessing, or preaching. Your greatest service, whatever your vocation, is to be your priestly intercession. God has ordained to work through the prayers of His people. He is waiting for your intercession. You were not only created to pray; you were redeemed, justified, and sanctified to pray.

Your Mutual Commission With Christ

What is Jesus' greatest personal prayer assignment in this age? Perhaps it is to pray for the church. However, only one command regarding Christ's intercession for the churches is recorded in the Bible. It is found in Psalm 2:7–8: "I will proclaim the decree of the Lord: He said to me, 'You are my Son; today I have become your Father. Ask of me, and I will make the nations your inheritance, the ends of the earth your possession.'" Is that why Jesus intercedes today?

Jesus is commanded by the Father to ask for the nations. His great commission to the church, His last request to the church, is to go to the nations (Matt. 28:19–20). His second return will be delayed until adequate witness is given to the nations (Matt. 24:14). If He is a God of infinite love, His heart is yearning for the nations. Certainly one of the priorities He places on every Christian is to intercede for the evangelization of the world.

Since Jesus ever lives to intercede, any time you pray—day or night—Jesus is already interceding. Every time you go to prayer, you can be Jesus' prayer partner. Paul makes this very clear: "By grace you have been saved. And God raised us up with Christ and seated us with him in the heavenly realms in Christ Jesus. . . . For we are . . . created in Christ Jesus to do good works, which God prepared in advance for us to do" (Eph. 2:5–6, 10). You are already seated with Christ in the heavenly realms. Where is Christ seated? On the throne of the universe beside God the Father. You are to be sharing Christ's throne already and doing what Christ is doing—interceding.

Jesus—Your Divine Prayer Partner

Note the important ways your prayer partnership with Christ affects your praying:

What reverent caution it places on you as you pray! If you are Jesus' partner in intercession, you must be sure to pray in harmony with Jesus' prayers, and not in contradiction to them. What kind of prayer partner would you be if you kept disagreeing with Him? How urgent it is, not only to seek to know God's will, but to pray constantly the words Jesus taught us to pray: "Your will be done on earth as it is in heaven" (Matt. 6:10). Just as Jesus prayed in Gethsemane, so you must pray, "Yet not as I will, but as you will" (Matt. 26:39).

What strong confidence it gives to your prayer! If you are praying for His will to be done, if you are joining your prayer to the intercession of Jesus, with what full assurance of faith (Heb. 10:22) you can draw near to God. "In him and through faith in him we may approach God with freedom and confidence" (Eph. 3:12).

If Jesus and you are praying together about a matter, what doubt is there that God is listening? Once, when praying, Jesus mentioned that He knew God the Father always heard Him (John 11:42). God's Word stacks assurance on assurance to encourage your intercession. "This is the confidence we have in approaching God: that if we ask anything according to his will, he hears us. And if we know that he hears us—whatever we ask—we know that we have what we asked of him" (1 John 5:14–15). The very next verse shows that the Holy Spirit especially had in mind your praying for others—in other words, your intercession.

What strong incentive it gives you to persevere in prayer! Jesus Himself urges you to hold on in prayer and not give up until the answer comes (Luke 18:1–8; 11:5–10). If you are praying in the will of God (see chapter 30) and your prayer has not yet been answered, you can be sure Jesus is still interceding for the need, so you too should persevere.

What an amazing story Jesus told to illustrate this truth! You are to keep praying with the same insistence as the widow who persisted in her plea to an unjust judge who was ignoring her and refusing to answer. God the Father, said Jesus, is not like that judge! But you should be like that widow!

The God of Amen

There is a beautiful picture in Scripture of Jesus' role as your prayer partner. "These are the words of the Amen" (Rev. 3:14), meaning that Jesus is the "Amen." What does this mean? The Hebrew rendering of Isaiah 65:16 calls God "the God of Amen." The original meaning of the verb *to amen* is to regard someone as reliable, trustworthy, and truthful. It is therefore used in the Old Testament in two ways: (a) It echoes a leader's prayer or praise. That is, it means "Yes, indeed" or "May it be so in very truth." (For examples, see Ps. 41:13; 72:19; 106:48; 1 Chron. 16:36; Neh. 8:6) and (b) It is used as the assent of an obedient listener to a royal decree or purpose (1 Kings 1:36; Jer. 11:5).

When Scripture declares that Jesus is the Amen, it means that He is the divine "Yes" to all of God's will and to the prayers of God's people whenever they are in accord with God's will. "For no matter how many promises God has made, they are 'Yes' in Christ. And so through him the 'Amen' is spoken by us to the glory of God" (2 Cor. 1:20).

Now let the full glory of the scene in heaven dawn on you! In human pictorial terms, Jesus is seated on the throne, on the right side of the Father. You, sharing the throne of Jesus in Spirit, are seated beside Him. When you intercede according to the will of God, aided by the Holy Spirit indwelling you (who intercedes for you and through you), you turn to Jesus and make your plea for His glory and for His sake. By your authority "in Christ," you hand the request to Jesus. He joins His almighty intercession with yours and turns to the Father to present your united intercession (Jesus' and yours!) and then seals it by saying His royal "Amen," being in His very essence your enthroned "Amen." Because of who Jesus is, because of what He accomplished at Calvary, because He agrees with you in prayer (Matt. 18:19), He is the sovereign "Amen" of your prayer.

Is not this the time to sing the doxology? And is it not a time to fall on your knees and join the heavenly beings exclaiming in adoration: "Holy, holy, holy!"?

"What is man that you are mindful of him, the son of man that you care for him?" (Ps. 8:4). "O Lord, what is man that you care for him, the son of man that you think of him?" (Ps. 144:3). "Oh, the depth of the riches of the wisdom and knowledge of God! How unsearchable his judgments, and his paths beyond tracing out! . . . For from him and through him and to him are all things. To him be the glory forever! Amen" (Rom. 11:33, 36).

6

Your Indwelling
Prayer Partner

The Holy Spirit, the third Person of the Trinity, is not only enthroned in heaven; He has been sent by Jesus (John 16:7) and the Father (John 14:26) to indwell the believer (John 14:17). Thus your inner nature as a believer becomes a temple of God through the indwelling Holy Spirit (1 Cor. 3:16–17). What does the Holy Spirit do for you as He indwells you? He sanctifies (2 Thess. 2:13), empowers (Acts 1:8), guides (John 16:13), witnesses through you (1 John 5:8; Acts 1:8), and helps you pray (Rom. 8:26).

The Holy Spirit is the Spirit of prayer. He prays directly, speaking with the Father and the Son. He also prays indirectly, praying through you, the believer. It is the nature of God the Son and God the Spirit to pray. They ever live to pray. Just as God has ordained that you join Christ in intercession for His will to be done on earth, so He has ordained that the Holy Spirit should enable, guide, and empower your intercession.

To say it in another startling way: God the Son is your enthroned Prayer Partner and God the Spirit is your indwelling Prayer Partner. Just as God the Father remains invisible to your human eyes, so God the Spirit remains invisible. But just as surely as you can know the Fatherhood of God and the Saviorhood of Christ, even so you can know when the Holy Spirit is working within you. To be filled with the Spirit is to be filled with the Spirit of intercession.

When the Holy Spirit fills, prayer becomes your very

spiritual breath. The Holy Spirit loves to do within you that for which He indwells you—to accomplish God's will on earth. God has ordained that the prayer of the believer is one of the major ways He accomplishes His will, so the Holy Spirit desires to make intercession a major expression of your spiritual life.

The Holy Spirit Enables and Transforms Your Prayer

The Holy Spirit increases your desire to pray. Just as it is natural for a child to talk to its father, so it is natural for the believer to pray to the heavenly Father. Though a child must learn to talk, a new believer can pray as soon as he is born of the Spirit, born again.

The Holy Spirit is present from the moment of spiritual birth to encourage and increase the desire to pray. It is a sign of spiritual ill health for any Christian to lack this desire. A carnal believer finds many excuses to neglect prayer, for Satan is always ready to try to rob us of communion with God, the Source of power. But a believer who is Spirit-filled can expect the Holy Spirit, the indwelling Prayer Enabler, to draw him to prayer.

The Holy Spirit brings Scripture to your memory as you pray. One of the ministries of the Spirit, as your Prayer Partner, is to bring to mind things of spiritual importance. He delights to remind you of verses of Scripture, for Scripture is the sword which enables you to stand against the evil powers of this world (Eph. 6:17). He reminds you of Scripture verses filled with praise, so you can quote them in your prayers. He reminds you of Scripture promises to strengthen your faith.

Memorizing Scripture—hiding it in your heart—will enable you to incorporate God's Word into your spiritual life (Ps. 119:11). Memorize some of the praise psalms, the doxologies of the New Testament, and some of the verses of prayer and promise. These can be used repeatedly, for you will find they express the deep desires and the deep joys of your heart. Oh, what a blessing to use God's own words as your prayer!

46

The Holy Spirit brings spiritual goals to your attention. The Spirit loves to place before you the image of Jesus and to deepen your desire to be more like Him as you read about Him in the Word, realizing that you fall far short of His Christlikeness. The Holy Spirit also delights to hold before you Bible characters, outstanding godly people in the history of the church, or people whom you have met or known. Using their examples, the Spirit helps you set goals for spiritual growth. There are many passages of the Bible which the Spirit can use in this aspect of His ministry. Therefore, it is very important to spend adequate time reading God's Word systematically day by day. The Spirit will also bring goals to your attention as you pray for your church, your missionary organization, your nation, and indeed your world.

The Holy Spirit brings needs to your attention. The Holy Spirit can give you eyes to see what others may fail to see. He can help you discern when people are discouraged, sad, or defeated. He can point out to you spiritual neglect, the need for revival, for new vision and greater obedience. He can inspire you to pray for the growth of the church, for the youth about you, for specially used servants of God.

His bringing of needs to your attention is His call to you to pray. Satan does not object to your recognizing the needs, but he wants you to criticize and ridicule. The Holy Spirit, as your indwelling Prayer Partner, wants to make you prayerful, not critical. Satan wants you to talk about people and their needs; the Holy Spirit wants you to intercede in prayer for them.

At times, you should share these concerns with others in order to join in prayer about them—widespread concerns of your community, your nation, and your world. The tremendous need for the advance and spread of the gospel calls you to unite in prayer for maximum prayer power. The Holy Spirit is always ready to assist you at such times, and Christ promises that He will be present with you (John 14:16).

The Holy Spirit places prayer burdens upon you. God's heart is pained by the sin, the indifference, and the godlessness of our age. Our loving Savior and the tender Holy Spirit plead in interceding prayer for the broken lives, broken homes, and the tragedies of sin and injustice throughout the world. They long for you to join them in daily intercession for the hurting, the broken, the lost, and those being destroyed by sin.

God the Father wants someone to intercede for everyone in need. God hears the cry of the orphan, the sob of the broken-hearted, the angry words of the violent, and the screams of their victims. God feels the woes of the prisoners and the refugees, the hunger pangs of those starving for food. He is touched by the sorrow of those who mourn, the helplessness and hopelessness of those chained by habits of sin. He understands the spiritual darkness and the vague but deep dissatisfaction of those who have never received the gospel.

Surely Jesus still weeps over our cities as He wept over Jerusalem, for His heart is the same yesterday, today, and forever (Heb. 13:8). He loves with deepest longing every atheist, communist, or terrorist. He cherishes every human being, no matter how sinful he is.

It is the special role of the Holy Spirit to give you a prayer burden for all these needs and all these needy ones. God wants to express His longing love through you as you pray. Such loving, longing intercession should be a part of your prayer time each day. The more faithfully and sincerely you pray for these needs, the more deeply the Holy Spirit will be able to burden you with these things which break the heart of God. The Holy Spirit wants to call you to weep with those who weep (Rom. 12:15). Your weeping is usually not in public, but in your secret place of intercession (Jer. 13:17).

The Holy Spirit will call you to prayer at crisis moments. There are crisis moments in the lives of all people—moments of danger, moments of decision, moments of special opportunity. There are times when the Holy Spirit is convicting someone of sin (John 16:8), and He may call you to pray during that spiritual crisis. There are times of illness or special discouragement when the Spirit may select you to bear a special prayer burden for someone. Learn to be very sensitive to His voice. (For a more detailed discussion of this important role, see chapter 11.)

The Holy Spirit will add special depth, power, and faith to your prayer. He will not only direct you to pray for special needs, but He will also guide you in how to pray for them, will strengthen your faith as you pray, and will anoint and empower your praying. In addition, as your Prayer Partner, He will join you in praying and interceding at a depth not possible to you alone (Rom. 8:26–27).

We are weak in ourselves and our prayers are weak as compared to His. He sees the urgency far better than we do. His infinite Personality feels an infinite depth of love, sorrow, compassion, and yearning. He sees the tremendous potential and possibilities beyond anything we could ever understand.

The Spirit's prayer, says Paul, transcends any possible prayer on your part. This is not so much His intercession through you, but above and beyond that it is His intercession for you (v. 27). He intercedes for you and for those for whom you intercede. He has led you to share His heartcry, His burden, His love. But He does not leave you to pray alone. He joins you as your loving Prayer Partner, adding infinite understanding, desire, and power.

The Holy Spirit wants you to have a worldwide prayer ministry. The Holy Spirit, your indwelling Prayer Partner, longs for you to share His heartbeat for the whole world. Since He is the Creator God, He loves all His creation equally.

About half of the people of the world have never heard the name of Jesus; or if they have heard it mentioned, they have not heard enough about Him to enable them to make an intelligent decision to receive Christ. These peoples live in a kind of poverty not often recognized or publicized. It is a poverty of intercessory prayer, for the intercessors in these heathen nations are few.

Who will pray for them? Who will pray for the outcast, the atheist, the communist, the terrorist—if not the

Christians in our nation? The Holy Spirit, who prays for them with deep hunger each day, longs for you to share His intercession for the rapid advance of the gospel. How tragic if our reluctance to pray and our failure to reach these lost ones are factors contributing to the delay of Christ's return (Matt. 24:14).

God forgive us! Why not stop right now and ask forgiveness, promising that through the Spirit's enabling power, you will begin to assume your full role as His prayer partner. Undoubtedly there are whole cities, nations, and world leaders waiting for your prayer. How long must they wait?

The Holy Spirit may call you to fast. We as a church have largely neglected the method of fasting as a means to more powerful praying and greater prayer results. From time to time the Holy Spirit will call you to add fasting to your prayer. (A more lengthy discussion of fasting is found in chapter 13.)

The Holy Spirit wants to multiply your eternal reward. Christ will greatly reward all His intercessors for their faithfulness. Far more depends on the faithful exercise of prayer than most Christians realize. Significant prayer battles are being fought again and again. You are in danger of missing the greatest opportunities of your Christian life. Christ and the Holy Spirit long for you to be their effective prayer partner. They need your intercessory help.

God the Father has ordained that much depends on your prayer. Don't fail your divine Prayer Partners. Don't fail your world. The Holy Spirit longs for your prayer life to become powerful and effective. He wants you to receive your full and glorious reward. Don't miss the intercessor's crown He has waiting for you!

7

Your Invisible Prayer Expediters

God's holy angels are your invisible prayer expediters. Scripture teaches that the total number of God's angels is beyond human numbering (Heb. 12:22). Their primary responsibility as created beings is to worship and serve Christ (Heb. 1:4, 6–7). Secondarily, they are assigned by God to serve "those who will inherit salvation" (Heb. 1:14). Angels have a keen interest in all that concerns us, because we are important to Christ. We are His church, His bride.

How Angels Helped
Answer Prayer in Bible Times

The Bible teaches how God used His angels to help answer the prayers of many of the great biblical heroes. When Abraham prayed for his nephew Lot during the time he was living in the pagan city of Sodom, God sent angels to deliver Lot before destroying the city (Gen. 19). Undoubtedly Jacob was praying fervently as he fled from his father-in-law Laban, for God instructed him to return to his own relatives (Gen. 31:3, 11–12) and sent a group of angels to protect him (Gen. 32:1–2). When Elijah was fleeing from the wrath of Jezebel, praying in desperation, God sent His angels twice to provide food for him (1 Kings 19:5, 7). When enemy forces surrounded Elisha, God sent multitudes of angels to protect him (2 Kings 6:17).

When Hezekiah and Isaiah cried out in prayer to heaven, the Lord sent an angel to deliver Jerusalem from her enemies (2 Chron. 32:20–21). After Daniel, the prayer warrior, was thrown into the lions' den, he testified, "My God sent his angel and he shut the mouths of the lions" (Dan. 6:22). When Daniel sought to understand his vision, God sent Gabriel to interpret for him (Dan. 8:15–16). Again Daniel prayed, with fasting, and again Gabriel was sent to him (Dan. 9:3, 20–23). Another time Daniel spent three weeks in prayer and partial fasting; this time Gabriel appeared and reported that Michael had helped him bring the answer in spite of demonic opposition (Dan. 10:2, 13). During the prophet Zechariah's vision and prayer, one of God's angels gave him the answer (Zech. 1:8–9).

In New Testament times God sent an angel to Zechariah, the father of John the Baptist, to tell him that his prayer for a son had been heard (Luke 1:11–13). It was angels who brought news of Christ's resurrection to the women who visited His tomb (Matt. 28:5). It was two angels who spoke to the disciples when Jesus ascended back to heaven (Acts 1:10–11). When the apostles were arrested by the high priest, God sent an angel to open the prison doors and to instruct them to tell the Good News (Acts 5:19–20). During the Samaritan revival, an angel directed Philip to go south on the road to Gaza where he met and witnessed to the Ethiopian eunuch (Acts 8:26). No doubt an angel was involved as well in transporting him miraculously from that place to other mission sites (vv. 39–40).

When the church prayed for Peter while he was in prison, God sent an angel to open the doors and lead him out (Acts 12:5–10). As the church continued to pray, God sent an angel to destroy their persecutor, King Herod (Acts 12:17–24). During the long, tragic Mediterranean storm when Paul and his shipmates were about to lose their lives, an angel sent from God assured him that, in answer to his prayer, all on board would be saved (Acts 27:23–24). No doubt angelic assistance was involved in getting them all to shore alive. When John prayed during his exile on Patmos, God sent His angel to give him the vision found in the Book of Revelation (Rev. 1:1).

Undoubtedly God's angels were far more active throughout Bible times than we realize. Jesus, too, received angelic assistance. We know that at least twice when He prayed, angels came to strengthen and help Him (Matt. 4:11; Luke 22:43). The Bible implies that angels are just as active today.

We Are Important to the Angels

You should rejoice in the glorious fact that you are never alone. Even children seem to have an accompanying angel (Matt. 18:10). God's angels are always watching you (1 Cor. 11:10; 1 Tim. 5:21). Paul said, "We have been made a spectacle to the whole universe, to angels as well as to men" (1 Cor. 4:9). There is not a moment of your life when the eyes of the angels are not on you. No doubt they are the ones who keep God's books in which all your thoughts, words, and deeds are recorded (Rev. 20:12; Dan. 7:10), enabling God to reward your prayer and loving service to Him (1 Cor. 3:11–15).

God uses His manifold goodness to us, His providential coordination of our lives, and our service to Him to illustrate to the angels His perfect plan, will, and ways. Thus our lives become educational tools by which the angels can know God better. "His intent was that now, through the church, the manifold wisdom of God should be made known to the rulers and authorities in the heavenly realms" (Eph. 3:10).

Angels Are Usually Invisible

In God's infinite wisdom He apparently prefers to withhold the sight of angels from human eyes. We often recognize, however, that God has wonderfully protected us. How does God do this? Probably He has called on one or more of His angels. I well remember an occasion while on furlough from the mission field. En route to Christian ministry in Ohio, an oncoming vehicle went out of control at a curve and slid sideways toward my car. Just before the other car struck mine, it suddenly straightened out, narrowly missing me. Upon passing, the vehicle again slid out of control. Instantly I knew God's angel must have thrown a shield around my car.

On another occasion an approaching car veered across the center line toward me. I could see the driver's head roll to the side as if he were asleep or drugged. Suddenly, as if an unseen hand were placed on the steering wheel, that car pulled to the proper lane and safely passed by. I saw, to my horror, that the driver's eyes were closed. I thanked God, knowing again that He had used His angel to protect me.

Sometimes Angels Are Visible

Occasionally, however, God permits His angels to be temporarily visible. When Rev. Lawrence Schaper was hospitalized in Jefferson Barracks, an army hospital in St. Louis, Missouri, the third night after his operation he felt so ill that he prayed, "Lord Jesus, come and stay with me tonight." Rev. Schaper reports that he saw Jesus enter the room with two angels. Jesus sat on one chair and an angel on the other. Lawrence said, "Jesus, I'm so sick, You come sit on the bed by me." Jesus sat beside him on the bed. When Lawrence awoke the next morning, the heavenly beings were still there. Rev. Schaper told them good-by. "Jesus was the first in the room, and the last to leave." The crisis passed. Today, forty-eight years later at ninety-two years of age, Rev. Schaper is still loving and serving the Lord.

My mother was converted as a girl in a country church during special revival meetings. As she went forward and knelt at the front of the church, she saw angels beside her. In midlife she became very ill. For more than four years she suffered attacks of pneumonia, pleurisy, partial paralysis, and heart trouble, one after another. During that time she could lie on only her right side, could not use her left side because of the paralysis, could not endure any sound—even of moderate intensity—and could not bear normal light. For four years we carried on conversations in whispers in the home, stopped the clock from ticking, padded doors with cloth, and kept heavy, dark fabric around her bed to close out the light.

One day Mother felt led to ask her brother's family and another Christian family to meet in our home to pray for her. Suddenly she heard a voice, "Look, the windows of heaven have opened for you." Opening her eyes, she saw angels beside her. Instantly she leaped to her feet, completely healed. She lived for more than thirty years after that.

When Sadhu Sundar Singh, beloved barefoot Indian evangelist, was sacrificially proclaiming the gospel amid the snow and cold of the windswept plateau of Tibet, he had many wonderful experiences of God's protection and aid. One of his amazing experiences was his visit to the town of Rasar. The head Buddhist lama had Singh arrested and sentenced him to death for preaching Christ. He was thrown into an empty, deep well—one of the two main forms of execution.

Sundar Singh sank into this charnel pit of bones and rotting flesh of those who had died there before him. The stench seemed unbearable and, for three days and nights, he was at times only partially conscious. Wherever he touched, there was rotting flesh. On the third night as he prayed, he heard a key grating in the lock of the lid overhead. To his surprise the lid was removed. At that moment a voice called down to him to grasp the rope being lowered and, as he did so, he was gently drawn out. The lid was replaced and locked again, and instantly Singh's deliverer vanished.

Sundar Singh praised God and the next day resumed his preaching in the town. The lama again had him seized and angrily demanded to know who had stolen the only key and released him. Upon search, the key was found on the lama's own belt. In fear of the evangelist's God, he asked Sundar Singh to leave the town before they were all killed by this mighty power!

God's Angels Are Important to You

God's angels are always on call to God and to you when you pray. They are sent to help accomplish God's purpose for you, particularly in the area of expediting your prayers. It is always correct to say God gives the answer to prayer, for angels act on God's behalf. They are His personal representatives. There is no limit to what they can do for you if it is in accord with God's will. If more than one angel is required, God can dispatch enough to meet your need.

Angels seem to be able to travel at the incredible speed of the world of spirit. They are not hampered by a physical body, but when God so wills, they can use physical strength or increase your strength (Dan. 10:18–19; Luke 22:43). If God wills, they can instantly assume a bodily form and function through this body.

Remember these important points about the angels:

1. God's angels are always with you.
2. God's angels can go anywhere at any time. They are where you need them when you need them.
3. God's angels are instantly available at God's command.
4. God's angels have superhuman strength.
5. God's angels are probably God's chief agents for answering your prayers.
6. God's angels delight to do God's will.
7. God's angels have a permanent assignment to help you.
8. God's angels love you because you are loved by God.
9. You can ask God for the help of His angels at any time.
10. God's angels are only God's servants, assigned to you. You do not pray to them; you pray only to God and ask Him for their help.
11. God's angels will rejoice with you in heaven and will probably explain to you how your prayers were answered on various occasions.

One reason you should be so thankful for angelic help is the constant opposition of Satan and his demonic forces to God's will, God's ministry, and God's people. He seeks to strike back at God by attacking mankind, the object of God's love and plans. Satan has mobilized his forces against you. They are constantly opposing you, hindering you far more than you realize (Eph. 6:12).

But rejoice! Take courage! God alone is almighty, omniscient, and omnipresent. Satan is present at only one place at a time. He must depend on his demon helpers to work for him.

God has far more holy angels than Satan has demons. Spiritual warfare is won by prayer, with the help of God's angels (see chapter 28). "If God is for us, who can be against us?" (Rom. 8:31). "Don't be afraid. . . . Those who are with us are more the those who are with them" (2 Kings 6:16). "Do not be afraid or discouraged . . . there is a greater power with us" than with those who oppose us (2 Chron. 32:7).

The Angels and Your Prayer

Whether the angels assist in answering your prayers as a special assignment from God or simply in the normal course of their duty, you are not required to ask for their help. In fact, you should never pray to angels. Pray to God, realizing that He may choose to assign angels to help meet the needs for which you pray. Under certain circumstances you may legitimately request the assistance of angels in meeting needs:

1. *Needs Related to Evangelism, Church, and Missionary Work.* You may wish to pray for God's angels to speed the granting of permits; to coordinate weather; to provide traveling mercies; to help with complex arrangements; to ensure that equipment works properly; to give favor with local or other government authorities; to attract the attention of key people; to motivate people to attend important meetings; to distract the opposition, or to silence and remove the opponents; to help you to answer questions and objections; to help break sinful habits.

2. *Needs Related to Defeating Satan.* You may need the assistance of God's angels to bind Satan's influence; to disrupt his plans and check his control over certain people; to dispel satanic darkness and drive back his demons; to help Christians in times of temptation, giving them power to resist Satan, and uniting them against Satan and his forces.

3. *Needs Related to Protection.* At times, angelic protection is imperative. Under God's direction, angels

may protect from accident, storms and other natural calamities; from insects, wild animals, disease germs and infections; from enemies motivated by Satan or from outright demonic attack; from Satan's temptation. Angels also may be empowered to distract the attention of your foes, causing your presence to go unnoticed in times of danger. They may then coordinate providential circumstances to aid in your escape from enemies.

4. Personal Needs. You may feel the need of angelic help in very personal matters: to protect your loved ones; to help you contact people, find solutions, give you special skills, help you locate items; to bring people to your aid, awaken you on time, bring things to your memory or attention; to guide in a difficult decision; to provide physical strength beyond your own; to remind others to pray for you, remind you of a Scripture verse or where to find it in the Bible; to help you understand others; to watch over your crops or livestock (Mal. 3:11); to help in business matters.

This is but a suggested list of situations in which you may need angelic assistance. Remember, God the Father, God the Son, and God the Holy Spirit can work directly, but they probably most often choose to work through the ministry and cooperation of angels. Thank God for the help of His angels whenever you suspect they have been involved. A multitude of these heavenly ambassadors is always instantly available to you, to be dispatched to the place or person in need. They are waiting to help you.

8

You Can Touch God's Throne Through Prayer

Prayer has a long arm. It can reach all the way to heaven. The Bible teaches this truth through beautiful symbolism—the raising of the hands in prayer. "Let us lift up our hearts and our hands to God in heaven" (Lam. 3:41).

Our first Old Testament example is found in an account of a strategic battle with the Amalekites, when Moses instructed Joshua to lead God's people while he lifted his hands in supplication. We read: "As long as Moses held up his hands, the Israelites were winning, but whenever he lowered his hands, the Amalekites were winning. When Moses' hands grew tired, they took a stone and put it under him and he sat on it. Aaron and Hur held his hands up—one on one side, one on the other—so that his hands remained steady till sunset. So Joshua overcame the Amalekite army with the sword. Then the Lord said to Moses, "'Write this on a scroll as something to be remembered'" (Exod. 17:11–14). What is the explanation of this great victory, and why should it be remembered? Moses answers in verse 16: "Hands were lifted up to the throne of the Lord."

Visibly our hands are lifted up; spiritually they touch the throne of God. You can pray prayers that go no higher than your head, that never go beyond the room you are in. But when you pray in the Spirit, in the will of God, and in Jesus' name, your prayer can reach all the way to heaven!

Moses wrote the truth. His hands touched God's throne. Yours can, too, if you follow God's principles of prayer.

Paul exhorts us in 1 Timothy 2:8: "I want men everywhere to lift up holy hands in prayer." Does this mean that we must literally hold up our hands whenever we pray? Certainly not. God is more concerned that we lift up our hearts and our souls to Him. "To you, O Lord, I lift up my soul" (Ps. 25:1; 86:4; 143:8). Whether we raise our hands literally or not, it is of the very spirit and essence of prayer that we lift up our spiritual eyes and heart to God. And during times of earnest intercession or intense spiritual warfare, we may, in the privacy of our prayer place or even in public (almost without realizing it), lift our physical hands toward God. "Hear my cry for mercy as I call to you for help, as I lift up my hands toward your Most Holy Place" (Ps. 28:2).

You Can Touch Another through Prayer

Not only can your prayer reach heaven, but the arm of prayer can also span the miles to any part of the world, and you in your place of intercession can touch someone who needs you, even thousands of miles away. This is not make-believe. This is spiritual reality.

I shall never forget the two-week period in India many years ago when I felt a continuing prayer burden for our son. It came to a climax one Sunday afternoon when I was alone in our house, so lost in prayer for him that for a while I did not notice the passing of time or the existence of space. As I prayed on and on it suddenly seemed that I was kneeling beside John with my hand on his shoulder, praying for him. I know not how long I prayed, or what I said, but I know my arm of prayer had spanned the land and oceans for thousands of miles and my hand was on John's shoulder. It was as real as if I were by his side. Then assurance came, and I rose from my knees and later gave my Sunday evening message.

Because of missionary responsibilities I did not find opportunity to write John till after lunch the following afternoon. I went to my office and was sitting at my typewriter. "Dear John," I wrote, "I don't know what this means to you, but I am sure it means something. For days I have been having a special prayer in concern for you, and yesterday afternoon as I was kneeling in our bedroom, it suddenly seemed I was kneeling by your side, with my hand on your shoulder." I was just ready to write the second paragraph when our doorbell rang. I went to the door and found a messenger from the telegraph office. He handed me a cablegram.

I stepped inside, closed the door, and opened the cable. It read: "God is my Captain. Quiet but sure decision. Thanks for heritage, love and prayer. John." I dropped on my knees as the tears coursed down my cheeks. God had permitted me to touch heaven's throne with one hand and our son's shoulder with the other. After the necessary days had elapsed John's letter had arrived. At the exact time when I was in prayer in Allahabad, India, John in the USA, kneeling alone in the darkness, had given his heart to the Lord.

You Can Be Touched by Someone's Prayer

I recall another occasion when, in June of 1962, I was summoned to Los Angeles for a special meeting of the OMS Board of Directors. During my last day in Landour, six thousand feet high in the Himalayas, I began to feel ill. My throat became raw, my body ached, and I was hot with fever. As I worked in my office trying to clear my desk of correspondence, I prayed that my family would not notice how ill I felt, for I feared they would not want me to leave that evening for Delhi and the USA. The family walked with me down the mountainside to the bus stand and did not notice my illness.

As the bus pulled out I waved good-bye to them, but as soon as it rounded the corner, I lay my head on the back of the seat in front of me, too ill to hold it up any longer. As I felt so feverish, the eighteen-mile ride down the winding road to Dehra Dun was very difficult. At Dehra Dun I caught the train to Delhi. For some reason that night the fuse was out and the fans and lights in our coach were not working. My fever rose as I struggled with nausea and headache. I thought, "If I could only find one Christian and ask him to pray for me!"

Suddenly, as the train sped on in the darkness, I felt as

if a human hand with a cool, wet washcloth had wiped my brow. Instantly my fever, headache, nausea, and sore throat were gone and I felt completely well. Immediately I thought, "Who prayed for me?"

There were stopovers in Hong Kong and Tokyo, with a day of prayer scheduled with our Chinese and Japanese co-workers in both cities. Each time, before my message, I told about my recent experience. "I am here today because someone prayed for me. I don't know who it was, but I felt that one's hand."

The OMS board sessions lasted several days in Los Angeles. One day when the mail was brought, there was a letter for me. I opened it and read that at about 9:15 P.M. on the day I left Landour, the person had felt a heavy burden of prayer for me. Yes, that was the time and day. Whether I had felt the actual hand of the pray-er, or whether it was the hand of an angel in answer to the prayer makes no difference. Prayer spanned the miles and left its healing touch on a speeding train that hot June night.

Why don't we experience such a prayer touch more often? Perhaps too few people have developed a listening ear to the still, small voice of the Spirit. Perhaps too often we are not close enough to the Lord to be sensitive to His guidance. The reality, however, remains. Prayer has a long arm. It can touch heaven, and it can touch anywhere on earth at any time. In some wonderful sense prayer makes you a mediator of God's blessings.

God's Trinity of Intercession

Jesus is the only Mediator between God and men in salvation. Any mediation of blessing that our God permits us to do now is on the basis of Christ's mediation at Calvary and Christ's mediation today on the throne. But the same Paul who wrote in 1 Timothy 2:5 that there is "one mediator between God and men, the man Christ Jesus," also wrote three verses later, "I want men everywhere to lift up holy hands in prayer."

God wants us to join the trinity of intercession that He has ordained. God the Son always lives to intercede for us (Heb. 7:25). He is interceding for us now at God's right hand (Rom. 8:34). God the Spirit Himself intercedes for us with groans too deep for words to express (Rom. 8:26). Although God the Son and God the Spirit are constantly interceding, God's trinity of intercession is incomplete until you join them in prayer.

The praying Christ is on the throne of heaven, face to face with the Father. But we weak, finite human beings, saved by the grace of God, are given the almost unbelievable privilege of reaching our hands to heaven and also touching God's throne! Then the prayer team God ordained is complete. In some sacred sense we share with Christ in mediating God's blessings. In some sacred sense God blesses the world through our prayer. Prayer enables us to touch God's throne with one hand and the needy world with the other!

9

Prayer Can Give You Entrée Anywhere

Prayer can give you instant entrance into any home, any hospital, any government office, any courtroom in any part of the world. Just as distance cannot hinder your reach or touch in prayer, neither walls nor "no entry" signs can halt your presence or stay your hand in prayer.

Through prayer you can steady the hand of a surgeon during crisis moments as he operates on a friend or loved one. Through prayer your unseen prayer-presence can be with the loved one throughout the operation.

When Rev. Bud Robinson was almost fatally injured, suspended for several days between life and death in a hospital in San Francisco, he experienced excruciating pain in his leg. The ministers' conference of his denomination was called to pray; interrupting their session, they knelt as a group and engaged in earnest, prevailing prayer for him. At that exact time his pain left him. A day or two later he lost consciousness for a time and had an amazing vision of heaven. Interestingly, as he talked with Jesus in the vision, he saw two ministers—one standing on each side of him. They were two of his best friends, who were in Los Angeles, interceding for him at that very moment! Though miles away physically, through prayer they were at his side!

Present in Spirit

Paul, the apostle of prayer, prayed constantly for his converts and the churches he founded in many places throughout the New Testament world. Indeed, his prayer was so real and earnest he actually believed that, though physically separated from them, his spirit was with them as he prayed. Is this not in effect what Paul was talking about when he wrote the church in Corinth: "When you are assembled in the name of our Lord Jesus and I am with you in spirit, and the power of our Lord Jesus is present" (1 Cor. 5:4)? Nor did Paul hesitate to tell them that his very spirit, through prayer, would meet with them when they handled a case of church discipline (v. 5). Paul was maintaining spiritual contact through prayer.

Again, Paul wrote in similar words to the Colossian church: "Though I am absent from you in body, I am present with you in spirit and delight to see how orderly you are and how firm your faith in Christ is" (2:5). This church lived so vividly in Paul's prayer that it was as if he were right there with them.

There is a lot of cheap joking by some people who do not attend a worship service but later tell the minister they were "present in spirit." Such talk can be almost sacrilegious. Others may sincerely say to absent friends or loved ones, "We'll be present with you in spirit," but mean little more than that occasionally their thoughts will be with them. Paul meant far more than this casual comment. He so loved the Colossian Christians, so identified with them, so prayed for them in prevailing intercession that he knew it was a spiritual fact that he could be with them through prayer. This was true although he had never visited Colossae! That depth of identification in prayer is not common today. But it is gloriously possible if we walk closely with God.

Developing Your Prayer-Presence

It is fully possible for any praying Christian to achieve such unity of love and holy desire through prolonged intercession that God will grant a special unity and identity of spirit and a reality of "prayer-presence."

For some twenty years whenever I returned home from college, missionary deputation, or on furloughs from India, it seemed every time we had family prayer my mother would begin to weep tears of longing love as she prayed for the mission fields, especially China and India. That was also the way she interceded for me, and I believe her praying spirit was often with me.

That was why God could call her to intercession at the exact hours when I was confronting danger during my service in India, even though she had no knowledge that I was in trouble. She was a real prayer warrior who spent several hours a day in true intercession and often experienced the prompting of the Holy Spirit. Through her prayer identity with me, she was reaching India for Christ!

Such faithfulness results in great opportunities for serving God. Through prayer you can enter halls of justice and place your affirming hand on the shoulder of the judge. Through prayer you can place your restraining hand on the arm of a criminal or terrorist anywhere in the world. Through prayer you can place your guiding hand on the steering wheel of a car.

But you cannot breathe a half-minute prayer once a month for someone and do that. Your heart must be beating with the heart of Jesus as He intercedes. Your love must be flowing day after day with the love of the Holy Spirit. If you yearn deeply enough, if your prayer ministry is constant enough, if you are living in the Spirit and praying in the Spirit, you mediate God's blessing as truly as if you were there in body.

You probably cannot attain that unity of spirit, love, and heartbeat so as to share deeply the ministry of a large number of people. But you can come to share with at least one, or perhaps several. Shortly after we reached India my wife, Betty, received a letter from a school-teacher in South Africa. "I have always longed to be a missionary," she wrote, "but God did not permit. As I read your missionary magazine and saw your picture, God said I was to do my missionary work through you." That was God's call to her. To whom has God led you to be a prayer partner through intercession?

Who Failed to Pray?

When my wife and I were first married, we lived temporarily in my parents' home before beginning our pastorate in another state. One night each week my parents drove several miles to a country schoolhouse, where my father conducted a Bible study and prayer meeting. One evening, while they were away, my wife and I were alone in my parents' home, praying on our knees, when a sudden premonition of terrible danger swept over me. I began to plead God's mercy, lifting my hands in agony of prayer. I did not know what the danger was and thought perhaps a robber was outside our window. For ten minutes or more I could only plead the blood of Jesus and claim the name of Jesus.

Then the burden lifted. My wife could not understand what had happened to me, and said my face was as white as a sheet. She asked me what I thought it was. I replied that I did not know, only that I was sure God had delivered from some great danger.

About twenty minutes later there was a knock on our bedroom door. It was my mother. Her first words confirmed my earlier apprehension: "Oh, Wesley, God has been so merciful to us tonight! When Papa and I were driving home on the highway, the bright light of an oncoming car blinded our eyes. The car was coming at high speed straight at us. At the last moment it swerved and just missed us. When it was past, we realized that we were on the wrong side of the road!"

Explain it as you will. Perhaps it was the hand of prayer that guided the steering wheel of the speeding car and swerved it to avoid a collision. Perhaps I had touched heaven's throne, and God sent an angel to handle the situation. I do not know. But this I do know: God alerted us to intercede and at the very time of danger spared the lives of my parents to many more years of ministry. Thereafter, when I hear that a valuable servant of God has been killed in an accident, I ask myself: "Who failed to pray?"

This Amazing Privilege

There is indescribable sacred reality in prayer. We have only begun to learn the ABC's of intercession. We have hardly begun to understand what it means to be a royal priest to God (1 Peter 2:9; Rev. 1:6), a co-intercessor with Christ. God has given us the amazing privilege of projecting our love, our touch, and our presence through prayer. This is not mystical fanaticism. The people referred to in this chapter are not unreal super-saints, given to the visionary. They are down-to-earth, ordinary people, but they are great intercessors.

We must not make a hobby of the visionary or the spectacular. Neither should we fail to take advantage of the amazing privilege granted us by God. The power of prayer is still largely undiscovered and little understood by many of His dear children. We live so far below our spiritual capacity, our privileges and rights as children of God!

"Let us know, let us press on to know the Lord. His going forth is as certain as the dawn" (Hos. 6:3 NASB). "I consider everything a loss compared to the surpassing greatness of knowing Christ Jesus my Lord. . . .I want to know Christ and the power of his resurrection" (Phil. 3:8, 10).

What is your deepest desire? How intense are your spiritual yearnings? Is your consuming hunger to know Christ better, to know the sacred secret of His presence, His power, how to commune with Him and how to prevail with Him as you share His intercession? Then indeed you will begin to fulfill your role as His bride and His royal priest and co-intercessor.

10

Your King Gives You His Keys

Jesus Christ is the Sovereign of our universe. He is the Creator of everything visible and invisible—the physical world, mankind, and the world of angels (John 1:3; Col. 1:16). Every heavenly being, except the members of the Trinity, was created by Jesus. All spirit beings who fell into sin and followed Satan were once created by Jesus, and He is still their ultimate Sovereign. They do not bow to Him, but one day they will—not in submission, for it will be too late for that—but in acknowledgment that He alone is Lord. Satan and all his followers cannot exceed the bounds of the permission that Jesus gives (Job 1:10, 12; 2:6; 1 Kings 13:4). The day hastens on when Satan and all evil beings will be cast into the lake of fire and will no longer oppose God or man.

With all the newest technological tools at their disposal, men of science cannot discover the secret of the power that preserves the universe. What is the source of power that keeps the electrons in every single atom orbiting around the nucleus at a speed comparable to the speed of light? What is the power that steers myriads of stars in their heavenly courses, century after century? The Bible gives the answer. His name is Jesus (Heb. 1:3).

Jesus Christ is sovereign today. In His own words, "All authority in heaven and on earth has been given to me" (Matt. 28:18).

Jesus Holds the Keys of History

Jehovah (Jesus in His preincarnate form) twice announced in the Old Testament: "I am the first and I am

69

the last" (Isa. 44:6; 48:12). Jesus restates this truth in Revelation 1:17; 22:13. He is the First because He is the Creator of all. He is the Last because He has the final word in all. He is going to carry out His eternal plan in spite of all that men and demons may attempt to do to destroy it. Jesus is the Lord of history. He will never surrender this lordship to anyone. You can never make a mistake by placing your life in the hands of the Lord of history.

Jesus Holds the Keys of Death and Hades

Jesus is Sovereign over death and hades. He announces, "I am the Living One; I was dead, and behold I am alive for ever and ever! And I hold the keys of death and Hades" (Rev. 1:18). No disease germ, criminal, or terrorist has power over you unless Jesus permits. No storm or flood, no wild animal, no force or power can harm you without His permission.

This does not guarantee that your life will be free from suffering or that you are going to live to advanced old age. If you disregard God's laws of health and live carelessly, you will reap what you sow. You will be more prone to accidents; you will be more susceptible to disease. It does mean, however, that Jesus will not permit anything to harm the real "you."

John Wesley said, "I am immortal till my work is done." This means that as long as you are in the will of God, as long as you remain sensitive and obedient to the guidance of the Spirit, and as long as you seek to take care of your body, the ultimate control of your life and death is not in the hands of chance, natural events, other human beings, or Satan. Jesus will permit nothing to touch you except that which He can work out for your eternal good. He plans to use you now and eternally. Praise God, Jesus holds the keys of death and hades. He will surrender them to no other.

Jesus Holds the Key of David

"These are the words of him who is holy and true, who holds the key of David. What he opens no one can shut, and what he shuts no one can open" (Rev. 3:7). Christ is the Lord of all doors. The doors He opens cannot be shut by men or demons. The doors He shuts will not be forced open, though all hell conspires to attempt it. Paul recognized that it was Jesus who opened doors for him throughout his ministry (2 Cor. 2:12; Col. 4:3).

If you seek "a great door for effective work," as Paul found (1 Cor. 16:9), remember that Jesus is the opener of doors. If you need some door slammed shut in Satan's face, remember Jesus holds these keys. People may force open doors that you and I have closed, or close doors that you and I have opened, but when Jesus steps into the picture, no one can change it. Jesus will never relinquish the ultimate sovereignty over the doors in your life. He keeps the key of David.

Jesus Will Give You the Keys of the Kingdom

Though there are some keys Jesus will never surrender to anyone, He is waiting to give to you and to me the keys of the kingdom. "I will build my church, and the gates of Hades will not overcome it. . . . I will give you the keys of the kingdom of heaven; whatever you bind on earth will be bound in heaven and whatever you loose on earth will be loosed in heaven" (Matt. 16:18–19).

Jesus entrusted the keys of the kingdom to the early disciples. His message was originally delivered to Peter who had just replied to Jesus' question: "Who do you say I am?" (v. 15). Upon Peter's affirmation of His lordship, Jesus gave him (and others who would follow) incredible authority for the purpose of spreading the work of His kingdom on earth.

How did Peter use the keys? How did he bind and loose? Jesus had just pledged that He would build His church. Since He would no longer be on earth in human flesh to do the building, He was committing this responsibility to Peter and the other disciples. Christ's concern in binding and loosing was not so much with the discipline of His church as with its building and advancement.

In the account of the growth of the New Testament

71

church in the Book of Acts, prayer and witness went hand in hand as the Holy Spirit worked through the disciples.

Christ gave a key to Peter on the Day of Pentecost, and Peter stepped forward in obedience, opening the door of the church to three thousand new believers. Christ gave a key to Stephen. Stephen obeyed, and walked right into heaven. But his martyr's death influenced Saul, who became the greatest soul-winner of the early church. Christ gave a key to Philip, who opened the door of the church to the Samaritans. He gave Philip another key and sent him to the desert. Philip obeyed and, on the Gaza road, opened the door to the Ethiopian eunuch and thus to the people of Africa.

Christ gave Peter another key, and he opened the door of the church to Cornelius and, subsequently, the door of salvation to the Roman Gentiles. Christ kept giving keys to Paul as He extended His kingdom, building the church in city after city—Philippi, Thessalonica, Athens, Corinth, Ephesus, Colossae, and on and on to many unnamed cities and towns. Paul kept obeying, preaching, praying, and building the church.

Jesus needs Christians to carry on His work in every age. So important is this truth that Jesus repeated His commission a little later in the Book of Matthew, using the plural form of the pronoun *you* to include all believers who would follow Peter: "I tell you the truth, whatever you bind on earth will be bound in heaven, and whatever you loose on earth will be loosed in heaven. Again, I tell you that if two of you on earth agree about anything you ask for, it will be done for you by my Father in heaven. For where two or three come together in my name, there am I with them" (Matt. 18:18–20).

Thus, Christ continues to build His church today as His followers use the keys entrusted to them—opening doors for the salvation of others, loosing the bonds of Satan by which he fetters the lives of people, and binding the power of Satan by which he seeks to destroy believers and the church. True, the leaders of the church are instructed by God to discipline the church to help preserve the purity of the church. While these passages may refer to matters of church discipline, they surely mean much more than that. The use of the keys, the binding and loosing, are closely related to prayer and to the agreement of believers meeting together to pray.

The Greek word for the verb *agree* is *sumphoneo*, from which we get our English word *symphony*. It means "to sound together in harmony" and refers primarily to musical instruments.

When two believers "harmonize" about a matter in the unity of the Spirit, unity of desire, and unity of prayer, it sounds like the music of a beautiful symphony in the ears of God. God the Father will surely ratify and answer such a request. Why? Because where even two or three pray together in Jesus' name, Jesus Himself will be there praying with them, agreeing with them, and amen-ing their prayer.

Christ is always ready and waiting to give keys to any believer who will use them. Some seize them and get to work; others sit back and lose their opportunities. Step by step, Christ is extending His kingdom yet today. He wants to use us more fully than we have ever been used before. You and I can reach some people by our obedience. We can reach many, many more by prayer.

Christ, the Lord of history, is building His church today as fast as He can find prayerful, obedient helpers. If you and I are not faithful in using the keys of obedience and prayer, He will cease to give us new keys.

Heaven or Hell?

The initiative is now yours. But you must be aware that the eternal destiny of others—either heaven or hell—depends upon your using the keys Christ has given you.

As Jesus met with His disciples for the first time after His resurrection, He blessed them, showed them His hands and side, and said: "As the Father has sent me, I am sending you" (John 20:21). Then He breathed on them and said, "Receive the Holy Spirit" (v. 22). Immediately He gave these disciples, and all who would follow them, a most awesome responsibility: "If you forgive anyone his sins, they are forgiven; if you do not forgive them, they are not forgiven" (v. 23).

But how can this be? you ask. Is not God the only One who can forgive sins? Yes, of course. Did not Christ pay the price so that anyone who calls on Him can be forgiven? Yes, thank God! Then how can it be that the forgiveness of others is in your hands instead of God's hands?

Simply this: Christ has chosen us to bear His message to the world. He has already paid the price for all; but the only voice He will use to tell the world now is yours and mine. If you reach your friend, he can be forgiven. If you don't, he can't. If you and I reach our world, it can be saved; if we don't, it will be lost forever. Heaven or hell is now in our hands. Christ's part is done; ours is not.

This has a direct relevance to prayer. At present, many people have no chance for any Christian to reach them before they die. This is why Jesus commanded you and me to pray the Lord of the harvest to send reapers to them. Many others will have only *one* chance in their lifetime to hear, believe, and be saved. Will they miss it? Will they fail to understand? Will prejudice cause them to disregard the message? Your prayer and mine must bridge the gap. God has made us the only hope of their salvation.

Certain Muslim and communist lands are closed to missions. In these regimented and repressive societies, the gospel witness is almost entirely nonexistent. The only way people in these countries will hear the gospel message is through radio. But without the joyous witness of openly professing Christians, they may not understand its meaning. Since there is no Christian voice on their local radio station, they may never discover a Christian broadcast. Will they? Your prayer may be their only hope. Your prayer can help guide them as they touch the radio dial. Your prayer can help remove their prejudice. Your prayer can help them understand. Your prayer can help shut out Satan's suggestions of doubt. Your prayer may be the only key to unlock the door to their salvation.

Christ gives to you through prayer the keys to the salvation of more people in your circle of acquaintance and around the world than you realize. One day Christ will ask you what you did with the keys He held out to you. For how many people will you have unlocked heaven's door? For how many will you have shut out and locked the door to Satan's deceptions? Christ's only plan for building His church, for extending His kingdom is to give us the keys to heaven. Will you use them faithfully?

11

You Can Be Part of God's Emergency Prayer Network

God is constantly both receiving and issuing emergency calls. Some events, which you could not have foreseen, call for God's immediate intervention. Other situations develop to a point of crisis. While God is never surprised, for He foresees all, you and I interpret these as emergency needs.

Christ is enthroned at God's right hand today, ruling the world through His intercession and the intercession of His earthly prayer partners. When such needs arise, God at times chooses to prepare for them in advance by calling His children to pray. At other times He sends an emergency call at the exact hour of need.

God's Children Constitute
His Emergency Prayer Network

This emergency prayer network is constantly available to you and me. It is also dependent upon you and me. Usually God alerts someone who already knows you to pray for you, thus strengthening that person's faith as well as your own.

Let me give you an example. During my college days I was counseling and praying with another student concerning an urgent situation known only to this student and me. An oppressive spiritual darkness weighed heavily upon my friend. For several days I spent every spare moment in prayer and counseling, but, for some reason, it was a real prayer battle for which there seemed to be no victory.

During that time I received a brief postcard from an evangelist who knew me well. He wrote: "Dear Brother Wesley, As I was praying for you I suddenly seemed to see you on your knees in prayer. I could see Jesus standing in front of you with His arms outstretched to you, but you did not seem to see Him. I thought to myself, how often is God so near to us, anxious to answer our prayer, and we don't realize it." God had alerted him to pray just when I needed it.

Sometimes we do not know why we are burdened, only that we have received a special prayer constraint from the Lord, a sense of call and responsibility to pray at a given time.

In August of 1962 I concluded ministry in Australia with four days of meetings in the Scarborough Baptist Church in Perth. God began to burden me to spend all day Saturday in prayer and fasting. Early Saturday morning I found a secluded spot on Scarborough Beach and began my time alone with God. As the day progressed I entered into a tremendous prayer battle with the powers of darkness. I knew not why, but the Holy Spirit led me into real militancy of prayer against Satan, and in the service that night I felt led to speak on "The Power of Satan and the Power of God."

En route to the service, my voice suddenly left me. I had prayed silently all day, so had not abused my voice, and I had no cold. When I rose to my feet to speak, I moved my lips but could not make a sound. The congregation gasped. Seizing both edges of the pulpit with my hands, I strained and strained. After a little while my voice began to return, but it seemed as if I were pushing every word over the pulpit where it fell to the floor. There was no liberty or blessing, and at the close of the service, the people silently left the church.

One woman, a stranger to me, stayed behind. She told me she knew she had been born again six months before. Having practiced black magic, however, she now felt the demons would not leave her alone. They visibly gathered around her bed each night and hooted at her. In righteous indignation I prayed with her and claimed victory. She was completely delivered from Satan's oppression.

In the service the next morning, it seemed as if all heaven opened to us. The spiritual needs of many were met, and some were called to the mission field. At the close a demon-possessed man, trembling from head to foot, was delivered as the pastor, deacons, and I prayed. He was the husband of the woman set free the night before. Unknown to me, for the past six months, the deacons had had a covenant of prayer for that man. The Holy Spirit called a prayer alert at the crisis time. Satan tried to interfere, but Jesus won the victory. To Him be all the glory!

How to Join God's S.O.S. Prayer Network

1. Be sure you are filled with the Spirit. This assurance is foundational to everything in the spiritual life. While any Christian can be led and used by the Holy Spirit, it is so much easier to hear His voice when He is in complete control of your life. Every born-again Christian is indwelled by the Holy Spirit (Rom. 8:9), but not every Christian lives a Spirit-filled, Spirit-controlled life.

You cannot live such a life until you enter into it. The believer must make a "total surrender" (the term Andrew Murray preferred)—a total consecration of himself and his all to God (Rom. 12:1–2)—and must ask for the Spirit's fullness (Luke 11:13), trusting for His cleansing, empowering, and filling (Acts 15:8–9). Any Christian living today can be as Spirit-filled as the early apostles, if the same commitment is made (Acts 2:38–39). This is not a matter of special manifestations of the Spirit; it is a matter of surrendering your will.

Whenever you see a believer struggling with the will of God, defeated by carnal longings and ambitions, hampered by a stubborn self-will, and reacting carnally toward his family or others, you know he is not living a Spirit-filled life. Either he has never been filled with the Spirit or, through disobedience and withdrawal of consecration, he is not now living in the fullness of the Spirit. Normally, once you have been filled by the Holy Spirit, the Spirit will fill you again and again as you have need.

2. *Develop a deep prayer life.* The more you experience the life of prayer, the more God is able to use you at special times of need. God is constantly needing real prayer warriors. You learn to pray by praying. Though book knowledge about prayer is beautiful, you gain confidence and strength in prayer only as you pray. Put into practice the principles of prayer, and the Spirit will give you increasing liberty and boldness in intercession as well as increased opportunities.

3. *Develop a conversational relationship with the Lord.* Repeatedly tell the Lord how you love and adore Him. Punctuate your day with praise. Share your joy with Him. In the quiet of your soul thank Him for each blessing of the day—sunshine, beauty, smiles, friends, song, His help in your work. Ask God to bless people you notice, pass, or meet. As you do your work, walk along the way, or drive your car, whisper to the Lord in your heart, without others knowing anything about your frequent communication with your wonderful Lord. Live in His presence.

4. *Develop a listening ear.* It is your privilege as a child of God to be led by the Holy Spirit (Rom. 8.14). Have you developed the habit of listening to God? No Christian ever masters this lesson, but God can help you develop a listening ear. May God make these suggestions a blessing to you:

a. Make sure you maintain your commitment to the Lord each day and live in the Spirit's fullness.
b. Ask God to teach you how to listen to Him. Prayer is not true communion if you do all the talking.
c. As you begin each day, ask God to speak to you whenever He desires throughout the day. Ask Him to help you recognize His voice.
d. Read your Bible, expecting God to speak to you and bless His Word to your heart. Read it for personal blessing and His suggestions as to how you can please Him more and how you can do His will more fully.
e. Ask God to guide and help in even small things. Anything that is important to you is important to

Him. Ask Him to help you be a blessing to others as you meet them, speak to them on the phone, or write letters. Ask God to show you little things to do for Him and others. You can ask Him to guide you in your purchases, your attitudes, your contacts, your work, as well as in your prayer life.

f. Relax and trust Him to guide you constantly (Isa. 58:11). Don't be fearful, afraid you will miss God's will. You are His child; rest in His faithfulness. Don't jump to conclusions. Don't expect to hear a voice or a sign from heaven. God's guidance is such a normal part of His dealings with you that He is often at work when you are most unaware.

g. Observe how God coordinates providence for you. Do not fret if He permits delays or blocks your plans. His way is best. He wants to work all things together for your good and His glory. He always knows what is highest and best. Don't struggle against God's providence; just relax in His loving care for you. God can open a way where there was none before, but you will never have to force open a door.

5. *Ask God to keep you alert each day.* Each morning ask God specifically to bring to your attention any person or situation for which you should pray. Keep prayer lists, for God may impress you to add others with special needs. The lists will serve, also, as a chronicle of answered prayer! Daily be sensitive to any new prayer assignment God may point out to you. As you go through your day, pray immediately for anyone or anything God brings to your mind.

6. *Accept responsibility for any special prayer burden God gives.* Assure the Lord each day that you will try to be faithful to bear any prayer burden He gives you. Treat it as a special trust from the Lord.

How to Recognize God's Prayer Assignment

God may impress someone indelibly on your mind. This may happen at your prayer time or at some other time during the day. If you have told God of your willingness, and a person keeps coming to your mind, that person probably needs prayer. This may happen only occasionally, but the more closely you walk with God and become attuned to His voice, the more frequently God will use you in this way.

You may feel a special presentiment or apprehension of danger or need. Go at once to the Lord. If at all possible, pause in the midst of whatever you are doing. As you pray, God may bring some person or situation to your mind. If not, just pray for God's help and mercy for whatever the need may be. As I mentioned in chapter 9, God called me to prayer on one occasion when my parents were in danger, though I had no idea what the danger was.

On December 12, 1939, while praying about the outcome of World War II, I became especially burdened for a particular situation. The *Graf Spee,* a German merchantman that had been converted into a "pocket battleship," was sinking many merchant ships with much loss of life. That night I felt God's special authority as I asked Him to intervene. The next day radio news announced that the *Graf Spee* had been chased into the harbor of Montevideo, Uruguay. After several days, the ship was brought outside the harbor and scuttled. No life was lost except that of the commander, who chose to go down with the ship. God probably put the same prayer burden on the hearts of many others at the same time He gave me that burden. But I had the joy of knowing that God had called me to prayer alert and that He had specifically answered that prayer.

Mrs. Hulda Andrus, the mother of Corporal Jacob DeShazer, one of the men shot down in the Doolittle raids over Tokyo during World War II, has recounted how God burdened her to pray. She did not know where her son was stationed. "I awakened suddenly one night with a strange feeling like unto being dropped down, down, down through the air. Oh, the terrible burden that weighed my soul! I prayed and cried out to God in my distress. Suddenly the burden was gone." Later she was informed that her son had been shot down and was in

Japanese hands. Comparing the time, she found that God had alerted her at the exact time her son parachuted from his falling plane.

At another time, God gave her a great burden for the salvation of her son. Again, as she prevailed in prayer, God reminded her of the promise of Isaiah 55:9. At that very time God spoke to Jacob in his prison cell, and he surrendered his life to Christ.

One day the news reports announced that these prisoners were going to be executed. As she cried to God, He seemed to say, "his angels watch over him," and again the burden lifted. Of the four men captured, three were executed by a firing squad, but DeShazer was spared through God's miracle. God not only saved her son, He called him to preach. After the war, DeShazer went back to Japan, where he was greatly used by God as a missionary.

God may give you a sense of urgency for a need you know well. You may have prayed repeatedly for a particular need, but now you are impressed that God must answer prayer without further delay. The prayer burden may be for a physical healing, the salvation of an unsaved person, the restoration of unity to a group of divided people, or revival in a particular place. God may keep a general burden on your heart for days and then at some point guide you to set apart a special time for prolonged urgent prayer.

One of the members of the Board of Directors of OMS International had a backslidden son who had once been an OMS missionary. The son had left the field and gone into secular work, where he remained unrepentant and far from the Lord. Our leader carried a deep prayer burden for his son for some months. One day he was in deputational meetings in a distant state. The prayer burden became so heavy that he asked his hostess not to disturb him that day or call him for meals. He shut himself in his room and prayed hour after hour. In the afternoon there was a knock on the door. With apologies for interrupting him, she said, "There is a long distance call for you." The father went to the phone, and the first words he heard were: "Dad! I've come back to the Lord!"

God may progressively deepen some prayer burden until it becomes your permanent assignment. God needs permanent intercessor-watchmen for churches, missions, cities, nations, and ministries. "I have posted watchmen on your walls, O Jerusalem; they will never be silent day or night. You who call on the Lord, give yourselves no rest, and give him no rest till he establishes Jerusalem and makes her the praise of the earth" (Isa. 62:6–7). God announces that He has posted prayer watchmen. Undoubtedly, Isaiah himself was one of these, for he says in verse one, "For Zion's sake I will not keep silent, for Jerusalem's sake I will not remain quiet, till her righteousness shines out like the dawn, her salvation like a blazing torch." You can be one of God's prayer watchmen.

Every full-time Christian worker needs a prayer team standing with him, strengthening him, and covering him with intercession. Every Christian ministry needs a burden-bearing team of prayer warriors. The effectiveness of any such ministry will depend upon the godliness of the team and the power of prayer that is marshaled behind it. God will bless any person or ministry as prayer support is deliberately enlisted and the prayer partners kept carefully informed and guided in prayer. Blessed is that person or ministry that has not only enlisted the aid of prayer helpers, but has intercessor-watchmen who carry a continual burden for the ministry.

This was the secret of the ministry of Charles G. Finney, whose ministry resulted in hundreds of thousands turning to the Lord and whose meetings in 1858–59 were called a direct cause of one of the world's greatest revivals. Finney was himself a mighty man of prayer and had many praying for his ministry. In his twenty-two famous lectures, "Revivals of Religion," four of them are on the role of prayer.

As Finney traveled from place to place, he was accompanied by two elderly men known as Father Clery and Father Nash. When he went to Britain for several weeks of special meetings, these two men of ordinary means went also, rented a dark, damp basement room for twenty-five cents a week and stayed there on their knees, prevailing in prayer. Their tears and groans in prayer prevailed. They were Finney's intercessor-watchmen.

When Evan Roberts was so mightily used of God in the great Welsh revival of 1904–1905, he had behind him a small group of young people who served as his intercessor-watchmen. One of my treasures is a post card from Evan to one of the young people on this burden-bearing team.

How to Make Your Prayer Burden Effectual

When God entrusts you with a special prayer burden, accept it with joy and be faithful to it. It is a special commission from the Lord.

1. Give the prayer burden priority over all else. If at all possible, put aside what you are doing and give yourself entirely to prayer for this need. Often time is of the utmost importance; do not delay. If you cannot immediately set yourself apart for this prayer burden, keep praying for it every spare moment until you are free to cease all else and go to prayer.

2. Be prepared to pray for hours. This is not always necessary, but be so diligent in prayer that you intercede as long as it takes to receive the assurance of God's answer.

In the 1930s a dear friend of mine, a barber in Oklahoma, was a zealous witness for the Lord. One afternoon he felt strongly impressed to pray for the salvation of the deputy sheriff of his county. He closed his barbershop in the middle of the afternoon, pulled down the blinds so people could not see inside, and went to an inner room to pray.

All the rest of the afternoon, through the supper hour, and into the night George Sherrick prayed on. At about two o'clock in the morning someone pounded on the door. No one knew George was in his shop at that hour of the night. When he went to the door, there stood the sheriff for whom he had been praying, under deep conviction of the Holy Spirit. That night George Sherrick led him to the Lord.

3. *Pray until God lifts the burden or gives you assurance He has heard.* In about 1949 a group of retired missionaries from China, with a few faithful praying friends, met for their regular missionary prayer meeting in Adelaide, South Australia. A great prayer burden and sense of urgency came on them as they gathered together. All felt especially burdened for Hayden Melsap, then assigned to the China Inland Mission. They unanimously decided to drop all preliminaries and go "straight to prayer." They prayed until they all felt a sense of peace and relief.

A few years later, when Hayden Melsap was on deputation in Australia, the missionaries asked him if he recalled any unusual occasion at that time. To their amazement, they found that on that day and hour Hayden and at least two other missionaries were backed against a wall in a courtyard in China, with communist guns leveled at them. Just as the officer was about to issue the command to fire, the door of the courtyard opened and a higher official entered. Shocked to see what was about to happen, he shouted, "Stop!" He then stepped up, put his arm around Melsap, and led him and the others to safety. I heard this testimony from Hayden Melsap himself and also have it in writing from an Australian friend.

4. *God may lead you to enlist the prayer of several others.* Many a miracle has been brought to pass by the Holy Spirit in answer to a chain of prayer or the prayers of a specially convened group. Many local churches have arranged S.O.S. prayer chains. When an emergency prayer request comes in, five or six people are immediately called. Each, in turn, calls the next person on his list. In a matter of minutes, many are at prayer. We have such an arrangement among our OMS headquarters staff.

During the Mau Mau uprising in Kenya in 1960, missionaries Matt and Lora Higgens were returning one night to Nairobi through the heart of Mau Mau territory, where Kenyans and missionaries alike had been killed and dismembered. Seventeen miles outside of Nairobi their Land Rover stopped. Higgens tried to repair the car in the dark, but could not restart it. They spent the night in the car, but claimed Psalm 4:8: "I will lie down and sleep in peace, for you alone, O Lord, make me dwell in safety." In the morning they were able to repair the car.

A few weeks later the Higgenses returned to America on furlough. They reported that the night before they left Nairobi, a local pastor had visited them. He told how a member of the Mau Mau had confessed that he and three others had crept up to the car to kill the Higgenses, but when they saw sixteen men surrounding the car, the Mau Mau had left in fear. "Sixteen men?" Higgens responded. "I don't know what you mean!"

While they were on furlough a friend, Clay Brent, asked the Higgenses if they had been in any danger recently. Higgens asked, "Why?" Then Clay said that on March 23, God had placed a heavy prayer burden on his heart. He called the men of the church, and sixteen of them met together and prayed until the burden lifted. Did God send sixteen angels to represent those men and enforce their prayers?

Heaven will reveal many wonderful accounts of how God has used special prayer burdens to advance His cause and protect His people.

12

You Can Sow with Tears

"Those who sow in tears will reap with songs of joy. He who goes out weeping, carrying seed to sow, will return with songs of joy, carrying sheaves with him" (Ps. 126:5-6).

Tears are precious in the sight of God when they are tears of longing, shed in intercession, or tears of joy as you praise God for answered prayer. The Son of God knows what it means to weep in prayer. The shortest verse in the Bible, "Jesus wept" (John 11:35), not only speaks volumes about the love and compassion of Jesus; it also explains the relation of tears to the intercession of Jesus. He who weeps *with* us wept *for* us as He wrestled with the powers of darkness in the Garden (Heb. 5:7).

Let us make very clear that we are not talking about tears of self-pity. Such tears can be basically carnal. They may give relief from tension, for "a good cry" often helps the mood of a discouraged or depressed person. But recurring tears of self-pity give no testimony to spiritual depth or power. We are here discussing the power of tears resulting from deep spiritual desire.

You should never be ashamed of tears shed in loving intercession. In fact, they testify to God of the depth of your identity with those for whom you intercede, the intensity of longing which underlies your intercession, and serve as a testimony of the Holy Spirit praying through you. Tears add a personal and private dimension of poignancy and power.

Such weeping intercession is much more likely to

occur when you are alone with God. Normally, our private prayer can be more deep and intense than our public prayer. Tears are so intensely personal that the praying soul can weep more naturally and freely when only God is the witness to the tears. It is possible, however, to have a weeping spirit even when no literal tear runs down your cheek. God looks on your heart above all else (1 Sam. 16:7).

Your tears, like your words, are very important. However, God sees and knows you as you really are (2 Sam. 7:20; John 21:17). God knows the secret depths of your longing even better than you can express it. By deeply identifying with those for whom you pray, seek to deepen your heartcry to God. But do not seek to produce outward tears. That would be hypocritical. Welcome the tears when the Holy Spirit gives them, but seek only to feel in your innermost heart the depth of yearning which the Spirit feels.

When It Is a Time to Weep

At times, God calls us to weep (Eccl. 3:4). This is His call to empathy, to vicarious intercessory identification with others. At such times, we must be sure to pray "us" prayers and not "them" prayers. We must identify with those in need, rather than condemn and accuse. Instead of praying, "Lord, forgive them for being so cold," we should pray, "Lord, forgive us as a church for being so cold. Help us to be more loving, help us to pray more, help us to be more effective for You."

For several reasons, I believe our current world situation is one that calls for weeping:

We should weep because humanity has forsaken God! The nations have forgotten God (Ps. 9:17). They do not want to retain the knowledge of God (Rom. 1:28). They show contempt for God's constant kindness, tolerance, and patience (Rom. 2:4). Often they are hardened by God's judgments and their reaping of what they have sown (Rom. 2:5; Rev. 16:21). We should weep for our world: "Lord, forgive our wayward race!"

We should weep because sin is multiplying! Evil people are going from bad to worse, deceiving and being deceived (2 Tim. 3:13). The sins listed in 2 Timothy 3:1–5 are all too evident: loving self rather than loving God, boastfulness, pride, abusiveness, disobedience to parents, ungratefulness, unholiness, lovelessness, unforgiveness, slander, lack of self-control, brutality, despising the good, treachery, rashness, conceit, love of pleasure more than love of God. All these, combined with the gross sins of sexual perversion, rape, and pornography, have hardened our national conscience. Crime has escalated. Terrorism, sadism, and calculated cruelty have reached unimaginable proportions. War is ever more terrible, and peace seems constantly precarious. Man seems on the verge of destroying himself. How can we but weep: "Lord, have mercy on our sinful race!"

We should weep because as a church we are too lifeless and powerless! We can thank God for the dedicated believers in many parts of the world, and for what He is doing through them. But the world has lost its respect for the Christian church in general, for we do not bring glory to God as we should.

We have the "reputation of being alive," but all too often we are spiritually dead (Rev. 3:1). We lack the power that should witness to the world of spirituality and godliness (2 Tim. 3:5). There is a drifting or departure from sound doctrine, and false cults are multiplying (2 Tim. 4:3–4). Too often our spiritual condition is typified by the Laodicean church; we do not realize how lukewarm, pitiful, spiritually impoverished, spiritually blind, and spiritually naked we appear to God (Rev. 3:17). What a small percentage of good evangelical churches are really characterized by revival, by constant soul-winning by the majority of the membership, and by sacrificial involvement in missionary enterprise. We need to weep for ourselves: "Lord, revive us again!"

We should weep because we as God's people are spiritually asleep. "Do this, understanding the present time. The hour has come for you to wake up from your slumber. . . . The night is nearly over; the day is almost here" (Rom. 13:11–12). It is a shame that we have been sleeping in harvest (Prov. 10:5). We have largely lost the witnessing, soul-winning passion of the early church. We are upset by blatant sins, but fail to be disturbed by Christians who have never won a soul to Christ, by Christians whose prayer is mostly self-centered and who seldom weep for the world. Earth's largest and whitest harvest since Pentecost is here, and we live a life of "business as usual"; we tend only to play church and to treat missions as a mere hobby instead of as the major task of the church. May God move us to tears: "Lord, awaken me, and stir me and my church again and again!"

We should weep because Christ's coming is so near and our task so incomplete! Among the conditions stated in the Scriptures as necessary to occur before our Lord returns, only one appears to be lacking: "This gospel of the kingdom will be preached in the whole world as a testimony to all nations, and then the end will come" (Matt. 24:14). The great assignment Christ gave to His assembled disciples as the representatives of the church of the ages was to reach the whole world. Probably one-fourth of all the people in the world have never even heard the name of Jesus Christ. At least one-half of them would not be able to make an intelligent decision to receive Him as their personal Savior. Cold statistics may not move us, but we should remember that each number represents a real individual who will spend eternity in either heaven or hell.

Some years ago, while I was serving as a seminary principal in India, my students and I spent a field term going from village to village with the gospel message and Christian literature. We made it a practice to camp occasionally in the villages in order to witness and minister to the people.

One night at a village meeting, I read the Christmas story from Luke 2. As I began to speak, an old villager seated on the ground interrupted me. "How long is it since that great day when God's Son was born?" I told him it had been approximately two thousand years. He pointed an accusative finger at me. "You say you have known for nearly two thousand years! Who has been hiding that Book all this time?"

How would you have answered him? If he were your brother, what kind of excuse would you have accepted for his not having been given a single chance to be saved? What will God accept as an adequate excuse for our not making this an earnest daily prayer burden? The condition of our world should often drive us to tears. One of my most precious memories is of my mother weeping day after day as she prayed for the salvation of comparatively unreached nations. "Lord, give us tears as we pray!"

Those Who Have Wept

Job testified, "Have I not wept for those in trouble? Has not my soul grieved for the poor?" (Job 30:25). Moses and others of the children wept over the sin of their people (Num. 25:6). David testified as to how he wept and fasted for God's people (Ps. 69:10). Isaiah wept for the need of his people (Isa. 16:9). God told King Josiah: "Because your heart was responsive and you humbled yourself before the Lord . . . and because you tore your robes and wept in my presence, I have heard you, declares the Lord" (2 Kings 22:19). When Ezra wept for his people, they began to weep and pray also (Ezra 10:1). Nehemiah "sat down and wept [for Jerusalem]. For some days I mourned and fasted and prayed before the God of heaven" (Neh. 1:4).

Jeremiah was known as the weeping prophet because of the great prayer burden he carried for his people. "Since my people are crushed, I am crushed; I mourn. . . . Oh, that my head were a spring of water and my eyes a fountain of tears! I would weep day and night for . . . my people" (Jer. 8:21; 9:1). "If you do not listen, I will weep in secret because of your pride; my eyes will weep bitterly, overflowing with tears" (13:17). "Let my eyes overflow with tears night and day without ceasing; for . . . my people has suffered a grievous wound, a crushing blow" (14:17). "My eyes fail from weeping, I am in torment within, my heart is poured out on the ground because my people are destroyed" (Lam. 2:11). "Streams of tears flow from my eyes because my people are destroyed. My eyes will flow unceasingly, without relief, until the Lord looks down from heaven and sees. What I see brings grief to my soul" (3:48–51).

Paul, the great missionary apostle, was also known for his ministry of tears. "I wrote you out of great distress and anguish of heart and with many tears" (2 Cor. 2:4). "You know how I lived the whole time I was with you. . . . I served the Lord with great humility and with tears" (Acts 20:18–19). "Remember that for three years I never stopped warning each of you night and day with tears" (20:31).

God Calls Us to Pray with Tears

God called through the prophet Joel, "Return to me with all your heart, with fasting and weeping and mourning" (Joel 2:12). He calls Christian leaders to pray with tears for their people: "Let the priests, who minister before the Lord, weep between the temple porch and the altar. Let them say, 'Spare your people, O Lord.' . . . Why should they say among the peoples, 'Where is their God?'" (2:17). God knows and records our tears: "List my tears on your scroll—are they not in your record?" (Ps. 56:8). Our day is similar to that faced by Isaiah, "The Lord, the Lord Almighty, called you on that day to weep" (Isa. 22:12).

It will take more than tears to make prayer effective; but a burdened heart, a soul crying out to God, is the very essence of intercession. It is a spiritual crime to be calloused while the world goes to hell. It is spiritually criminal to pray casually, dry-eyed and burdenless, while a world is in sin and pain. It is Christlike for your heart to weep with those who weep (Rom. 12:15). It is Christlike for you to be so filled with loving compassion that you pray with tears for those broken, fettered, and destroyed by sin.

Prayer is not recreational or arbitrary for the Christian. Prayer is the very business of Christ's kingdom. Prayer is joining with God the broken-hearted Father, Christ the weeping High Priest, and the tender, interceding Holy Spirit by sharing their heartbeat and bearing with them the same burdens which they carry in their loving hearts.

To pray with tears is to make an eternal investment. To pray with tears is to sow your tears for eternal harvest. No tear shed in burdened intercession for others is ever forgotten by God, unrecorded, or in vain. Intercession watered with your tears is one of the most powerful forms of prayer known. As surely as God is in heaven, "Those who sow in tears will reap with songs of joy. He who goes out weeping, carrying seed to sow, will return with songs of joy, carrying sheaves with him" (Ps. 126:5–6). Let this poem I wrote while in India speak to you.

Give Me Tears

Give me tears in my eyes, loving Lord,
    I pray;
Give me tears when I intercede.
Give me tears when I kneel at your
    throne each day;
Give me tears till I learn to plead.

Nail-pierced Lord, break this cold stony
    heart of mine;
Melt my heart with Your holy fire.
Flood my soul with the passion of love
    Divine;
May I hunger with Your desire.

Take the callousness all from my
    heart again
Till I hunger and thirst and yearn,
Till the longing for souls of sin-ruined
    men
All-consuming within me burn.

Fill my heart with Your tears; there
    unveil Your cross
Till all else of this world has died,
Till all else in this world I shall count
    but dross
Save the cross of the Crucified.

May my heart be a crucified heart always,
That it bleed for the souls of men.
May the burden for souls melt my soul
    each day
Till I share Your travail again.

Give me tears when I preach of Your
    dying love;
Give me tears when I plead with men.
Give me tears as I look to Your
    throne above.
Love of God, melt my heart again.

13

You Can Deepen
Your Prayer
by Fasting

Why has the mouth of the church so often been closed on the subject of fasting? How has Satan managed to silence so many Christian leaders today on this subject? Though fasting is clearly taught and practiced in both the Old and New Testaments, I do not recall having ever heard any other person give a full message on this subject.

Moses twice fasted for forty days (Deut. 9:9, 18) till his face shone with the glory of God. Joshua fasted after the defeat at Ai (Josh. 7:6). In the time of the judges (Judg. 20:26) and in the time of Samuel (1 Sam. 7:6, 12), all Israel fasted. David fasted before he was crowned, when his child was ill, when his enemies were ill (Ps. 35:13), and because of the sins of his people (69:9–10). Jehoshaphat and his people fasted till God said, "You will not have to fight this battle" (2 Chron. 20:17). They won by fasting and praise, without one hour of fighting or bloodshed. Elijah, Ezra, Nehemiah, Esther, Daniel—all were known for their fasting.

Fasting was a powerful God-blessed strategy of the early church, and in the lives of many of the leaders God raised up. Paul prayed with fasting in every church (Acts 14:23). One cannot found New Testament churches in any other way.

Epiphanius, Bishop of Salamis (born A.D. 315), wrote: "Who does not know that the fast of the fourth and sixth days of the week are observed by the Christians throughout the world?" In the thirteenth century, Francis of Assisi went through the streets of Italy singing, preach-

95

ing, testifying, praying, and fasting until thousands of the youth were saved. Martin Luther was criticized for too much fasting. John Calvin fasted and prayed till most all of Geneva was converted, and there was not a house without at least one praying person. John Knox fasted and prayed until Queen Mary said she feared his prayers more than all the armies of Scotland. Latimer, Ridley, Cranmer, in fact, most of the reformers, were known for their fasting added to their prayer.

John Wesley fasted twice weekly until tea time in the pattern of the early church. He urged all of his followers to do the same. He said he would as soon curse and swear as not fast, for "the man that never fasts is no more in the way to Heaven than the man who never prays." Jonathan Edwards was mighty in fasting and prayer. Some say he fasted to the extreme until he was almost too weak to stand in the pulpit, but he moved New England for God. Charles G. Finney, mightily used of God in revival in the 1800s, fasted regularly each week. Whenever he detected some diminution of the Spirit's presence in his meetings, he would spend three days and nights in prayer and fasting. He reported that, afterward, the Holy Spirit would again invariably move in power and the revival would proceed. Dwight L. Moody, at times feeling a special need in his campaigns, would send word to Moody Bible Institute to call faculty and students to a day of fasting and prayer. Often they would pray until two, three, four, or even five o'clock in the morning. "If you say I will fast when God lays it on me, you never will," he said. "You are too cold and indifferent. Take the yoke upon you."

Fasting is rather widely practiced on our mission fields today. Like every other God-ordained religious practice, fasting can be misused or abused. This will be discussed in later paragraphs. But fasting is still God's chosen way to deepen and strengthen prayer. You will be the poorer spiritually and your prayer life will never be what God wants it to be until you practice the privilege of fasting.

This is a time of spiritual warfare for people and nations, but carnal Christians prefer a parade. It is a time for unity, but carnality pulls for self. We need Spirit-energized action, but the carnal self prefers speeches. It is a time of fasting, but our people prefer feasting (Isa. 22:12–13).

The Christian age began with people counting nothing their own (Acts 4:32), but great power and great grace fell upon the church. Today we grasp for more and more for ourselves; we want to have the latest conveniences and material possessions. We do not understand the spirit of fasting or the bearing of the cross of Christ. For the joy of harvest, Paul toiled, prayed, and fasted and shook the Roman Empire for Christ. For the joy set before Him, Jesus endured the cross (Heb. 12:2) and provided eternal salvation for all who would believe in His name.

The Spiritual Role of Fasting

Biblical fasting is a form of self-denial for the sake of Jesus and His kingdom. It is a deliberate abstinence from some or all food for a spiritual purpose. It demands a deep level of commitment and sacrifice. While fasting for health reasons can at times be physically beneficial, that is not what we mean by Christian fasting. Fasting in the biblical sense is choosing not to partake of food because your spiritual hunger is so deep, your determination in intercession so intense, or your spiritual warfare so demanding that you have temporarily set aside even fleshly needs to give yourself to prayer and meditation.

The spirit of fasting can also be applied to sleep. Christ often fasted from sleep in order to spend more time alone with the Father. You can fast from sleep for the same reasons you fast from food. Many of the 105 OMS church-planting teams today fast from food monthly or even weekly, but many also fast from sleep in an all-night of prayer at least once a month. At times they are joined by their new converts. The same spiritual hunger, burden, and concern that inspire fasting from food underlie fasting from sleep.

A deliberate withdrawal from the fellowship of friends and family for a time in order to devote yourself more fully and exclusively to fellowship with God and intercession is true fasting. When our fellow believers in Korea fast for a period of forty days, they often go apart to a special mountain "prayer house" or "prayer retreat center." There they combine fasting from food, fasting from normal social intercourse, and often fasting from sleep, at least part of the time.

All-day prayer retreats could combine fasting from both fellowship and food, that is, if the time is primarily spent in prayer. Unfortunately, the only kind of prayer retreat many people know about is characterized by singing, listening to messages, and eating, with only a token time of intense intercession. Christ sent His disciples away at times to give Himself more exclusively to prayer (Matt. 14:23). At other times He excluded all but the three (Peter, James, and John) or all but the Twelve (Matt. 17:1; Luke 8:18).

In an even broader sense, fasting is any deliberate self-denial and abstinence for the purpose of becoming spiritually stronger and advancing the work of the kingdom of God. You can fast from your own ambitions, desires, and plans, from legitimate pleasures, rights, and joys, and from comforts and luxuries. John Wesley, while being shown through a nobleman's house, admired the expensive works of art and other symbols of wealth and culture. "I too could love these things," he said. "But there is another world."

At the heart of the gospel is a cross. The spirit of Christ is a spirit of self-sacrifice. The cross, self-sacrifice, self-denial, and fasting are all interrelated. It is the spirit of putting God first, of seeking God's kingdom first, of putting priority on God's will and eternal goals, of taking up your cross daily and following Christ. At the heart of the sanctified life is a crisis of crucifixion, of self-surrender, and of total commitment followed by a crucified life. The Spirit-filled believer should find joy in fasting for kingdom goals.

Fasting Can Be Abused

At times in the history of the church, there have been false ascetic emphases, and we must continue to guard against mistaken motivation or even excesses. Evangelical churches, however, are in far greater danger of neglecting the will of God and the blessings of fasting as a means of grace than they are of going to excess. Any means of grace can become a danger if it becomes an end in itself.

Do not fast to earn God's blessing. There can be a subtle danger in thinking that if you pray enough, God will be sure to answer, or if you fast enough, God will pay attention to your prayer. God's ear is always open to you; God's heart is always gracious. You can never earn the salvation of another, God's blessing upon your work, or revival in the church. These cannot be earned by ritual acts or by frantic activity; they are the gifts of His grace and mercy.

Do not fast as a substitute for obedience. Isaiah 58:1–11 clearly presents God's exhortation to His people who were fasting as a means of bribing Him. Instead, they were encouraged to stop quarreling, to correct injustice, to help the poor and needy, and to lift the burdens of others if they expected God to answer when they prayed and fasted. "You cannot fast as you do today and expect your voice to be heard on high" (v. 4).

If God convicts you of some sin of omission or commission, that sin will block your prayer until you make it right. Your fasting cannot bribe God to overlook disobedience. God prefers obedience to sacrifice, but obedience plus sacrifice pleases Him even more.

Do not fast to impress others. Zechariah's message to Israel echoed that of Isaiah: Fasting does not automatically bring God's blessing, and injustice and lack of mercy and compassion can invalidate fasting. The children of Israel had been observing this practice more to impress men and God than as a means of seeking God.

Christ taught that when you fast (please note, not "if" you fast, but "when" you fast), you are to do it secretly, and not like the hypocritical Pharisees who did not wash their faces or put oil on their faces in order to impress others with their piety. Fasting is to be done unto the Lord. Other people may or may not ever find out.

Do not let fasting become a mere form. Just as baptism, the observance of the Lord's Supper, the reading of the Bible, or tithing can become empty rituals for many Christians, so prayer and fasting can become mere form. Any means of grace can degenerate into an end in itself. The remedy is not to stop the practice, but to do all out of deep love and devotion unto the Lord.

Do not fast as a form of legalism. Any practice taught by the Bible can become legalistic bondage. You can be bound by the amount of time you spend in prayer, by the amount of money you give to God's cause, or even by your attendance of church services. The answer lies, not in discontinuing the practice, but in loving the Lord so much that you want to use every means possible of drawing closer to Him.

Self-discipline is not legalism. Self-discipline can help you establish specific times for prayer, an approximate minimum amount of time spent in prayer, the use of prayer lists, and times for adding fasting to prayer. Be prepared, too, for Spirit-directed times of fasting and prayer which will be unscheduled and unexpected. These can be among your richest experiences. If you only pray when you feel like it, or fast when you feel like it, you will grow spiritually weak and miss the great blessings God longs to give you.

How to Fast unto the Lord

1. Fast to please the Lord. Fast because you want to draw nearer to the Lord. Fast because He is so precious to you that you want to give Him a costly gift. Fast because He suffered so much for you that you gladly choose to enter into the spirit of His cross. Fast because you love Him and want to love Him more and more. In Zechariah 7:5, God asked, "Was it really for me that you fasted?" God treasures your fast when you fast to please Him.

2. Fast in response to God's call. In both the Old and New Testaments, fasting has been a distinguishing mark of piety among men and women, lay persons and special servants of God. In the Old Testament the prophet Joel exhorted: "Declare a holy fast" (Joel 1:14; 2:15). In the New Testament, Jesus Himself made it clear that He expects His people to fast (Luke 5:33–35).

We are called to worship God, and fasting is specifically called "worship" in Luke 2:37 and Acts 13:2. If you never fast, something may be lacking in your worship.

3. *Fast to humble yourself before God.* In the Bible, fasting is often associated with repentance (1 Kings 21:27; Ps. 35:13). But there is more to fasting than its use in the initial stage of repentance; you will need to humble yourself before the Lord again and again as David did (Ps. 35:13). Fasting can enable you to feel the emptiness of your heart, your inadequacy, your need of God. "God . . . gives grace to the humble" (James 4:6). Fasting is one way to humble yourself under God's mighty hand (1 Peter 5:6).

4. *Fast to seek God's face more fully.* You are to love God with all your being — all your heart, all your soul, all your understanding, and all your strength (Mark 12:30, 33). "You will seek me and find me when you seek me with all your heart" (Jer. 29:13). Fasting is a sacred way to seek God with all your heart.

Christ taught us that, in order to receive heaven's answers, we must "ask . . . seek . . . knock" (Matt. 7:7). Each word indicates a deeper level of intensity. Fasting, too, indicates an intense desire to seek God. The hunger to see God and His mighty work can be so great that one loses the desire for food. It is also possible by deliberate fasting to intensify the desire of your heart, even though you may experience physical hunger.

5. *Fast as a holy discipline of your soul.* John Wesley also believed and taught that we may seek God's face through prayer and fasting. He placed such emphasis upon putting method into one's walk with God that Wesley's early followers were called "Methodists."

A disciple of Jesus is a disciplined follower. Regular habits of prayer and fasting are a natural part of the spiritual life of those who follow Him. They provide a regular method for drawing near to God, examining yourself before God, and entering more fully into the life of intercession. It is a precious way to take up your cross and follow Jesus (Matt. 16:24).

Remember that the apostolic methods are still valid today. Satan hates fasting, but God honors fasting. In this missionary age in which a militant church must win strategic battles for the Lord, accept again God's strategy of adding fasting to prayer.

14

You Have
Prayer Authority
through the Cross

Christians should rejoice again and again in the glorious triumph of Christ on the cross. Not till we reach heaven, however, will we fully realize the eternal significance of the cross for ourselves and for the whole world. In God's plan the cross of Christ ceased to be an instrument of torture and shame and became His greatest glory.

Do you remember how Jesus showed His disciples the nailprints in His hands and feet and the spear mark in His side (John 20:20, 27)? In His resurrected body He still wears these marks of the price He paid for our salvation. I believe that you will someday have the joy of fellowshiping personally with Jesus and that He will show you, as He did His early disciples, His nail-pierced hands. Revelation 5:6 assures us that, throughout all eternity, Jesus will continue to bear the evidence of His sufferings on the cross as His unique badge of honor.

Let me share with you something of the glory of Christ's triumph. It is essential that you understand so you can more effectively bind Satan in your prayer battles and win new victories over him.

The Kingdom of Satan

Satan, the archenemy of God and the church, has his own evil kingdom. He rules over fallen angels, demons, and sinners who, from God's viewpoint, are children of the Devil (John 8:44). The fallen angels are not permitted to be active today. They are imprisoned in the darkness of Tartarus (the Greek word for "hell" in 2 Peter 2:4), bound with everlasting chains (Jude 6), awaiting their judgment day.

The demons, however, are very active today. The Greek word for demon, *daimon*, is completely different from the word used for a fallen angel, *angelos*. Demons are also called unclean spirits, *pneumaton akatharton* (Acts 5:16), and evil spirits, *pneumata ta ponera* (19:12–16). We do not know their origin, but God does not create evil beings; so they, like the fallen angels, were obviously holy at one time, becoming sinful by their own choice.

In his inveterate opposition to God and man, Satan is very dependent on the demons. God is omnipresent, while Satan can be in only one place at a time. God is omniscient, while Satan must depend upon information he receives from his demons. But Satan is the deceiver of the whole world (Rev. 12:9), the father of all lies (John 8:44). Just as he teaches his demons to lie, no doubt *they lie to him*, for Satan often seems to act on inaccurate information. God is omnipotent, while Satan has limited power and usually has to work through one or many demons.

Satan is anti-God, anti-Christ, anti-church, anti-Christians, and anti-mankind. He does not love his own; he despises and hates them. His only way to strike back at God is to harm someone loved by God, so he constantly tries to hinder, harm, and damn people. When we speak of binding Satan, we mean binding Satan's power, which is usually exercised through demons.

How Satan has organized the demons in his kingdom of evil we do not know. Scripture uses a number of terms for spirit beings, and often in a way which indicates they are under Satan's dominion. Here are some of the terms in the Greek, along with references where they may be found:

archai	rulers (1 Cor. 15:24; Eph. 1:21; 3:10; 6:12; Col. 1:16; 2:10, 15)
exousiai	authorities (1 Cor. 15:24; Eph. 1:21; 3:10; 6:12; Col. 1:16; 2:10, 15)
dunameis	powers (Rom. 8:38; 1 Cor. 15:24; Eph. 1:21)

kuriotēs	dominions, lordships (Eph. 1:21; Col. 1:16)
thronoi	thrones (Col. 1:16)
archōntes	leaders, princes (1 Cor. 2:6)
kosmokratōres	world rulers (Eph. 6:12)

These terms may refer to different ranks of authority, different backgrounds, or different assignments under Satan. The important thing is that all these beings are limited in power, knowledge, and scope of activity. All were defeated by Christ at the cross. All know they are awaiting their judgment, to be followed by their eternal punishment (Matt. 8:29).

Satan and All Evil Spirits Were Defeated at the Cross

Have you realized how total was Christ's victory at Calvary? It was a victory for us because Jesus took our place, bearing our sin on the cross. He paid the price for our redemption. He fulfilled the Old Testament prophecies and all the Old Testament types. Every sacrifice for sin from Adam onward was accepted by God upon the condition of the final, perfect, and holy sacrifice of Christ on the cross. So every sacrifice accepted by God from a repentant sinner was like one more debit, one more promissory note which Jesus guaranteed to pay. Praise God! On the cross He paid it all! Calvary was an eternal victory for whoever wills to receive it (Rev. 22:17).

It was also a victory for God's plan. His original plan for eternal fellowship with man will one day be reinstated on a new and righteous earth (Rev. 21:1). All that man lost in the Fall will be restored because of Calvary. Sin, suffering, tears, death, the curse—all that entered the world through man's fall into sin—will be removed forever (21:4–5, 25; 22:3, 5).

God's eternal plan was interrupted by Satan. This interruption has lasted for several thousand years. That seems a long time to us from the viewpoint of our life on earth, but from God's viewpoint, it is but a brief moment. This satanic interruption will be terminated by the triumphant return of Christ. His second coming will be possible because of Calvary. The vast unending ages of eternity will so outdistance and overshadow the interruption of Satan and sin for these few thousand years of time that, when we reach heaven, sin's reign will seem like a bad dream.

But for Satan, Christ's victory at Calvary was a devastating, total, and eternal defeat. At first, Satan thought he had won; that shows how limited his knowledge and understanding are. In reality, the cross destroyed Satan, sin, death, and all of Satan's kingdom. It did not annihilate Satan or his fallen spirits, the multitude of demons. They will be tormented forever and ever in the lake of fire (Rev. 20:10). Hell was prepared for Satan and his evil beings. Man goes to hell only because he allies himself with Satan and refuses to repent and be delivered from sin by the atonement Christ provided at Calvary (vv. 14–15). Let us note the pictorial language the Bible uses to illustrate Satan's ignominious defeat at Calvary:

At the cross, Jesus drove out Satan, "the prince of this world" (John 12:31–33). Today Satan is a usurper. The cross passed initial judgment on him. His claims were destroyed; his claimed authority was invalidated. His defeat was so complete that he has lost his place and authority. The Greek word *ekballō* means "to drive out, expel." The cross doomed Satan to ultimate expulsion from our world, though he is still active and desperate in his anger and futility. He is the *archōn*, the ruler of this age only until God enforces the judgment of the cross after Christ's return.

At the cross, Jesus "disarmed the powers and authorities" (Col. 2:15). The word *disarmed* is from the Greek *apekoyo,* a double compound meaning "to put off completely, to undress completely and thus render powerless." At the cross, Christ undressed all demon authorities. It is a picture from the ancient oriental custom of stripping the robes of office from a deposed official. At the cross, the leaders and authorities of Satan's forces and kingdom were stripped of their authority and honor. They now have no authority to oppose, intimidate, or harass you.

But that is not all; there is even more in this picture. Paul says Christ "made a public spectacle of them, triumphing over them by the cross" (v. 15). This again is an illustration taken from ancient history. When a conquering emperor returned from a great victory, he was often given a triumphal procession. The victor and his army marched through streets lined by cheering thousands. While the musicians played, chariots and soldiers carried the looted treasures of the defeated king, and he and his general or other selected prisoners were led in chains, their shame openly displayed.

The Greek word *edeigmatisen* means "to make a public exhibition." During the interval between Christ's death and resurrection, when He announced (*ekarussen*) Satan's defeat at the cross to the evil spirits in prison (1 Peter 3:19), in symbolism Christ marched triumphantly through the spirit prison, with Satan and his demonic rulers chained in inglorious defeat behind Him. He made a public spectacle of their defeat, says Paul, and now every demonic being knows his cause is defeated forever, his satanic lord's authority stripped from him, and his own doom waiting for the appointed time (Matt. 8:29).

At the cross, Satan and his unclean spirits were destroyed (Heb. 2:14). The word *destroy* is from the Greek *katargeo*, which means "to put out of action, to make useless." It is used repeatedly to show how through the death and the return of Christ (*parousia*), the powers of destruction that threaten man spiritually are put out of action. In 1 Corinthians 15:24, this includes all dominion of demonic authority and power. In verse 26, death itself will be the last enemy to be rendered useless. All these are "coming to nothing," including Satan himself (Heb. 2:14) and his demonic leaders (1 Cor. 2:6).

As a result of Calvary, the Resurrection, and the Ascension, Christ is enthroned. "He is raised far above all rule and authority, power and dominion. . . . And God placed all things under his feet" (Eph. 1:21–22). These terms for heavenly beings may include both the holy angelic beings and the fallen ones, now the demons. The term "footstool for your feet" (KJV) emphasizes that the unclean spirits are also included, for this phrase is a quotation from Psalm 110:1 in which they are termed Christ's enemies. Christ is seated at the right hand of God, far above all heavenly beings of whatever rank, and certainly above all fallen spirit beings of whatever rank. Potentially, these fallen beings are "under his feet," for they have already been defeated. But they are bluffing as if they were still undefeated, trying to assert their dominance over us.

The metaphor of the footstool is illustrated by Joshua 10:24, which depicts a scene in which Joshua's commanders placed their feet on the necks of the defeated enemy kings before they were slain. Jesus will one day place all these defeated spirits under His feet, and under ours also, since we are His victorious warriors. Then He will have them cast into hell.

These demonic beings know they are defeated and what their end will be; that is why they fear us and our prayer so much. They know we have authority from Jesus. But when you resist them in His name and power, they will not only back away, they will actually flee from you (James 4:7).

In summary, Satan may roar like a raging lion, trying to frighten you, but he is a defeated usurper. He has no right, standing, authority, or legal place in your life.

a. He is being expelled, driven out by Jesus (John 12:31).
b. He is disrobed and disarmed and has been made a public spectacle as a defeated foe in Christ's triumphal procession. Christ has displayed the disgraced Satan as His prime trophy, revealing to all beings in heaven and hell that Satan has lost (Col. 2:15). The counterfeit roaring lion has been defeated by the true Lion of the tribe of Judah, Jesus Christ, Son of Man, beloved Son of God (Rev. 5:5).
c. His power is destroyed, and he and all his forces are put out of action as far as any true power is concerned (Heb. 2:14; 1 Cor 2:6; 1 Cor. 15:24).
d. He and all his demonic cohorts are put under Jesus'

feet potentially and will soon be put there absolutely (Eph. 1:21–22). In fact, he will be actually crushed (*syntribo*) beneath your feet also (Rom. 16:20). *Syntribo* means "to break to pieces by crushing"—a total, crushing defeat.

Thus, Jesus says to us, as He said to His disciples, "I have given you authority . . . to overcome all the power of the enemy; nothing will harm you" (Luke 10:19). Unworthy though we are, we should humbly but confidently accept this authority, acting upon Christ's glorious victory at Calvary as we defeat and bind Satan's power in His name.

15

You Must Use
the Command of Faith

Mountains are used in Scripture to symbolize strength and stability. They are also used to represent massive difficulties and seeming impossibilities. While God promises to move or overcome some mountains for His children, there are others that God commands you to move. He will not move them until you give the command. Thus, there are two types of "mountains" in Scripture.

Some mountains of difficulty are meant by God to bless you. "I will turn all my mountains into roads" (Isa. 49:11). These are God's mountains. He permits them. He directs you along a path that leads to them. They are intended for your spiritual good. They may slow down your progress, but they will build your spiritual muscle, strengthen your faith, and develop your skill in prayer as you learn to prevail until God's answer comes. Some are so massive, so difficult, that they may only be moved when several believers unite with you in a prayer of agreement.

These are God's mountains, even though they do not seem that way to you. He has permitted them temporarily to block your way. He will teach you deep spiritual secrets as you face them, persevering in prayer. At times you may grow weary as you pray, but at the proper time—God's perfect time—you will reap if you faint not (Gal. 6:9).

One of my beloved Bible teachers had an oft-repeated saying: "God's clocks keep perfect time." God is never early, never late. His schedule is always best. After God's mountain becomes His highway you may discover why God delayed in answering your prayer. In some cases you must wait till you reach heaven before your questions are answered. Trust God; He knows what He is doing. But you may be sure of this: When God permits a mountain to block you from reaching His destination, He is preparing a miracle. God turns all His mountains into roads.

Satan often erects roadblocks which become mountains barring your way. This is a very different kind of mountain from the one described previously. The longer you pray about these mountains, the more convinced you become that the delay is not of God. The more you pray, the more certain you become that you are involved in a spiritual conflict with the demon powers of darkness. It is Satan and his forces that block your way in an attempt to hinder the work of God and dishonor the name of Jesus.

You can almost hear Satan taunting you, mocking you; you can almost see him opposing you. But can Satan stop a child of God? Yes, he may be able to delay you for a time. Repeatedly he prevented Paul from reaching Thessalonica (1 Thess. 2:18), but eventually Paul returned to minister there (Acts 20:1–2).

God may permit Satan to delay you in order to work out some higher purpose, but God does not want Satan to stop you altogether. God wants you to move the mountain. He does not want you to abandon the place He gave you or the advance steps He pointed out to you. These are demonic mountains, not God's mountains. They are to be moved.

But how are you to move them? You would naturally expect Jesus to tell you that, when you face such mountains, you should pray until God removes them. There are some problems which may only be resolved through prayer (Mark 9:29). But Jesus has given us another tool which, when combined with prayer, will remove obstacles. He says: "I tell you the truth, if you have faith as small as a mustard seed, you can say to this mountain, 'Move from here to there' and it will move. Nothing will be impossible for you" (Matt. 17:20).

111

This truth was so strategic for His kingdom's advance that Jesus repeated in even stronger words: "I tell you the truth, if you have faith and do not doubt, not only can you do what was done to the fig tree, but also you can say to this mountain, 'Go, throw yourself into the sea,' and it will be done. If you believe, you will receive whatever you ask for in prayer' (Matt. 21:21–22).

In the first instance (Matt. 17:20), a father had brought a demon-possessed boy to the disciples while Jesus was on the Mount of Transfiguration. Because they were spiritually unprepared, the disciples were unable to cast out the demon, and their failure brought disgrace to the name of Jesus. In the second instance (Matt. 21:21), Jesus cursed the barren fig tree and it immediately withered up. The fig tree was a sham. Jesus was teaching that Satan's works—no matter how large or how small—need to be withered up.

The Command of Faith Is Biblical

The exercise of Christ's authority is sometimes referred to as "the command of faith." This truth is taught by symbol and example in the Word of God. God wants His children to use the authority He has given us. The staff of Moses was a symbol of his authority as the representative of God to Pharaoh. During Moses' conflict with the demonic powers behind the magicians and gods of Egypt, Moses sometimes prayed to God. At other times he was told merely to use his staff.

God told Moses to stretch out his staff and strike the water of the Nile, and the water turned to blood; to stretch out his staff, and the frogs came on Egypt; to stretch out his hand and strike the dust with his staff, and the dust turned to gnats; to stretch out his hand toward the sky, and the huge hailstones fell; to stretch out his hand, and the locusts came and devastated the land; to stretch out his hand, and for three days and nights, there was no light from sun, moon, or stars (Exod. 7–10). When Israel came to the Red Sea, Moses began to pray. "Why are you crying out to me?" (14:15), God asked him. He told Moses to stretch out his staff over the sea, and the waters parted and the people crossed over on dry land. Sometimes continued prayer indicates a lack of faith. God wants us to give the command of faith and go forward.

Elijah was a mighty man of prayer, but there were times when he was led to use the command of faith. He told the widow at Zarephath to prepare a meal for him first, and she would have a miracle supply of food that would last till the famine was over (1 Kings 17:8–16). He told Ahaziah's rude captain, "If I am a man of God, may fire come down from heaven" (2 Kings 1:10). The fire appeared and consumed the captain and fifty men. When Elijah and Elisha reached the Jordan River, Elijah did not pray. Instead, he smote the water and the Jordan rolled back like the Red Sea had done for Moses. When Elisha returned after Elijah's ascension, he also smote the waters of the Jordan, and they parted for Elisha too (2:14).

Jesus repeatedly demonstrated and used the command of faith. In Cana of Galilee, the scene of His first miracle, He simply commanded the servants to fill the water pots with water. He commanded the lepers, "Be clean." He touched blind eyes and said, "Be opened." He commanded deaf ears, "Be opened." To the paralytic, He said, "Get up." He touched feverish bodies, leprous bodies, even dead bodies, and the miracle happened. At the grave He commanded, "Lazarus, come forth." He rebuked evil spirits, and they came out. He rebuked the wind and said to the stormy waves, "Quiet, be still!"

The apostles also practiced the command of faith. At the gate of the temple, Peter commanded the leper, "In the name of Jesus Christ of Nazareth, walk." To the paralyzed Aeneas, Peter said, "Get up." To Dorcas, who lay in death, "Get up." To the sorcerer Elymas, Paul said, "You are going to be blind!" And he was. At Lystra Paul called to the man lame from birth, "Stand up on your feet." To the demon enslaving the girl at Philippi, Paul ordered, "In the name of Jesus Christ I command you to come out of her." The spirit instantly left her (Acts 16:18).

113

When Should You Use the Command of Faith?

The command of faith is not an optional spiritual power that you may use at will to make life easier for yourself, to remove all your trials, or to vent your spite on the Devil. It is a very deliberate exercise of Christ's own authority and name in a situation where His glory is at stake, where His kingdom is being hindered, or where Christ calls you to demonstrate His power to prove He is the living God. As an official representative of Jesus Christ, you may always use it, though implementing your command may require the help of His holy angels.

But may it not be used in cases of self-protection? Yes, there are legitimate emergencies when God's children have rebuked a person intent on robbery, rape, or physical attack. Because you are the child of God, you are under His protection. Similarly, you may be led of God to command the elements in Jesus' name as did John Wesley when an approaching storm threatened to disrupt his preaching to an open-air crowd. Notice, however, that Wesley did not appropriate this power for his own comfort or convenience, but for the purpose of promoting the gospel.

The command of faith is not an alternative to prayer. It is an additional step of obedience which normally grows out of prevailing prayer or prayer warfare. In an emergency you may not have time for protracted prayer, but must call instantly on Jesus' name. Normally, however, the command of faith is an element of offensive prayer warfare as you invade Satan's territory, attack Satan's roadblocks, or confront satanic resistance. The following are examples of occasions when God may lead you to use the command of faith:

- To command Satan to be gone from an area
- To command Satan to stop agitating opposition to the gospel
- To command Satan to lift his demonic darkness with which he is blinding a person, family, or village
- To command Satan to stop binding the will of a person who is hesitating to follow Christ
- To command Satan to lift depression and leave a person in peace

114

- To command Satan to keep his hands off a person or family
- To command Satan to stop confusing a new believer
- To command Satan to quit oppressing a child of God
- To command Satan to stop afflicting a person with illness
- To command Satan to get behind you when he approaches you with vile temptations
- To command Satan to stop inciting division among God's people
- To command Satan to cease working his counterfeit signs, wonders, and miracles
- To command Satan to stop frightening believers with his lionlike roar
- To command Satan to restrain his demons
- To command demons to leave a person
- To command illness to depart
- To command the elements to cease for a period of time
- To command a criminal to stop or go

You Can Give the Command of Faith

You need not be a supersaint to give the command of faith. Even new Christians may be empowered to perform miracles in the name of Jesus.

I have known of new believers in India who had never seen a demonstration of Jesus' power suddenly capable of casting out demons. In a cottage prayer meeting held by one of our new church groups, when no pastor or missionary was able to be present, a Hindu neighbor heard them singing and came to the door.

"We have visitors from out in the district," he said, "and they have a demon-possessed woman with them. Can you do anything to help us?"

"Bring her in," the Christians replied instantly. "Our Jesus casts out demons."

The demon-possessed woman was brought in, the new believers cast out the demon in Jesus' name, and the Hindu group left.

A month later a messenger arrived from the Hindu

115

village about sixty miles away, requesting that the Christians send someone to teach them. "We have never heard of a God with power like this," they said. Our evangelists responded, and many were won to Christ because of the evidence they had seen with their own eyes. On one day more than eighty new believers were baptized. I had the personal joy of dedicating the mud-walled church building that they erected for worship.

F. J. Huegel in his splendid book, *The Enthroned Christian*, tells of a Christian boy, the son of a national pastor, who in the absence of his father cast out a demon from a person who was brought for help. He explained he had seen his father do it, so he knew how. The demons had to obey the command of even a Christian child when he commanded in the name and authority of Jesus.

Don't let the Devil convince you that you have no power or right to use the God-ordained command of faith. Huegel goes so far as to suggest that Christ's teaching on the command of faith is so clear that it should hold the same place in the life of the ordinary believer as prayer!

Prerequisites for Using the Command of Faith

There are essential prerequisites before anyone can safely and successfully execute the command of faith. The unregenerate, nonbelieving sons of Sceva tried to use it and were physically attacked and wounded by a demon-possessed person (Acts 19). The prerequisites are very simple:

You must be a true child of God. Any born-again believer has the authority to use Christ's name in prayer, praise, and command. Christ gives this authority to His own children only.

You must have in your life nothing grieving the Spirit of God. This authority is executed under the supervision of the Holy Spirit. Your lips speak the words, but the Holy Spirit and God's angels actually enforce them over Satan, his demons, and whatever else must yield to God. If angelic help is needed, God will take care of that. But if you hide unforgiveness or some other sin in your heart (Ps. 66:18; Matt. 6:15), do not expect the Spirit's help.

116

Your command must be in harmony with the will of God. You must not attempt to use this power for selfish ends. As a member of Christ's kingdom, you may reap the benefits, but your goal must be to glorify God and advance His kingdom. The only exception is an emergency when your safety is threatened. You and your body belong to God, so you are free to use Christ's name to protect yourself from imminent danger.

How can you know the will of God? Some life situations such as trial, sickness, or persecution may or may not be the clearly revealed will of God, though God may permit them for His ultimate glory. You may be sure, however, that other things are always in God's will—the salvation of a sinner, the growth of His church, the penetration of Satan's darkness by the gospel light. In those situations in which we are not sure, it is as we prevail in prayer, perhaps even wrestling with the powers of darkness, that we come to a Spirit-given clear conviction of God's will. If we then perceive that Satan is hindering, we are authorized to rebuke him through the command of faith.

How to Prepare Your Heart for More Effective Commands

1. Be filled with the Spirit. You can realize your greatest spiritual potential only when you are filled with the Spirit. As explained in chapter 11, this experience demands total commitment of the self to God, trusting Him to fulfill His promise. As you continue to live in the Spirit, you can be refilled again and again.

Too many Christians live in the flesh and are powerless to live a consistently victorious Christian life. God may help such defeated believers in emergencies, but to live the enthroned life and to be instantly ready to give the command of faith requires daily living in the fullness of the Spirit. If you have reneged on your commitment to Christ, you need to renew your consecration and be filled with the Spirit once again.

2. Face your mountain. Don't try to pretend it doesn't exist. Accept the reality of the mountain and focus your

117

attention on the nature of the obstruction. Recognize the hand of Satan behind it. Perhaps the Devil is using good people whom he has deceived. Your enemy is not flesh and blood, but the demonic forces behind the problem. Perhaps you see a pseudo-mountain of Satan, or a pseudo-growth like the fruitless fig tree that Jesus rebuked. The Spirit can wither all false growth that encumbers and disguises the true situation. Don't fear Satan's bluff. Face your need and expect God's answer.

3. *Live in the spirit of faith.* Don't be afraid. How many times Christ said, "Fear not!" Doubt gives the Devil a foothold; do not give him that advantage (Eph. 4:27). God's promises are for you. God knows the situation better than you do. Live in an attitude of expectancy, just waiting to see how God is going to handle the problem. The mountain may have taken you by surprise, but God is never surprised nor unprepared.

Remember, Satan has already been defeated at Calvary. You have not only died with Christ and been resurrected with Him, but also have spiritually ascended with Christ and are now enthroned with Him. "And God raised us up with Christ and seated us with him in the heavenly realms in Christ Jesus" (Eph. 2:6).

Don't look up at your mountain with fear. Look down on it from your place beside Jesus! Look down from the throne upon Satan, your defeated enemy. "The God of peace will soon crush Satan under your feet" (Rom. 16:20). Rejoice in your victory in Christ; live in the triumph of faith. Expect God to take charge of the situation and guide you in moving the mountain.

4. *Discern the will of the Lord.* You need God's wisdom and guidance in dealing with the entrenched forces of Satan. Don't rush into battle until God has given you His plan. Before each battle David looked to God for fresh directions. God rarely works in exactly the same way twice. In 2 Samuel 5:18–20, David in effect asked, "Am I the one to attack? Is this your assignment to me?" Again he asked, "When and how should I attack?" Each time God directed him (2 Sam. 5:22–25).

Pray until you feel you have discerned God's will as to

how to confront the mountain, when to confront the mountain, and at times with whom to confront the mountain. It may be a situation in which God wants several of you to agree in faith before you issue the command of faith.

As a Spirit-filled believer, you have a right to God's guidance (Rom. 8:14). The Lord can guide you constantly (Isa. 58:11). He wants you to understand His will (Eph. 5:17). It is more important to Him than to you that you take every step correctly.

5. *Take a special step of faith.* You are already living in faith, seated with Jesus far above all the forces of Satan. God has given you His directions. Now it is time to take the initiative; it is time to act on your faith. Don't tremble before your "Red Sea." March across it on the dry land the Lord will provide for you (Exod. 14:15).

Don't falter before your "Jericho." March around it in faith, expecting God to tell you when to give the shout of faith, and your "Jericho" walls will come tumbling down (Josh. 6:20).

Jesus said, "I will build my church, and the gates of hades will not overcome it" (Matt. 16:18). Actually, this statement can be interpreted in two ways. It is true that in Christ you are so secure that Satan can never run over you, trample you, seize you, or destroy you. All the demonic forces that he might send out of the gates of hell cannot overcome you.

But it is also true that God wants you to do more than sit in your fort or hold your battle line against Satan. He wants you to attack. This verse can also be interpreted to mean that the gates of hades will never be able to hold out before you. God does not intend you to be passively trustful; He wants you to be militantly believing! He wants you to storm the very gates of Hades and rout the Devil. He wants you to dislodge the forces of Satan from their long-entrenched positions.

Satan will attempt to intimidate you as long as you will let him. Lay down your barrage of prevailing prayer, and then take the initiative and drive Satan out of his stronghold—whether that be in the life of a person, a family, or in any other kind of situation. Don't stay on the defensive; take the offensive for Jesus. Advance, praising the Lord!

6. *Give the command of faith.* Jesus instructs us clearly as to the words we are to use in issuing this command. "I tell you the truth, if anyone says to this mountain, 'Go' . . . it will be done for him" (Mark 11:22–23). Speak to your mountain in Jesus' name. Take the authority Jesus has given you as His official representative. Speak from your position with Jesus on the throne. You have prayed and have determined God wants the mountain to be moved. You are sure it is His time. God has given you the steps of faith. Go forward and speak boldly to the mountain; command Satan to take his forces and go.

Tell Satan he is guilty of shedding the blood of Jesus. He has sinned the unpardonable sin. He has sinned against the Son of God. He has sinned against the armies of heaven. Millions of angels are ready to attack him. He was defeated at the cross; he is forevermore defeated. Tell him so. Just as Jesus said, "Out of my sight, Satan!" (Matt. 16:23; Mark 8:33), so you must tell him to be gone.

Demons fear Jesus' name. Use it. Praise His name till the demons fall into such confusion that they hinder each other like the enemies before Jehoshaphat's army (2 Chron.20:22–23). Use Jesus' name as your mighty weapon. Dare to penetrate the darkness and dislodge Satan by the name of Jesus and the command of faith.

Be God's Zerubbabel. "What are you, O mighty mountain? Before Zerubbabel you will become level ground" (Zech. 4:7). Be God's David. David told the giant Goliath, "I come against you in the name of the Lord almighty . . . whom you have defied" (1 Sam. 17:45). Others may flee from Goliath; you face him in the name of the Lord. God says of your mountain, "I am against you, O destroying mountain. . . . I will stretch out my hand against you" (Jer. 51:25). You have God's promise. Now tell the Devil you come in the name of Jesus Christ, the Son of God, who defeated him at Calvary. In that almighty name, command him to leave.

16

Your Prayer Can Help Prove That Christ Is God

In nations where other religions have been dominant for centuries, Christ needs to prove that He is truly the living God. An individual or a family hearing the gospel for the first time might well be confused. How are they to know which is the truth? In some ways their plight may be compared to that of persons living in Old Testament days at the time Israel had backslidden into idolatry. When God raised up a prophet, how were the people to know that he was sent by God?

False prophets contradicted true prophets; false gods competed for the allegiance of the hearts of people. Jehovah often validated the true prophet or the truth he taught by means of miracle. These were basically of two kinds—miracles of knowledge (prophecy) and miracles of power.

Today Christian pastors, evangelists, missionaries, and even new believers are again facing this dilemma. When the gospel penetrates a new non-Christian area, how are the people to be made willing to listen to the message? How can they be aided in leaving the religion of their fathers and turning to what others may consider "the foreigner's God"? Such a decision often results in open persecution for the new believer—social ostracism, loss of home and job, denial of further education, and even physical harassment and threatened death.

In these circumstances, Christ must somehow prove Himself to be the living God. As in Bible times, when pagan religions were a major influence, demonstrations of Christ's supreme presence and power are necessary before converts can be won. Your prayer has a vital role in helping Christian workers in such difficult places. Your prayer can join with theirs for the opening of the eyes of the non-Christians to the reality of Christ. Your prayer can help bring those answers to prayer which will make the non-Christians willing to listen to the gospel and believe.

The Contest in Bible Times

In Egypt, when God's people were living in bondage to the Pharaoh, the power encounter was between the magicians and gods of Egypt on the one hand and Moses and Aaron as the representatives of Jehovah on the other. Using Moses and Aaron as His spokesmen, God sent ten overwhelming demonstrations of His power, the ten plagues, to prove that He was the only true and living God. The Egyptian magicians countered with tricks of their own. Were these seemingly paranormal demonstrations sheer chicanery, or were they demonstrations of limited demonic power? From what we know on mission fields today, these displays may well have been demonic.

God knew that the Israelites needed tangible evidence of divine power to lead them out of the idolatry in which they had been ensnared. The plagues were followed by supernatural manifestations of God's power until Israel was settled in Canaan. There was the miraculous parting of the Red Sea, the daily provision of manna during the forty years of wandering in the desert, the miraculous supply of water from the rock, the amazing revelation of God's power at Sinai, the visible reminders of God's presence with them in the pillar of cloud that led them by day and in the pillar of fire each night. God condescended to meet the need of the children of Israel on their own level. He knew that they needed miracle, and He gave it to them.

Samuel, Elijah, and Elisha were validated as true prophets of God by supernatural demonstrations of His power. Even in the time of the Old Testament kings, He did not hesitate to prove Himself the living God.

In the time of Christ, God validated His Son by the voice from heaven and, later, through miracles performed by Jesus. Jesus told His listeners that if they would not believe His words, they should at least believe because of His miracles (John 14:11). In the New Testament church Jesus continued to confirm His reality by miracles as the apostles and Paul confronted pagan religions and demonic power.

You and I may not need miraculous signs and wonders in order to believe the gospel. In our nation there has been a long history of gospel light. But the followers of other religions are in a completely different situation with which it is hard for us to identify. Christ is prepared to come to them and validate His gospel. He does not hesitate to prove to needy people that He is the only true and living God.

The Prevalence of the Demonic in Non-Christian Religions

The Bible teaches that the origin of false doctrines (1 Tim. 4:1) and the origin of all false religion is demonic (1 Cor. 10:19–20). This explains the frequency of demon possession among people of false religions and the strong demonic opposition to missionary work in so many places throughout the world.

In a sense, all sinners are children of the Devil (John 8:44); hence, they are much more susceptible to Satan's suggestions, often without even realizing it. It is not surprising, therefore, that Satan takes advantage of "natural" human emotions. He kindles the anger of family and friends against a new convert, whom they believe has been deceived by a false or foreign religion. He arouses suspicions, jealousies, hatred, and all forms of opposition against gospel workers penetrating a non-Christian society with the gospel. He precipitates persecution, threats, and even murder.

Added to this is the demonstration of actual demonic power through the words and works of witch doctors, voodooists, and some of the leaders of non-Christian religions. This power is present at times in some of the cults in our own country, but usually not to the same extent as in ancient non-Christian religions.

Such people by their occult and demonic powers try to curse Christian believers and workers in an attempt to hinder, injure, or destroy them. Your prayer is needed to claim Christ's protection for these Christians who become special targets of Satan.

An illiterate OMS convert in Indonesia, on fire for the Lord, taped his testimony along with a brief Bible exhortation. He then returned to his home island, playing the cassette tape from door to door as a form of personal evangelism. This aroused intense opposition and threats to his life.

One day, as the new Christian sat in an open-front shop with his cassette player, he saw a ball of molten metal flying through the air. The object entered the shop and fell at his feet. (This phenomenon is not unknown among the practitioners of black magic in his area and is usually fatal to the one against whom it is used.) He waited till the red-hot metal had cooled and then picked it up and went to the house of a worker of black magic, who he knew greatly opposed his Christian witness. He confronted this man, opening his hand and showing him the still-warm mass of metal. The magician leaped to his feet and shouted, "Tell me the secret of your power!" The convert immediately testified that Jesus had all power, power over all demonic forces.

During our first term in India, it seemed that every time I left home for an extended evangelistic or ministry trip, Satan attacked my family through accident or illness. These incidents became so frequent that my wife would say as I left, "Well, I wonder what will happen this time." I would assure her that God would protect the family, that Christ's blood would cover them, and not to fear or worry. But invariably, each time I was away, something would happen. This continued until some time later, when a church in London prayed one night. Afterward, the chain of incidents stopped for fifteen years. Other missionaries have given similar testimonies.

Such happenings are hard to explain, but they remind

us that we are in a constant state of spiritual warfare. Your prayer is daily needed by God's faithful ambassadors on the front lines of missionary service.

Answers to Prayer Can Prove That Christ Is God

When a missionary, national co-worker, or believer witnesses to followers of other religions, how are these people to be convinced that Christ is truly the only living God?

One of my senior Indian co-workers never used the name of God alone when speaking or witnessing. He always said "the living God"—"the living God says...," "the living God sent His only Son," "the living God answers prayer." He felt it must always be clear that the God about whom we witness is like no other god or concept of God.

For those who have had so little opportunity to know Him, the living God is willing to demonstrate His reality. One of the ways He chooses to do this is through answered prayer. Pastors, evangelists, and other believers in many nations are seeing God prove His miracle power in answering the needs of the people to whom they are witnessing.

Each month I receive reports from our evangelistic teams telling how non-Christians have come to them, asking for prayer for special needs. As God proves His living reality, the word gets out that the Christian's God answers prayer. Again and again this opens the door for the gospel, and many are saved. As I read these reports, I often feel I am back in New Testament times.

For example, there are accounts of the miraculous healing of illness and infertility. Though we hold no healing campaigns, when such requests for prayer are made, our teams honor them. Many non-Christians, seriously ill for prolonged periods of time, have as a last resort come to our missionaries. They report that they have made pilgrimages from temple to temple, but have gotten no better. When prayer is offered by some member or members of our team, healing comes. This dramatic occurrence often leads to the evangelization of whole families as they become convinced that Christ is God and that God answers prayer.

Every home in India wants a child. Often the couple has prayed and made offerings in the pagan temples, sometimes traveling great distances, all in vain. Again and again we hear their pleas, "Can your God help us?" The team goes to the home, holds a prayer meeting, and asks God to bless that home with a child. And repeatedly there are reports that, in due time, a child is born and the whole family turns to Christ. Our co-workers never hesitate to accept such a challenge to prove that Christ is God.

One of the most dramatic proofs of God's sovereignty is in the casting out of demons. In these ancient societies, the non-Christians are very conscious of the reality of demons. In the case of longstanding instances of demon possession, it is widely known that the pagan religions and religious leaders have been unable to help. At times the demons cause the indwelled persons great distress. In desperation these demon-possessed people are brought to our evangelistic teams, and their non-Christian friends and relatives plead for any help our Jesus can give. When the demon is cast out, one or many of the amazed onlookers turn to Christ.

These kinds of supernatural answers to prayer, in which Christ encounters and defeats satanic forces, are often called "power encounters." Christ proves He is alive by answering prayer as no other god can do.

Your Prayer Can Help to Vindicate Christ

An effective prayer life is one of the most important qualifications for any missionary, pastor, or evangelist in front-line missionary endeavor. But your intercessory prayer supporting their work is their greatest need. Christian witnesses in unreached and unresponsive areas must be covered by prayer so that God's presence may be demonstrated and prayers answered in such ways as to bring salvation to many. The Christians needing this prayer partnership work in some of the most difficult places in the world.

While stationed in central India, an Indian soldier was led to Christ in one of our new churches. Later he was transferred to Kashmir in the northwest corner of India, a state where Christian work has been slow and where there are very few churches.

When the Christian soldier reached his new post, he learned of a Muslim lady who had been demon-possessed for several years. Relatives had taken her from one reputed Muslim holy spot to another without any results. When the soldier learned of her condition, he was moved by Christian compassion and asked permission to pray for her in Jesus' name. She was instantly set free. The Muslims were overwhelmed.

A Muslim with a severe heart problem was then brought to him, and he was asked to pray for the man in Jesus' name. He did, gladly, and the man was healed. A woman with a huge goiter was carried in to him and again the soldier prayed. Within two weeks the goiter had disappeared.

Soon the Muslims, who believe that God is honored by a place dedicated to Him, approached the soldier. "You need a place to worship your God." So the Muslims gave him three acres of land in a prominent spot on a mountain side and offered to help him build a little church.

Since there was no other Christian church or worker for miles, the soldier accepted, but sent an urgent message to the pastor of the church where he had found the Lord. "I'm just a soldier. The people here want to become Christians. Someone must come and help!" Today we have a small Christian congregation because Jesus vindicated Himself through the prayer of a Christian soldier who was only trying to show Christian compassion.

How can your prayer assist in proving to non-Christians that Christ is God? Let me suggest some ways that you should pray:

1. Place "power encounter" on your daily prayer list. Remember each day those who are laboring in these difficult areas where there are few Christians and where

serving and following Christ is costly. Pray for all those facing challenges to prove that Christ is the loving God and that He answers prayer.

2. *Pray for Christ to be manifest in miracle power.* Pattern your prayer after that of the Jerusalem church: "Now, Lord, consider their threats and enable your servants to speak your word with great boldness. Stretch out your hand to heal and perform miraculous signs and wonders through the name of your holy servant Jesus" (Acts 4:29–30). When the people of that church united in praying this prayer, God's power shook the place where they were assembled. Your prayer can help shake spiritually untold numbers of people and places for Christ.

3. *Pray for God to keep the Christian workers spiritually victorious and empowered by the Holy Spirit.* Satan tries in every way possible to afflict workers in these pioneer ministries with discouragement and temptation. They must stay very close to the Lord and live in the Spirit so that Christ's power may rest mightily upon them. This was the secret of Paul's ministry, and it must be the secret of theirs also (Rom. 15:18–19; 1 Cor. 2:4; 2 Cor. 12:9; Eph. 3:7, 20; 2 Tim. 1:7; Acts 15:12). Pray for God to clothe them daily with His Spirit.

4. *Pray for daily guidance for these Christian workers.* Pray for God to bring to their attention the people with the needs God wants to meet, and to open the door for their Christian ministry. Pray for guidance in winning those for whom Christ exerts His miracle power.

5. *Pray for God's protection for these Christian workers.* Satan becomes very angry with those God is using and makes them the special target of his attacks. Pray for God to protect the workers spiritually and physically, to keep them free from fear of threats against them, and to guard their families.

"Power encounter" is an important aspect of Christian ministry and spiritual warfare in many places. Your prayer can empower those in front-line ministry. Pray that the name of Jesus will be honored and that God will bring the harvest for which He died.

17

You Can Defeat
and Bind Satan

Because of Jesus' triumph at Calvary, you and I have an amazing new authority. What does that include? Is it really the plan of Jesus that you and I bind and restrain Satan and his demons? Jesus said, "If I drive out demons by the Spirit of God, then the kingdom of God has come upon you. Or again, how can anyone enter a strong man's house and carry off his possessions unless he first ties up the strong man? Then he can rob his house" (Matt. 12:28–29).

This teaching is so important that it is repeated by both Mark (3:27) and Luke (11:21–22). The strong man to whom Jesus referred is Satan. The possessions which are to be taken from Satan are the people who are enslaved by him—even those who are possessed and indwelled by demons. The power Jesus used included His own inherent authority and the power of the Holy Spirit.

But does Jesus expect you to seize Satan's possessions? Yes, God wants you to rescue those whom Satan has seized or bound in any way. Jude 23 urges, "Snatch others from the fire and save them." Proverbs 24:11 commands, "Rescue those being led away to death; hold back those staggering toward slaughter." Second Timothy 2:26 teaches that sinners are made captive by Satan to do his will. Jesus and His followers are commissioned "to proclaim freedom for the captives" (Isa. 61:1; Luke 4:18).

But do we really have authority to bind Satan? Remember the words of Matthew 16:18–19: "I will build my church, and the gates of Hades will not overcome it. I will give you the keys of the kingdom of heaven; whatever you bind on earth will be bound in heaven, and whatever you loose on earth will be loosed in heaven." Commentators interpret this passage in several ways, as we have discussed in a previous chapter. Whatever the full meaning may be, it is related to building Christ's church.

This teaching was so important to Christ that it is repeated and amplified two chapters later. Here, it is related to prayer in Jesus' name and is strengthened by agreement in prayer. "I tell you the truth, whatever you bind on earth will be bound in heaven, and whatever you loose on earth will be loosed in heaven. Again, I tell you that if two of you on earth agree about anything you ask for, it will be done for you by my Father in heaven. For where two or three come together in my name, there am I with them" (Matt. 18:18–20). Whatever else Christ may have had in mind, certainly He was teaching the following truths:

a. He is determined to build His church.
b. This building will be dependent on both His power and our obedience.
c. Binding and loosing has something important to do with building His church.
d. He expects us to participate in this binding and loosing.
e. Heaven's authority and power will back our binding and loosing.
f. This binding and loosing can be related to agreement in prayer.
g. Those agreeing in prayer need not necessarily be a large group, for Jesus Himself will be there joining in their prayer agreement.
h. Binding and loosing is primarily accomplished through our prayer.

It was prophesied that Jesus would crush the serpent's head (Gen. 3:15). Jesus' victory over Satan is implied by symbolism here and in the following passage: "I have given you authority to trample on snakes and scorpions, and to overcome all the power of the enemy" (Luke 10:19). The primary reference is not to physical snakes and scorpions. It is to be interpreted spiritually. Christ gives us, His disciples, authority over all the power of Satan, our chief enemy. "The reason the Son of God appeared was to destroy the devil's work" (1 John 3:8). Binding Satan's power, restraining his diabolical work by the authority of Christ, is certainly in the will of God.

But please remember: This is not child's play. This is spiritual warfare. Even the archangels respect the awesome power of Satan and, in their warfare against him, do all in the name and authority of Jesus (Jude 9). When the seven sons of the Jewish chief priest Sceva tried foolishly to use the name of Jesus without themselves being in right relation to Jesus and hence not covered by His promise, they were physically assaulted and hurt by the demon-empowered man (Acts 19:13–17). Spiritual warfare is not for the spiritually defeated nor for those not covered by Christ's blood. You don't bind Satan by repeating a few words as if they were some magic formula. To use the name of Jesus, you must be "in Christ" and must be living in harmony with His holy nature and will.

Paul says clearly, "We struggle" (Eph. 6:12). Prayer warfare is serious spiritual conflict. However, every scriptural injunction in this connection is for you to be bold, to have faith, and to expect Christ to prove His sufficiency and authority. You need not fear defeat by Satan when you use the name of Jesus scripturally.

How to Bind Satan

Since prayer warfare is so urgent and Satan so powerful, we are urged to use all the armor and all the weapons God provides to win victory. We are to put on "the full armor of God" (Eph. 6:13). This passage found in Ephesians (vv. 10–20) refers to all spiritual warfare, but primarily to prayer warfare (vv. 19–20). The full armor includes all the separate pieces listed in this passage. The purpose of the armor and exhortation is "so that you can take your stand against the devil's schemes" (v. 11).

The Christian in this warfare is expected to do "everything" made possible by God (v. 13). This implies that there will be various aspects to your prayer warfare.

As you live a Spirit-filled life and daily fulfill your role as a fellow intercessor with Christ and the Holy Spirit, there may come unexpected emergencies when you are confronted by a manifestation of Satan's power and must, like Jesus, rebuke Satan instantly (Matt. 16:23; Luke 4:8). Do not hesitate to take the authority Christ gives you whenever you need it.

There are, however, other places and situations where Satan has been long entrenched. It is not so much an emergency situation as an urgent need. You may have prayed repeatedly and yet not seen God's answer to your prayer. God may lead you to spend a longer time in prayer until you feel the inner witness of the Spirit that your prayer has been heard and by faith you claim the binding of Satan. It is for such a longer period of intense prayer warfare that the following suggestions are offered. You may feel free to use any of them at any time as the Spirit leads, without regard to this specific sequence.

1. Rejoice in Christ's victory at Calvary over Satan and his demonic spirits. Strengthen your prayer by reading such Scriptures as Luke 10:19, John 12:31–33, Romans 16:20, 1 Corinthians 2:6, Ephesians 1:21–22, Colossians 2:15, Hebrews 2:14, and James 4:7. Praise God for Christ's complete victory. Thank Jesus for paying the price. Perhaps some chorus or hymn will be the expression of your heart. My Indian co-workers often sang this chorus of triumph:

> He signed the deed with His atoning
> blood
> And ever lives to make His promise good.
> When all the hosts of hell combine to
> make a second claim
> They all march out at the mention of
> His name.
> They all march out at the mention of
> His name.

2. Rejoice in Christ's sovereign authority and almighty power. Praise God, Jesus has sat down "at the right hand of the Majesty in heaven" (Heb. 1:3). He is seated at God's right hand while God is putting everything beneath His feet (Ps. 110:1). "Of the increase of His government and peace there will be no end" (Isa. 9:7). He has power to bring everything under His control (Phil. 3:21). "Your God reigns!" (Isa. 52:7). Jesus is seated at God's right hand in heaven "far above all rule and authority, power and dominion, and every title that can be given" (Eph. 1:20–21). All authority in heaven and earth has been given to Him (Matt. 28:18). Our Jesus Christ is the same in power and authority yesterday, today, and forever (Heb. 13:8).

3. Plead the blood of Jesus. You have no merit of your own, but Jesus died for you. You do not place faith in yourself but in Jesus' blood (Rom. 3:25). When Jesus cried on the cross, "It is finished" (John 19:30), Satan's defeat was complete, the victory of Calvary was complete, the blood of the Son of God was now available as the basis of your plea for God's answer to your prayer. Now you can overcome Satan by the blood of the Lamb of God (Rev. 12:11). Plead the blood of Jesus as you advance and attack Satan's stronghold and his power.

4. Use the name of Jesus. Your prayer warfare is for His name's sake. It is for the glory of Jesus' name that you advance against Satan. Before Jesus every knee must bow, for He is Lord (Phil. 2:9–10). Jesus promised, "I will do whatever you ask in my name, so that the Son may bring glory to the Father. You may ask me for anything in my name, and I will do it" (John 14:13–14). "The Father will give you whatever you ask in my name" (15:16). "I tell you the truth, my Father will give you whatever you ask in my name. . . . Ask and you will receive" (16:23–24).

All power in heaven and earth is behind that name. Every demon from hell knows the authority of that name. Peter, Paul, the apostles, and the early church again and again proved the power of Jesus' name. Across the world today Satan is being driven back and forced to release his captives through the use of the name of Jesus. You are authorized to use His name. Take the authority God has given you.

Use the name of Jesus when you pray. Use it when you claim God's promise. Use it as you take the initiative to drive back Satan and his evil spirits. Use it to break the bonds of sin and hell and demand the release of Satan's captives. Use the name of Jesus to rout the Devil. Use it to bind Satan's power and authority. Use the name of Jesus now!

5. *Take the sword of the Spirit, the Word of God.* Quoting from the Old Testament, Jesus used the Word to defeat Satan (Matt. 4:1–11). The weapon which the Holy Spirit uses to defeat Satan, the Spirit's sword, is the Bible (Eph. 6:17). The entire Bible contains passages which can be mightily used to claim victory over Satan. You may use Scripture to point out to Satan how Christ is Conqueror over him. You may, like Jesus, use the Scriptures to rebuke Satan to his face. Refer to the Scriptures, quote Scripture passages, and you may even at times symbolically want to hold the Scriptures in your hand or place your hand on the Word of God as you pray or rebuke the Devil.

While he was president of Union Biblical Seminary in India, Dr. Frank Kline visited the village home of a new convert to share in a joyous service of cleansing the home of its former idols. He was chosen to be the one to enter the house and bring the images outside.

The Indian pastor instructed him: "Call on the name of Jesus, hold your Bible in your hand before you, and go in and bring out the images." This was a new experience for Frank. With the Bible at his side and forgetting to use Jesus' name, he started toward the door of the house. To his amazement, at a certain point he was stopped by an unseen power. Try as he would, Frank, who is a strong man, could not advance another step.

"Hold your Bible before you, Frank, and use the name of Jesus!" the pastor called. Suddenly realizing the seriousness of Satan's power against him, Frank held out his Bible before him and, in Jesus' name, walked right into the house and brought out the idols. I myself have faced experiences in India when I wanted the Bible in my hand to symbolize my strength and confidence. Bible truth is literally the sword of the Spirit.

6. *March forward, praising Him.* Praise is not only a method of worshiping the Lord, bringing joy to the heart of God and expressing your love and thanks, but praise is also a mighty spiritual weapon. Perhaps Jehoshaphat is the only king who won a literal war by praise instead of by weapons (2 Chron. 20). Judah had been invaded by a vast army from Ammon, Moab, and Mount Seir. Jehoshaphat called the nation together to fast and pray at Jerusalem. They came from every town "to seek help from the Lord."

King Jehoshaphat stood and led the nation in prayer, first rejoicing in God's sovereignty, and then interceding for the men, women, and children who were all standing before the Lord in prayer. The Holy Spirit came upon one of the Levites in the middle of the congregation and He prophesied that they would not need to fight; the battle was the Lord's (v. 15). He told them not to fear, but to go out and face the enemy, and the Lord would be with them. The whole nation fell on their faces before the Lord in worship, and the Levites praised the Lord "with very loud voice."

Early the next morning they all arose; Jehoshaphat exhorted them to believe God, and then they appointed singers to lead the army into battle, praising God. "As they began to sing and praise, the Lord set ambushes" against the enemy (v. 22). While the Israelites praised the Lord, the enemy began to attack one another, and they were all destroyed. For three days Judah gathered the loot from the defeated enemies.

On the fourth day they had a praise gathering, and then the king led the whole nation in a triumphal procession back to Jerusalem and into the temple. We have no record that Jehoshaphat ever again was attacked by another nation. Satan was absolutely routed.

Use praise to defeat the Devil. Praise strengthens your own spirit of faith. Praise brings the angels of God to help you. Praise clears away the dark clouds with which Satan would like to engulf you. Praise angers and frightens Satan and his demons. The name of Jesus is powerful in prayer, powerful in commands you give to Satan, and powerful in striking terror into the ranks of Satan.

Advance against the demon opposition, praising the Lord. Shout the praise of the Lord in the Devil's face. I have several times been used by the Holy Spirit to cast out a demon just by calling praise to Jesus in the ear of the demoniac as the demon convulsed him. Praise to Jesus routs the unclean spirits.

7. *Command Satan in Jesus' name.* I cannot overemphasize the importance of speaking directly to Satan in Jesus' name. "Satan, you were defeated at Calvary. By the authority of the name of Jesus I command you to go. By the name of Jesus I bind you and all your working."

When casting out demons, if the demon's name is known, use it in ordering the demon to leave as you command by the authority of Jesus' name. In cases of demonic pressure, oppression, or opposition, do not hesitate, if God leads you, to command Satan and all his demons to obey your command. (Other examples and more detailed instruction on the command of faith were suggested in chapter 15.)

Through Christ, You Can Defeat Satan

Thank God, the Christian is able to resist Satan and cause him to run from the field of battle (James 4:7). Sometimes you must drive him away by prayer and praise. Sometimes you must command him to leave. Sometimes you must bind his power. Sometimes you must rob him of his captives and in Jesus' name set them free. You have full authority in Jesus' name to defeat Satan on any field of combat. You are not to run. You are to force Satan to run.

You are to invade the Devil's territory and set his captives free. Satan is nothing but a usurper. Through Him who loved us and gave Himself for us, through Him who goes with us and covers us with the protection of His blood, through Him who has armed us with the authority of His conquering name, you are to battle and defeat Satan again and again.

Some battles may be more prolonged than others; sometimes Satan is deeply entrenched. In some battles you may need the backing of an interceding, fasting group of believers who agree with you in prayer. But Jesus is Victor now and forevermore. Stand in His victory. In yourself you are nothing, but in Christ and His name you are more than conqueror.

18

Your Praise Can Rout
the Devil

There are many times when it is more important to praise God than to continue in petition. Praise lifts your eyes from the battle to the victory, for Christ is already Victor, and you have the Victor in your heart that you might have His victory in your life and in your prayer. Normally, all prayer should begin with praise (Ps. 100:4). The Holy Spirit often wants to lead you out of burdened intercession into victorious praise. Burden-bearing is scriptural, but praise is even more so.

Have you ever realized that God's answers to your prayers are at times delayed because you do not praise Him enough? Have you realized that mountains of difficulty often remain before you because you have failed to praise Him? Did you know you can often rout Satan faster by praise than in any other way unless it be by the command of faith? Or that the command of faith is often related to a praise barrage? Did you know that depression can be lifted by the sacrifice of persistent praise? Praise pierces the darkness, dynamites long-standing obstructions, and sends the demons of hell fleeing.

Mrs. Charles E. Cowman, author of *Streams in the Desert* and co-founder with her husband of OMS International, pointed out that Christians often repeat the familiar statement, "Prayer changes things." God taught her the deep spiritual truth that after you have prayed and believed, it is often praise that changes things. Prayers that have been repeated for a long time with no seeming response from God are rapidly answered when the intercessor turns from pleading to praise. Mrs. Cowman emphasized that two wings are necessary for the soul to reach God's throne—prayer and praise. Why is it that we put more emphasis on prayer than on praise when the Scripture gives far more exhortations to praise than to pray?

There are three levels of praise that can bless your life and add effectiveness to your prayer: (1) praise for what God has done, (2) praise for what you expect God to do, and (3) praise for who God is. Such praise is not only worthy worship; it is powerful spiritual warfare.

How God Uses Your Praise

Praise renews your strength. Waiting on God and hoping in Him renew you spiritually and often physically also (Isa. 40:29–31). Praising God is often even more effective than prayer in refreshing, reviving, and empowering you. Every Christian at times experiences a sense of spiritual dryness. Certainly, after a spiritual battle, there is mental and emotional exhaustion. Again and again we need an outpouring of the Spirit. Praise brings a change of mood. Praise opens an artesian well of faith and joy. Praise is one of God's means for your inner renewal (2 Cor. 4:16; Ps. 103:1–5) When you are sincere in your praise of God, praise is holy, God-pleasing, and powerful.

You will be far stronger spiritually if you build praise into your daily walk with the Lord. You will be healthier physically by making praise to the Lord a part of your lifestyle. As you praise the Lord, worry flees. Praise drives away frustration, tension, and depression. Praise drives out the darkness and turns on God's light. Praise cleanses the atmosphere of Satan's suggestions of doubt, criticism, and irritation. Praise gives you a heavenly transfusion.

A. B. Simpson called praise both a physical tonic and a wholesome stimulant. Praise will change the atmosphere of your life, your home, and your church. A word of praise or a chorus or hymn of praise can make a home devotional time come to life. You will be daily growing in spiritual strength if you plan and practice praise constantly. Spurgeon said, "When we bless God for mercies, we prolong them; and when we bless Him for miseries, we usually end them."

Praise clarifies your vision. Satan will try to inject his perspective into your mind before you realize it. He delights in painting things black. He magnifies molehills into mountains, darkens your sky with gloom, and makes difficulties seem like impossibilities. He wants you to evaluate yourself wrongly. He accuses you of being unimportant to God, too weak to be used by God, a failure. He makes his forces of evil seem much larger, much wiser, and much stronger than they really are.

Begin to praise God, and you can shake off Satan's suggestions. Praise God, and the Holy Spirit will clarify your vision. Satan's perspectives are always deceitful; he only wants you to see part of the picture. Praise the Lord, and the Holy Spirit will begin to give you heaven's perspective. Praise cuts the Devil down to size and helps you recognize the falsity and hollowness of his bluster.

Praise gives you the Holy Spirit's overview of how God has been working and how God's answer is nearing. Praise lifts you above the dust of the battle and lets you look down upon it from Jesus' perspective as He sits enthroned at the right hand of the Father. Praise gives the lie to Satan's claims and shows you what God's angels see.

Praise cleanses your soul. You would be amazed to know how much prayer is hindered by the self-life of Christians. Carnality keeps thousands of prayers from rising higher than the ceiling. "If I had cherished sin in my heart, the Lord would not have listened" (Ps. 66:18). Sinful thoughts, carnal attitudes, and self-centeredness destroy the power of prayer. These close God's ear to our words and desires.

Scripture often speaks of people praying and God not hearing. According to James, our relation to God must be true and our motive pure before God will hear us (4:3). Pride cancels many prayers (4:6). A critical attitude, unforgiveness, and bitterness hidden in the heart block prayer. If you want your prayers to be answered, let the Holy Spirit purify you (4:6–10).

You can be preserved in purity by the spirit of praise. When Satan comes with such suggestions to your mind, cleanse your thoughts by praise. Praise turns your eyes away from yourself to Jesus. Praise washes away negativism, self-pity, self-centeredness, and the beginnings of self-idolatry. Praise makes you so beautifully clean that God accepts you as you approach the throne of grace.

Praise empowers your prayer. Psalm 50:14–15 suggests that in your day of trouble a sacrifice of thanksgiving is the proper prelude to your prayer for deliverance. In other words, praise makes your petition more effective. God has done so much for us already for which we have so often inadequately thanked Him, that adoring praise warms the heart of God and prepares the way for speedy answers.

If there was ever an expert in spiritual warfare, it was Martin Luther. He was very aware of the demonic forces fighting against him. Luther wrote: "When I cannot pray I always sing." Praise brings heaven's power upon you. God has delivered people from sinful habits through praise. Every time the temptation returned, they praised the Lord some more until the pressure lifted. Other people have been healed while praising the Lord. John Wesley, too, knew the secret: "Praise opens the door to more grace."

Praise multiplies your faith. As you begin to praise the Lord, the focus of your attention is drawn from the complexity of the problem to the adequacy of God's resources, from the urgency of your need to the power of the Lord to meet your need. As you praise Him, you begin to remember how He has helped you on other occasions and your faith rises in expectancy. You begin to lay hold of God's availability and willingness to help you now. The more you praise, the smaller the mountain you are facing appears in the light of God's greatness.

Praise lifts your eyes to Jesus and almost unconsciously you cast your burden on the Lord (Ps. 55:22).

141

Praise helps you realize how comparatively insignificant Satan and his demonic helpers are, how fully defeated and fearful they have already become because of Calvary. Praise gives you courage to stand in Jesus' name and rebuke them. Praise not only is the way to multiply your faith, it also becomes an evidence of your faith.

Praise unites you in spirit with the angels. Spiritual battles are won in the invisible world by prayer and by the active assistance of God's angels who are assigned to be your helpers (Heb. 1:14). Gabriel told Daniel that he and Michael had to defeat the opposing evil spirits before they could deliver Daniel's answer to prayer (Dan. 10:12–13).

The great joy of the angels is to praise and worship Jesus. When you begin praising God, the angels seem to gather around you and join in your praise and joy. You don't see them, but they are there. Again and again heaven seems so near as you begin to praise. God and His angels listen and are pleased.

Praise puts Satan on the run. Satan and his demons fear the presence and authority of Jesus. They know Jesus could banish them at any time to the lake of fire, which will be their final doom. The fear of that punishment and the holy presence of Jesus torture them (Matt. 8:29).

Praising Jesus puts the demon hosts to flight. Expect Satan to run from you (James 4:7). Luther once said, "Let us sing a hymn and spite the devil." When the battle against Satan seems unending and almost hopeless, start praising God, and Satan's hosts will flee.

We have praised God a little and occasionally during prayer. Let us praise Him more and more. We have used praise to worship the Lord; begin using it to defeat the Devil. Apart from all the other wonderful results, it is worthwhile to praise the Lord just because of the blessing you will feel in your own heart. But praise is the Christian's heavy artillery; praise is more effective in spiritual warfare than is an atom bomb in military battle. Praise is a strategic way to victory.

How to Praise the Lord

You can praise God in the solitude of your own soul without anyone else being aware. Begin your day in the office with silent praise. Enter a home when you make an evangelistic call, praising Jesus in your heart. If others are counseling a person while you are present, you can quietly repeat the name of Jesus over and over in praise and adoration. As you sit beside a suffering one in the hospital, you can silently praise the Lord until God's presence is near and perhaps even felt by the patient. How many, many times it is appropriate to praise Jesus in this way!

While praise is to flood your inmost being (Ps. 103:1) and can be sung in your heart (30:12), praise is also to be expressed in public (35:18), in the presence of others (34:3). Praise is to be declared (9:14), sung (33:1), shouted for joy (33:3; 71:23), expressed with music (92:1), and with the lips and mouth. "I will extol the Lord at all times; his praise will always be on my lips" (34:1). "Through Jesus, therefore, let us continually offer to God a sacrifice of praise—the fruit of lips that confess his name" (Heb. 13:15).

Praise can transform your daily life. Praise can transform your prayer life. Praise can speed victory in your prayer battles. There is no substitute for praise. Praise honors God, brings joy to the angels, and strikes terror in any evil spirit which may be around. Praise clears the atmosphere, washes your spirit, multiplies your faith, and clothes you with God's presence and power. "Praise the Lord, O my soul; all my inmost being, praise his holy name" (Ps. 103:1).

19

The Promise
Is for You

The Bible is one of God's greatest love gifts to you. It is
the world's greatest literary treasure. It is the foundation
of the church and of your faith. But there is always the
danger that you may forget how personally God wants to
give it specifically to you. He desires you to use it daily
as your spiritual food, your personal prayer resource, and
your weapon for spiritual conquest.

John is very clear in stating that he wrote his Gospel to
help *you* to believe (John 20:31). It is not just for people
in general; it is for you. That is true of all the Bible,
including the Old Testament.

The instruction is for you. Referring to the Old
Testament, Paul wrote: "Everything that was written in
the past was written to teach us, so that through endur-
ance and the encouragement of the Scriptures we might
have hope" (Rom. 15:4). The more you live in God's
Word, the stronger your spiritual life will become.

The examples are for you. After recounting how God
used Moses to bring Israel out of Egypt, Paul wrote,
"These things happened to them as examples and were
written down as warnings for us" (1 Cor. 10:11). God
intends for you to learn and apply personally the examples found throughout the Bible. For example, James, the
brother of Jesus, encourages your prayer by Elijah's
example: "Elijah was a man just like us. He prayed
earnestly that it would not rain, and it did not rain on the
land for three and a half years. Again he prayed, and the
heavens gave rain, and the earth produced its crops"

(James 5:17–18). Every example in God's Word is for you.

The food is for you. Jeremiah testified, "When your words came, I ate them; they were my joy and my heart's delight" (15:16). The psalmist added, "How sweet are your promises to my taste, sweeter than honey to my mouth" (119:103). The food of the Word is always a tremendous source of blessing as you begin any prayer time, particularly the times when you spend an hour or more with the Lord.

Jesus testified, "My flesh is real food and my blood is real drink. . . . The one who feeds on me will live because of me" (John 6:55, 57). To make His meaning very clear, He added, "The Spirit gives life; the flesh counts for nothing. The words I have spoken to you are spirit and they are life" (v. 63). You cannot maintain spiritual health and life apart from feasting on the words of Jesus.

"Eating" involves reading, understanding, and obeying. The Bible was given for you to "eat." Some writings have almost no food value for mind or soul. Others are worth tasting—but a taste is enough. The Scripture is essential diet; there is no alternative for the Christian. No Christian layman or Christian leader who does not read at least several chapters of God's Word daily can be a strong Christian, regardless of how many years he may have professed to be a Christian or what position he holds in the church. A devotional book may be helpful, but is unacceptable as a substitute for God's Word. There is no person mighty in prayer who neglects God's Word. This neglect explains pygmyish souls and feeble praying.

The promise is for you. Children sometimes sing a chorus that begins:

Every promise in the Book is mine,
Every chapter, every verse, every line. . . .

Is that true? God's Word is given to *you* to use. While the Scripture was initially spoken or given to persons in specific situations centuries ago, its basic truth is as true today as ever, and as true for you as for anyone. Peter said

145

to the thousands listening on the Day of Pentecost, "The promise is for *you* and your children and for all who are far off—for all whom the Lord our God will call" (Acts 2:39, italics added). To what promise was Peter referring? Probably several, going back to Isaiah 44:3. But to whom was Isaiah 44 spoken? It was originally delivered to Israel more than seven hundred years before Christ was born. Was the message really for them? Yes, for them, for the people at Pentecost, and for you.

God inspired the writing of Scripture to bless you. The promise Peter referred to was the promise Jesus called "the promise of my Father" (Luke 24:49). What the Holy Spirit accomplished at Pentecost in fulfillment of that promise was cleansing (Acts 15:9), empowering (Acts 1:8), and the infilling of the Spirit (Acts 2:4; 4:31). The Old Testament promise to Israel was fulfilled for the church, the spiritual successor to Israel, at Pentecost. You are a member of Christ's church. Therefore, says Peter, "the promise is for you."

Promises to individuals have their first and primary significance for that person, but what God was willing to do for any Bible character He is eager to do for you when you have need. The promise to Moses or to the disciples is generally also God's promise to you. The promises Paul gave to the churches are fully available for you. Paul's prayers in his letters to the churches are still being answered today.

The promise Malachi gave to Israel if they would be faithful in tithes and offerings was appropriate for that day—and for this: "I will prevent pests from devouring your crops" (Mal. 3:11). My father walked out into our garden one day and found that the gardens of several neighbors were being destroyed by potato bugs. Our garden was next in line. My parents had been faithfully tithing, so they had a right to claim this promise. Father walked into the middle of the potato patch and prayed, reminding God of His promise. The bugs stopped at the fence, and we did not have one potato bug in our garden. The neighbors lost their potatoes. Was it legitimate for my father to claim that promise? Yes, the promise was for him, and for you.

146

God's promise to help Moses bring Israel out of Egypt was for that time. But it illustrates the kinds of prayer God is still answering today, particularly if applied spiritually. On the night before we sailed for India in 1940, Mrs. Charles Cowman reminded us of a promise that God had given her for the opening of our OMS work in that country: "I will . . . do better unto you than at your beginnings" (Ezek. 36:11 KJV). I puzzled for years as to how that promise would be fulfilled. But now it is very evident that God did just that. The early years saw much fasting, prayer, and hard work on the mission field, with little results to show for it. Now God is rapidly multiplying the work in India.

Did Mrs. Cowman misuse Scripture? Can we spiritualize for ourselves today a promise given to others centuries ago? Yes, under these conditions:

a. Study Scripture carefully to understand what it meant to those to whom it was originally given. Your spiritual application must be made in the light of this literal meaning.

b. Recognize that if this is God's promise to you, He will not only deeply impress it on your heart, but will provide corroborating evidence through providence, opinions of other Christians, and deep heart peace.

c. Keep your motive primarily for the glory of God, not your own self-interest, even though you may be benefited by the fulfillment of the promise.

How to Use Scripture When You Pray

Scripture and prayer are interrelated and indispensable to each other. All prayer is based on our knowledge of God as revealed in the Bible. All prayer is strengthened by the examples of prayer and the answers to prayer found in the Bible. Given this foundation for praying, the following are some of the ways to use Scripture in seeking to make your prayer more effective:

1. Begin your regular prayer times with God's Word. Your prayer time will be the more effective if you listen to God through His Word before you pray. This was the great secret God taught George Mueller, the "Apostle of Faith." Reading Scripture first helps you realize God's immediate presence, helps you concentrate your thoughts, and often suggests things to include in your prayer. Spend as much time in devotional reading of God's Word and listening to God through the Word as you spend in prayer. Thus, if you spend an hour in prayer, spend half of the time with Scripture. There are exceptions when you have a special prayer burden.

2. *Apply to your life what you read.* What do you find that personally encourages you? How should this help you? What new spiritual instruction does this passage give you? How does it guide or correct you? How does it bless you today? Constantly apply to yourself what you find in God's Word.

3. *Personalize Scripture passages during your prayer time.* You can adapt praise or prayer passages and make them a part of your prayer. You can pray for the things God says to you through the Word. For example, "Enter his gates with thanksgiving and his courts with praise; give thanks to him and praise his name. For the Lord is good and his love endures forever; his faithfulness continues through all generations" (Ps. 100:4–5). You can pray these verses like this: "Lord, I enter Your gates with thanksgiving; this morning my heart is filled with praise. I thank You and praise Your name, for You have been so good to me, Your love has so surrounded me! You have been so faithful to me! Oh, I thank You and praise You!" Such a paraphrase of God's Word prepares your heart for praise and worship of Him.

Another example: "Though you have not seen him, you love him; and even though you do not see him now, you believe in him and are filled with an inexpressible and glorious joy" (1 Peter 1:8). As you read this verse, you can pause and lift your heart to God, "Lord, I can't see You with my eyes, but in my heart I see You. I know one day I will see You face to face. But Lord, You know I love You. You are so precious to me. And the more I love You, the more joy I feel in my heart. I do believe You; I believe Your promises. I love Your Word, and, Lord, I love You more and more. Praise Your name!"

One more example: "But thanks be to God, who always leads us in triumphal procession in Christ and through us spreads everywhere the fragrance of the knowledge of him. For we are to God the aroma of Christ among those who are being saved and those who are perishing" (2 Cor. 2:14–15). A sample personalized use of this verse might be: "Lord, I'm so glad You defeated Satan at Calvary. I'm so glad You are the Victor over all the powers of darkness. I'm so glad You are leading me step by step. Lord, I love to follow You. Thank You for leading me in Your triumphal procession. I know the world is watching. Lord, help me to show Your joy and triumph in my face today. Thank You, Lord, that as You put Your beauty in my face and in my life, and as I manifest a Christlike spirit regardless of what happens, that this is like a sweet perfume to the Father that reminds Him of You.

"Lord, I am not worthy of this. Help me to be more fragrant for You. And help me to be fragrant before the world also, that today whatever I say or do will be like a sweet perfume that reminds people of You. Make me a blessing, a fragrance to unsaved people today, too. Oh, Lord, I am so insufficient for these things. I depend upon You. Bless me, help me, and make me fragrant for You today."

4. Bathe your soul in Scripture to increase your faith. "Faith comes from hearing the message, and the message is heard through the word of Christ" (Rom. 10:17). This is not only true for unsaved people; it is true for the nurture and growth of your faith also. Your faith will never grow without immersing yourself in God's Word. The more you saturate your soul in God's Word, the stronger your faith will become.

5. Memorize verses of Scripture which will be useful in prayer. It is so important to memorize Scripture to be used in witnessing and prayer. By all means memorize the Lord's Prayer. You will want to pray this in your private devotional times again and again. In the next points you may find several verses to memorize, if you have not already done so. They will bless your heart as the Holy Spirit brings them to your memory.

6. *Use Scripture in praising and worshiping the Lord.*
The role of praise is discussed in chapter 18. Here are
some good sample passages to use in prayer: 1 Chronicles 29:10–13; Nehemiah 9:5–6; Psalm 8; 27:4; 36:5–9;
40:5; 71:14–19; 73:23–25; 103:1–5, 20–22; 108:1–5;
115:1; 118:28–29; 139:17–18; 145:1–21; Isaiah 25:1;
Jeremiah 32:17–21; Romans 11:34–36; Revelation
1:5–6; 4:8, 11; 5:12–13; 7:12; 15:3–4.

7. *Use Scripture to confess your unworthiness.* It is
such a blessing to tell the Lord how unworthy you are of
having your prayer answered! In the following verses
you may find phrases and passages of great prayer value,
especially as you adapt them to your situation: Genesis
32:10; 2 Samuel 7:18; 1 Kings 3:7; 1 Chronicles
29:14–16; Jeremiah 1:6; Luke 7:6–7; Acts 20:19; Ephesians 3:8.

8. *Use Scripture prayers and prayer expressions.* Often
you will want to use phrases or whole verses of Scripture
in praying for needs. These will say just what you want to
say. You will not have time to look up the verses each
time you pray. But if some of these are hidden in your
heart, God will make them a great blessing to you. In
your reading, adapt these sample passages to your
personal prayer:

- Prayer for cleansing: Psalm 19:12–13; 51:1–10
- Prayer for blessing on your Scripture reading: Psalm
  119:15–16, 18, 97, 103–105
- Prayer for blessing on your work: Psalm 90:16–17
- Prayer for fulfillment of God's promise: 2 Samuel
  7:25–26, 28; Psalm 119:81–82, 162
- Prayer for guidance: Psalm 5:8; 25:4–5; 31:3; 43:3;
  86:11
- Prayer of heart searching: Psalm 26:2–3; 139:1–10,
  23–24
- Prayer of hunger for God: Psalm 42:1–2; 61:1–5;
  63:1–8; 84:1–2; 123:1–2; 130:5–6; 143:5–8
- Prayer for God to listen and help: Nehemiah 1:5–6;
  Psalm 5:1–2; 17:1; 19:14; 27:8–9; 69:16–17; 70:1, 5;
  121:1–2; 130:1–2; 142:5–6
- Prayer of love for God: Psalm 18:1; 139:17–18

- Prayer for personal growth: Romans 12:1–2; Ephesians 3:16–21; 4:12–16; Philippians 1:10–11; 3:12–15; 4:4–8; Colossians 1:9–12; 3:12–17; 1 Thessalonians 5:16–24; 2 Peter 1:5–8
- Prayer for revival: Psalm 85:6–7; Isaiah 43:18–19; 44:2–3; 51:9; 54:2–4; 55:6–13; 57:14–15; 59:12–13; 62:1, 10; 64:1–5
- Prayer for assistance in prayer warfare: Ephesians 6:10–18

9. Claim the Bible promises when you pray. Oh, what a wealth of promises can be found in God's Word! We have already discussed how you can make them your own.

10. Use Scripture to rebuke Satan. God's Word is the sword of the Spirit (Eph. 6:17). Jesus quoted Scripture to defeat Satan and drive him away (Matt. 4:1–11). You have full authority to do the same. Do not be flippant when confronting Satan, but do not fear him. Use Scripture facts and promises to resist him. God's angels will enforce your use of Scripture and send him running (James 4:7).

20

Elijah Was
Just Like You

Scriptural biographies are selective and very condensed. The mighty examples of faith listed in Hebrews 11 and elsewhere in God's Word may not only bless you, they may sometimes cause you to wonder if perhaps these people belonged to some elite class of saints who lived on a higher level of humanity than the rest of us mortals. Do you at times suspect that there may be very few such saints of God living today?

There are two passages of Scripture with which God wants to challenge and encourage you: "The promise is for you" (Acts 2:39), and "Elijah was a man just like us" (James 5:17). Every precious word in the Bible about these heroes and heroines of sacred history is absolutely true. But it is also absolutely true that each of those persons was human like you.

The Bible does not camouflage the fact that every outstanding character recorded had one or more weaknesses, disappointed God on one or more occasions, and had need to appropriate God's grace and help. The only perfect person who ever lived was Jesus. He alone never sinned in thought, word, or deed. But He fully understands and sympathizes with you—not only because of His infinite, divine knowledge, but also because He by choice experienced all of life's temptations, hardships, and problems. Jesus understands you.

And Jesus prepared the plan of salvation for you. He planned for prayer partnership with you and prayer ministry by you. His tremendous plan is made to order for you; it is your size. It is for a human being just like you.

Did any human being ever accomplish as much through intercession as Moses? He wrote the beginning books of the Bible. He had no Scripture promises to lean upon until God gave them to him and he put them into writing. Moses is an example of love, patience, prayer, and obedience. He brought an idolatrous, stubborn, doubting nation out of slavery and into nationhood; out of idolatry into worship of Jehovah alone; out of Egypt, through forty years of desert wanderings, to the entrance of Canaan. Moses came to know God as no other human being ever did (Deut. 34:10).

Moses had one of the best-trained minds and was probably the most experienced world leader of his time, but he was an ex-criminal. He faced family problems, repeated rebellions, and occasions when his life was in danger. He repeatedly exhausted his resources. He came to the end of himself again and again. He often faced situations in which he did not know what to do next. At least once, in the latter part of his ministry, he greatly disappointed God. In spite of his brilliant role, his family was jealous of him. Aaron, his brother-helper, failed him; his wife failed to understand or support him; and his children were never heard of again. Moses was a normal human being just like you. But Moses knew how to pray!

Elijah was a normal human being also. Elijah got weary and discouraged, and he was ready to give up. He became so despondent he longed to die. He had neither wife nor brother to encourage or comfort him. He was lonely, despised, betrayed, and unappreciated. He was no great success in any way except as a prophet. Elijah, in fact, had a sinful human nature. But Elijah stands out in history for his powerful prayers.

David was unrespected and unappreciated as a youth. His father-in-law became his enemy and spent much of his time trying to find and kill David. His wife Michal did not understand his love for the Lord. Some of his chief helpers had no spiritual interests. On one occasion David sinned a tragic sin, though afterward he truly repented. But God was able to count David His close companion and call him "a man after my own heart" (Acts 13:22). Why? Because of David's prayer life. David was a man just like you, except for his constant communion with God and his life of prayer.

What about Peter? How truly human he was—sincere, outspoken, with a mouth that kept getting him into trouble. Only minutes after making his great confession of Jesus, he received the sternest rebuke ever given to one of the disciples. Yet Peter was one of Jesus' closest prayer partners. If Peter, the outspoken fisherman, could become a man of prayer, so can you.

Or take Paul as an example. Paul was a rugged, determined man of steel. He toiled, endured, and suffered almost beyond human comprehension. He loved his converts and the churches he founded with a tender, intense, and godly jealousy. He was undoubtedly uncompromising and very demanding of his helpers and co-workers. I doubt you would have wanted to be on his team. But what Christian ever left such a trail of blessing? He worked harder than all others, suffered more than all others, and probably loved more intensely than all the other early church leaders. What a man of God! But, oh how human! True, in many respects Paul was certainly not like you; yet perhaps in others, you might see yourself in Paul.

He was the greatest missionary who ever lived, the greatest theologian of the Christian church, and the greatest church planter who ever lived. Paul could never have accomplished all he did, suffered all he did, and built the church of Christ as he did had he not been mighty in prevailing intercession. Paul prayed day and night. He prayed for long lists of believers. He wept and prayed for his churches. He fasted and prayed for every church he founded or visited.

God's history may well reveal that Paul accomplished as much or more through his prayers as he did through his personal evangelism and preaching. His writings were born of prayer and were filled with prayer. Paul was just like you, except for his massive, unceasing prayer warfare. If ever any Christian fought and won prayer battles, it was Paul!

Kneeling, They Conquered

David Livingstone, John Knox, John Wesley—all were mighty men of God. Yet some today would like to rewrite biographies and dig up all the mud, tarnish the halos, and point out all the weaknesses of such great heroes of the faith. Despite their imperfections, however, God used all of them, just as He uses you and me. Their greatest role may ultimately not be that for which they were most famous.

Livingstone may have been greatest in prayer. He died on his knees.

John Knox was a rigid, unyielding leader, but he fought and won the spiritual battle for Scotland on his knees. It was his prayers, more than his sermons or actions, that saved Scotland.

John Wesley did not have a happy home life. How could he at the pace at which he lived? His wife did all she could to embarrass him. Yet this man turned England upside down for God, teaching holiness of heart. John Wesley often traveled on horseback sixty to seventy miles per day, preaching several times. For fifty-four years he averaged 5,000 miles on horseback per year, traveling a total of 290,000 miles, a distance equal to that of circumnavigating the earth twelve times. During his fifty-four years of ministry, he averaged fifteen sermons per week, plus many other exhortations and addresses. At times he addressed ten, twenty, and thirty thousand people in the open air without any kind of amplification.

Wesley's ministry is credited by some secular historians as having so transformed England that the country was spared a repetition of the bloody French Revolution. John Wesley made his mistakes. But John Wesley was a man of prayer. He said, "God does nothing but in answer to prayer." Of him it was said, "He thought prayer to be more his business than anything else, and I have seen him come out of his closet with a serenity of face next to shining." Wesley spent two hours each day in prayer.

Rugged Martin Luther, too, was intensely human, yet a man of prayer. He wrote, "I judge that my prayer is more than the devil himself; if it were otherwise Luther would have fared differently long before this. Yet men will not see and acknowledge the great wonders of miracles God works in my behalf. If I should neglect prayer but a single day, I should lose a great deal of the fire of faith."

People spoke of Luther as "the man who can have whatever he wishes of God." When they brought a demon-possessed girl to Luther, he put his hand on her head, prayed, and she was completely delivered. Luther's powerful prayers for healing brought people back from the brink of death.

Melanchthon's eyes were set, his speech and hearing seemingly gone. He recognized no one, and he had ceased to take any nourishment. When Luther saw his condition, Luther began to plead mightily with God, took Melanchthon by the hand and said, "Be of good courage, Philip, thou shalt not die. . . . Trust in the Lord who is able to kill and to make alive." While he spoke Philip began to move, breathe again, and was raised to health and strength.

In the last stages of tuberculosis, the beloved leader Myconius lay dying when Luther prayed for him. "May God not let me hear so long as I live that you are dead," Luther wrote him, "but cause you to survive me. I pray this earnestly and will have it granted, and my will will be granted herein, Amen." Myconius said it was as if he heard Christ saying, "Lazarus, come forth." Myconius was healed and outlived Luther.

All of God's saints were human like you and me, but became mighty in prayer. You will never be any greater than your prayer. But you can be great in prayer in spite of all else if you will walk with God. Probably most of God's greatest intercessors are almost unknown to all but Him.

Beware, however. You will never be great if it is your strong ambition to be great in the eyes of God. "Should you then seek great things for yourself? Seek them not" (Jer. 45:5). If you are willing to be disregarded by men, praised perhaps for a time and then forgotten, considered a failure by many human standards, you may, like John the Baptist, become "great in the sight of the Lord" (Luke 1:15).

The way to spiritual greatness involves Spirit-filled living, a humble walk with God, constant communion with God the Father, and a close fellowship with God the Son and God the Holy Spirit. God is seeking great intercessors. Intercession is usually a hidden role. It is a role undervalued by most Christians who so often walk only superficially with God.

If Moses could be one of the world's greatest intercessors, you too can be mightily used of God. If Elijah could be counted by God as one of earth's greatest prayer warriors, you too can enlist in His intercessors' legion. If David could overcome his sordid background of adultery and murder to be known as a man after God's own heart, you too can be beloved of the Father if you will truly give yourself to sweet communion and intercession.

You may not be able to duplicate Martin Luther's best three hours given to prayer each day—few do. You may not, like John Wesley, give your first two hours each day in prayer—few do. But what can you do? If President George Washington could arise at four o'clock each morning to have time to pray, perhaps you can rise earlier than the rest of the family in order to have quality prayer time. You may not spend nights kneeling and lying on the floor, weeping and calling repeatedly, "O God, give me Scotland or I die," as did John Knox. But you can begin to bear prayer burdens for others.

You can determine by God's grace to give priority to prayer in new and specific ways. You can form good prayer habits. You can learn to discipline your time and begin to schedule prayer. You can redeem moments throughout the day and give them to prayer if your heart is hungry enough for God.

There is a way for you to begin a new dimension of prayer. None of these great men of prayer began as giants of intercession. They developed their prayer life through a series of steps. They learned to constantly seek God's face. They learned to pay the price of prayer. Thus they became mighty prayer warriors.

God calls you to a new step in prayer. Take it today. Begin a new walk with God. Make some time today your prayer time. Make some place your prayer place. Begin to make your own prayer lists today. Elijah and other heroes and heroines of prayer were just like you. You, in your own busy life, in your own confining circumstances, can make room for more prayer, if you will. Will you?

21

God Needs You
to Prepare His Way

"A voice of one calling: 'In the desert prepare the way for
the Lord; make straight in the wilderness a highway for
our God. Every valley shall be raised up, every mountain
and hill made low; the rough ground shall become level,
the rugged places a plain. And the glory of the Lord will
be revealed, and all mankind together will see it. For the
mouth of the Lord has spoken'" (Isa. 40:3–5)

Our Greatest Need

Our nation needs a great spiritual awakening to sweep
across our land. Our people have largely forgotten God.
Sin, violence, and crime are destroying the potential of
our civilization. Our literature, our language, and our
media have been polluted. Our youth are growing up
with very little awareness or knowledge of God. For at
least a generation or two, many families have been
almost godless.

While thousands of us call ourselves "born-again
evangelicals," we are making far too little impact on our
educational system, our government, and our society. We
as a people need to return to God. When will God send
new reformation, new spiritual awakening, and such a
movement of God's Spirit that multitudes turn to God?
When? Only when we prepare the way of the Lord.

During past decades, nation after nation across our
world has been taken over by militant atheism in the
form of communism. Then when communism has consol-
idated its power, it begins to restrict the church and to

attack religion, evangelism, and mission work. In many Islamic nations, alarmed by the spread of secularism and materialism, Islam and other ancient religions are awakening, and religious fanaticism is increasing. The church is often subject to pressure and sometimes to attack and terror.

Given these conditions, how is the church to advance across our world, reaching our generation for God? How are the unreached peoples of the world to hear the gospel when necessary visas for Christian workers and missionaries are so difficult to obtain? How are small groups of believers to be established in hostile environments? There is only one answer to all these questions. There must be an adequate team of prayer warriors preparing the way, covering the gospel workers, believers, and ministry.

If we want to see closed areas open, the absolutely essential preparation is massed, militant prayer. If we want to see great harvest and spiritual revival, our greatest need is for great praying. This is the message of Isaiah for today: "Prepare the way of the Lord!"

Our Greatest Hope

Mighty works of God are done only after He has blessed adequate preparation. God planned to lead the children of Israel out of Egypt and into their new home in Canaan. He planned to deliver them from idolatry. He planned to make them into the people who were to receive God's revelation in the Old Testament and to be the people of the Messiah. But first God had to make great preparations.

He prepared Moses for forty years in the desert before Moses was ready to lead Israel. Through the miracle-judgments of the plagues in Egypt, He prepared that nation to release Israel from their bondage. Through those same events, Israel was prepared to accept the truth that Jehovah alone was God. It was necessary, too, for Israel to be prepared to receive the Ten Commandments and Old Testament law. For this purpose God used their experiences between Egypt and Canaan and His revelation of Himself to Moses at Sinai.

160

The coming of Jesus was also carefully orchestrated. God permitted the Jews to be scattered across the civilized world and to build synagogues in major centers so that these could be used by the first heralds of the cross in the decades after Pentecost. God permitted the Greek language to become the commercial or trade language of the Mediterranean world, including Palestine and Rome, so that the New Testament in Greek could be immediately usable throughout the whole area at the dawn of the early church. Roman roads, Roman rule, and Roman peace were also used of God to expedite the spread of the gospel. Babylonian captivity had at last cured the Jews of their repeated relapses into their besetting sin of idolatry. From that time until now the Jews have abhorred idolatry. Christ could not come until idol worship was utterly forsaken.

For four hundred years after Malachi, God raised up no prophet. Heaven seemed silent. The severity of Roman rule now caused the Jews to long for Messiah. Finally, everything was in readiness for God "in the fullness of time" to send Jesus. The last public preparation was that made by John the Baptist. When asked who he was, John called himself "a voice in the wilderness" to "make straight a highway for our God." This pointed back to the prophecy of Isaiah 40:3–5.

The reference in Isaiah was to the well-known historical fact that ancient kings would send pioneers or messengers along the route which they and their armed guards planned to travel. Aided by the king's forces, the people of the area were summoned to prepare "the king's highway."

Highways in that day were literally elevated roads, built higher than the surrounding countryside in many places. Passes were opened through mountainous areas, rough areas were leveled, the crooked was made straight, and all impediments were removed. It was painstaking work, requiring hard labor on the part of many. But it was essential preparation for a road worthy of a king.

Only God knows how many hidden intercessors prepared the way for Christ's first coming. Just as the intercession of Ezra and Nehemiah enabled the Jews to return to their homeland, so heaven's honor rolls (Exod. 32:32; Ps. 56:8; 87:6; Mal. 3:16) include many names of intercessors over the centuries who prepared the way for the Incarnation. Their role will be recognized at the judgment seat of Christ (2 Cor. 5:10). Their testimonies will be shared with us and will undoubtedly be researched by the historians of eternity.

Among these faithful intercessors at the time of Christ were Simeon, a righteous man (Luke 2:25–35), and Anna, a prophetess who, by her fasting and prayer, was serving the Lord (Luke 2:36–38). They were two of a much larger group (Luke 2:38) who were not only expecting but undoubtedly constantly interceding for the arrival of Messiah. Another of these was Joseph of Arimathea (Luke 23:51). What an honor it will be in eternity to have shared in this role of preparation for the coming of Christ! Now you and I have the privilege of helping prepare for His second coming by our intercession.

In every great revival or time of spiritual harvest in the Christian church, history records preparation by God's people. God usually makes use of some evangelists with prophetic messages, especially just before some mighty work. But by far the greater preparation seems to be shared by many people, often in hidden places. Theirs is the preparation of prayer. Often the extent of the prayer preparation is unrealized until after God's work of power when research uncovers the true facts.

This was true in the revival of the United Prayer Meetings which spread across America in the mid-1800s and brought perhaps a million people to Christ. It was true in the revival in Wales in 1904–1906 when over a million were swept into Christ's kingdom. It is true even today in many localities and cities across the world. Mission history proves that seldom is there a mighty work of God apart from the preparation of prayer.

Why Is Preparation Necessary?

Salvation, harvest, and revival are the supernatural work of the Holy Spirit. The most godly believers cannot produce spiritual results in their own strength. True, God always uses humans. It is His chosen method. But spiritual work is, nevertheless, a divine work. Our efforts cannot earn God's blessing. No accumulated spiritual merit obliges God to answer prayer.

We may perfect the structure and efficiency of our organizations. We may increase the number of people involved in our evangelistic efforts. We may increase our use of literature, radio, or other media. We may advertise widely—all without spiritual results. We may use all the right words, the right Scriptures, the right methods, and even the right people. But unless God gives His anointing, empowering, and help, our results will be only human results. Spiritually we will remain barren.

When God desires to do a mighty work of salvation and spiritual harvest, He calls His people to their knees. The Holy Spirit places a deep hunger in the heart of those of God's children who are close enough to Him to hear His voice. As their hearts cry out to Him, He leads them to spend more and more time in prayer. He leads them to join with others who share a similar prayer burden. God may lead them to add fasting to their prayer because their heart's desire is so intense that they want to take this extra, more costly step in seeking God's supernatural visitation.

Many times God uses pastors or other Christian leaders to issue calls for special prayer or to set aside days for prayer and fasting. More often God leads people, one by one, to take steps to deepen their own personal prayer life. Many a local revival visitation by the Holy Spirit was assisted by the prayer preparation of two or three people in one or more places, praying individually or together for months or even years. As they have humbled themselves before God, asking for God's mercy, claiming God's promises, they have been used by the Spirit to prepare for a mighty work of God. This is the role for which God needs you and your prayer.

22

How You Can Prepare the Way of the Lord

In a sense, the purpose of this book is to help equip you to more effectively prepare the way of the Lord to work in many places—whether in your local church, your community, your denomination, in one or more missionary societies, or on mission fields everywhere. You may be praying for all of these simultaneously, but there is a sense in which we should all carry a world vision, a world burden, and a world ministry of intercession.

Since chapter 32 is devoted to prayer for individuals, this chapter will be confined to prayer for larger groups or for some area of the world. The practical suggestions are applicable, whether praying for revival or for great evangelistic harvest.

Blessed is that missionary society, organization, local church, or denomination that not only has a widespread base of deeply committed prayer partners in its membership, but also has within the larger group some who pray with special faith and perseverance, holding on and believing for repeated outpourings of God's Spirit upon the group or organization. Are you willing for God to use you as one of His hidden intercessors who prepares the way of the Lord?

Preparing Your Own Heart

If you are eager for God to use you as one of His chosen hidden intercessors, there are steps you can take to prepare your heart for this ministry:

1. *Refresh and challenge your heart by reading the biblical and historical accounts of harvest and revival.* Read and reread the accounts of revival blessing on David (1 Chron. 28:1–29:25); Asa (1 Kings 15:9–24; 2 Chron. 14–16); Elijah (1 Kings 17–18); Jehoshaphat (2 Chron. 17; 19:1–20:33); Hezekiah (2 Kings 18–19; 2 Chron. 29–32); Josiah (2 Kings 22:1–23:30); and the New Testament church (Acts).

Books have been written containing thrilling accounts of revival in America, Wales, and other parts of the world. These testimonies will deepen your hunger and nourish your faith.

2. *Collect information and statistics to show the need of the world and the church.* Focus on the practically unreached two billion people of the world, the tragedy and spiritual darkness of non-Christian religions, the tremendous responsiveness of some areas, the overwhelming difficulties of others. Focus on the sins of the human race, the unrest, injustice, crime, immorality, terrorism, and other evils. Focus on the spiritual apathy of so many who claim to be Christians, the poor or declining attendance of so many churches, the need for new spiritual life and challenge everywhere.

3. *Meditate on Scripture passages in which God promises great blessing, harvest, and revival and passages in which God's children have prayed for revival.* Here are sample passages: 2 Chronicles 7:14, Psalm 80:18–19; 85:6; Isaiah 32:12–17; 35; Jeremiah 33:2–3; Lamentations 3:40–50; Hosea 6:1–3; 14:1–2; Habakkuk 3:2; John 7:38.

4. *Make sure there is nothing in your own heart which would hinder your prayer.* Remember that prayer can be blocked by sin cherished in the heart (Ps. 66:18), pride (1 Peter 5:5–6), unforgiveness (Luke 11:4), personal conflict with another (Matt. 5:23–24), or marital conflict (1 Peter 3:7).

Preparing the Way of the Lord

1. *Give prayer for revival and harvest a special place in your regular prayer list.* Make sure that you pray for this at some time each day.

2. *Make a list of specific prayer requests.* Whenever you have longer periods of prayer, devote time especially to the items on your check list. Pray for God to:

a. Deepen hunger in members of the group, Christians in the area, or others who care.
b. Reveal a new dimension of His holiness and power. This is always an important preparation for God's mighty working.
c. Produce a holy discontent with things as they are.
d. Quicken and strengthen faith that it is God's will to work in this way.
e. Give God's children new sensitivity to His guidance and voice.
f. Give God's children an eagerness to be used of God and to obey Him.
g. Give humility of heart before God, with confession of sin, giving all glory to God.
h. Give new awareness to His people of the urgency of this need.
i. Prepare the key individuals whom He plans to use.
j. Motivate and coordinate the prayer and faith of large numbers of Christians so they continue in earnest, prevailing prayer.

3. *Be prepared to accept God's timing, God's methods, and God's people.* Don't try to program God; trust Him to work in ways above and beyond anything you could think or plan.

4. *Look for opportunities to spend extra time in prayer.* How little we realize the potential of the unused moments we let slip by almost unnoticed. Every minute has the potential of blessing if used for the Lord. Moments lost are lost forever. Find moments to invest for eternity as you lift your heart to God in prayer for this need.

5. *Schedule special prayer times for yourself.* Minutes saved here and there and invested in prayer are of lasting value. Cry out to God again and again during the day. No sincere prayer is insignificant. Specially scheduled time for prayer, however, permits your prayer to become deeper and more intense. Pray both intensively and

extensively. If possible, find some day each week when you can plan to spend special time with God, preparing His way. If necessary, tell your friends you have a special appointment—it will be truly special, because it is with your Lord.

6. *Pray publicly for revival and harvest.* Make use of times of voluntary prayer in public services to pray for these needs. This can help increase and enlist the prayer concern of others.

7. *Mention your concern and encouragements in your testimonies.* When opportunity is given in prayer gatherings or in conversation for someone to give personal testimony, share how God is deepening your prayer and faith for revival and harvest. You may be able to share some special news of how God is blessing elsewhere. Trust God to guide you in encouraging others through your testimony.

8. *Use Christian tracts and leaflets to motivate others.* When you find available inexpensive literature, secure some and use it prayerfully—in your letters, in person as you meet your friends, for your prayer group, or as God may guide you. Circulate challenging books. Involve as many people as possible in the challenge to prepare the way of the Lord.

9. *Encourage the selection of harvest or revival as a theme for special occasions.* When you have opportunity to be a member of a program committee, or on other planning occasions, suggest revival or harvest as a topic for special emphasis.

10. *Keep files on revival and harvest.* When you find articles, poems, or reports on revival and harvest, cut them out and file them for possible later use.

11. *Add fasting to your regular prayer.* There may be times when the hunger of your heart, the urgency of a need, or the importance of a situation may motivate you to add fasting to your prayer. This may be even a partial fast for one or more meals. Remember, spiritual fasting strengthens your hunger for God. God sees and honors fasting, but we do not earn God's prayer answers by fasting (see chapter 13). The early church fasted on

Wednesdays and Fridays. John Wesley urged his followers to adopt this plan, too. When you schedule regular fasting, you should, if at all possible, spend the mealtime in prayer. Avoid telling others that you are fasting.

Suggestions Regarding Your Prayer Time

1. Begin your prayer time joyfully. Normally you should enter the Lord's presence with thanksgiving (Ps. 100:4). You may often feel deeply burdened as you continue week after week to seek to prepare the way of the Lord in harvest and revival, but don't neglect joyous prayer.

2. Be sensitive to the mood of the Holy Spirit. Remember that the Holy Spirit is a Person who indwells you, loves you, and desires to pray through you. It becomes physically exhausting to maintain any one emotional state for a prolonged period of time unless you have some change. The Holy Spirit weeps and groans under the burden of prayer (Rom. 8:26–27), but this does not necessarily mean that you will do so. As the Spirit prays through you, His mood at times may be one of burden; at other times, of joy.

When Praying Hyde, mighty prayer warrior of the Presbyterian missionary work in India, carried heavy prayer burdens before some of the great Sialkot Conventions, he prayed with great spiritual intensity for hours and even days. Often, however, in the midst of weeping under the weight of prayer concern, the Holy Spirit would impress on him one of God's promises, and he would begin to sing and praise the Lord and even laugh for joy!

3. Allow God's Word to speak to you. You may be reminded of some special passage or promise which will nourish your faith. The best plan, however, is to read the Bible through consecutively and regularly. All of God's Word is filled with blessing. Base your life on the whole of God's Word, not just favorite passages. You will often find that the very blessing you need is found in the portion you come to that day.

168

4. Use hymns and choruses in prayer. A verse of a hymn or a chorus may come to mind during your prayer. Quote it, sing it silently, or, if you are alone and desire to do so, sing aloud. The words may express the very hunger of your soul, the faith by which you seek God. Many people find blessing in keeping a hymnal at their place of prayer.

5. Pray with pencil and paper nearby. If other unrelated prayer needs come to your mind during your special time of praying for harvest and revival, jot them down so you will not forget them. If the needs are somewhat related to your main prayer concern, you may feel led to move right into praying for them too, and then back to your general topic.

God may bring to your mind steps of obedience you should take in helping answer your prayers. Make a brief note to remind you later. Perhaps there are letters you should write, or people you should help in some way. After you have noted on paper these suggestions God gives you, go back to your main prayer concern. Don't be diverted from your priority prayer burden.

6. Be very sensitive to any obedience which will strengthen love and unity. A mighty work of the Spirit has often been strengthened or begun when someone obeys God's prompting in prayer and seeks forgiveness for some wrong committed (Matt. 5:23–24). On the other hand, when interpersonal conflict is present and you do not obey this Scripture, it can block the answers to your prayer.

(Note: The question is not who is in the wrong, or who is most in the wrong. If you know that someone feels strained toward you, negative toward you, or wounded by you, this exhortation is your direct command from the Lord. Your prayer can be blocked until you obey the message of Matthew 5:23–24. But once you have humbly obeyed, your prayer channel is clear, regardless of how the other person does or does not respond.)

7. Close your prayer time with thanksgiving. The Lord's Prayer begins and ends with praise. Some of the "Hallelujah Psalms" do the same. When you have completed your prayer, tell the Lord again how much you love Him. Rejoice in His goodness and in His promises and go your way, knowing that God has heard your prayers and that you have contributed to preparing the way of the Lord.

23

You Can Experience
and Share Revival

It is God's wonderful will that you and His church experience maximum blessing. His loving provision of the abiding presence of the Spirit in each believer encourages us to expect the Spirit to be graciously present in the assembling of believers for worship and service. God is a bounteous Giver in the material realm; how much more He will provide for us in the spiritual realm (Luke 11:13).

Revival Is God's Universal Plan

Renewal seems to be God's uniform plan for man, nature, and the church. Food fuels our bodies and gives physical strength and renewal; sleep brings rest and restoration to both mind and body. For much of the earth, the cycle of the seasons provides for annual renewal. What a joy to see the spring buds burst forth on the trees after the barrenness of winter. In much of India and many other tropical lands, men and nature endure the long, dry hot season in anticipation of the coming of the monsoon rains, which revive the parched earth.

For Christians, too, God has ordained times of spiritual renewal characterized by new life and power, spiritual joy and blessing, and new fragrance and fruitfulness for the Lord. We commonly term this experience "revival." These periods of special blessing come all too seldom, and some church groups seem never to experience them. Even those pastors and people who seek to live in continuing revival tell of times of spiritual dryness which

171

they cannot trace to any specific disobedience or willful neglect. All Christians again and again need a fresh touch of God upon their lives. Indeed, "times of refreshing" come from the Lord (Acts 3:19).

Biblical symbolism of the Holy Spirit encourages us to expect an abundance of His presence and ministry. The anointing oil, symbolizing the Spirit, was poured on Aaron's head in such abundance that it flowed down his beard and onto his garments (Ps. 133:2). Water, symbolizing the Holy Spirit, is promised in abundance. God causes it to gush out (Ps. 78:20; 105:41; Isa. 35:6; 48:21). He gives streams and rivers (plural) of blessing (Ps. 46:4; 78:16; 126:4; Isa. 30:25; 33:21; 35:6). The supernatural river of Ezekiel miraculously deepened and widened (Ezek. 47:1–5), bringing life wherever it flowed (vv. 9, 12).

God "pours" out His Spirit on His people like life-giving water. "I will pour water on the thirsty land, and streams on the dry ground; I will pour out my Spirit on your offspring, and my blessing on your descendants" (Isa. 44:3; see also Isa. 32:15; Ezek. 39:29; Joel 2:28–29; Acts 2:17–18). The Holy Spirit is not only poured into God's children; He pours Himself out through their lives like streams of water, bringing blessing to others (John 7:38–39).

The more spiritual a person or work, the more urgent it becomes to have frequent visitations of God. It is the difference between mere survival and life abundant; between evangelical orthodoxy and evangelical vitality; between being content with the status quo and experiencing thrilling new anointings of the Holy Spirit and making thrilling new breakthroughs for God.

We all believe in renewal and revival. We know we need it. But do we really want revival badly enough to seek God's face, to pay the price to prepare the way for God's coming in revival? No one can predict revival, no one can program revival, no one can earn revival. We cannot generate revival by faithfulness, busyness, or spiritual activities. God is the only source of revival.

What Do We Mean by "Revival"?

A proper distinction is often made between evangelism and revival. Every extensive movement of God's Spirit among His people seems to be related to an evangelist, prophet, or human instrument. Yet most God-honored, God-directed evangelism, while bringing blessing and spiritual fruit, falls far short of revival. Just what is real revival?

Revival is a manifestation of the holy, sovereign, almighty God. It is God visiting His people with special and renewed blessing. Revivals usually bring a new God-consciousness, a new revelation of God, a new sensitivity to God, at times an awesome sense of God's holiness and righteous demands. These are times when God makes bare His holy arm in salvation, and His holy voice in the inner consciousness of people. Revivals are sudden interventions of the sovereign, supernatural working of God in the life and witness of the church. In some sense, they are a messianic foretaste of the final conquest of Christ. They are always the work of the blessed Holy Spirit.

Two theories present extreme Christian viewpoints concerning revival. One viewpoint acknowledges the reality of revival, but holds that revival is so sovereignly the working of God that it is entirely dependent upon Him and we can but wait until God chooses to visit us anew. The other extreme is to think that by our religious efforts we can bring revival. If we just pray enough, humble ourselves enough, and do God's will sufficiently, we will be able to see revival at any time. Scriptural truth and the experience of God's people repeatedly demonstrate that while God's people have a very vital role in preparing the way of the Lord, no person or group can program how, when, or where revival will come.

Some have interpreted John 3:8 ("The wind blows wherever it pleases") to imply the uncertainty of the work of the Spirit. I suggest that it illustrates that the Spirit retains His sovereign will regarding His divine working. It points to the invisibility of the work of the Spirit, not to the uncertainty of His working. It points to the mystery of God's working, not to His capriciousness. The Holy Spirit is not the wind. He is only symbolized in some ways by the wind. He is a God of purpose. He works according to His plan and for holy reasons. He is a God of promise. He is a God of unchangeable covenant. He is a God of power and holiness, and He desires that we have a part in His work.

God's covenants and promises tell us it is God's will to bless His people. These covenants and promises include God's stated conditions for this blessing—our response to His Word, His call, and His provision. His promises will be fulfilled. God has ordained it. But we must first humble ourselves, seek His face, and take some active steps of obedience.

The history of revival points to two special roles for God's children: prayer and obedience. Obedience can involve many things, but it always involves prayer. If there is one central key to revival, sometimes hidden, but always present, it is prayer. The obedience of prayer leads to all other necessary obedience.

When Should You Pray for Personal Revival?

How do you know when your own heart needs spiritual reviving? When do you know it is time to apply yourself to prayerfully seeking new refreshing and blessing from the Lord? Here are a few suggestions. Pray:

a. When you sense a spiritual listlessness, a continuing lack of spiritual appetite for the Word, prayer, and the fellowship of the church.

b. When God's Word seldom truly blesses you; when you only rarely hunger for more time to read and feast on God's Word; when you seldom sense the Spirit speaking to you as you read God's Word.

c. When you sense a lack of deep humility, Spirit-born graciousness, and loving patience.

d. When you lack real compassion for people suffering and in need; when you feel little true concern for people without Christ, and little sense of personal responsibility for God's presence and blessing in your local church or group.

174

e. When prayer is more of a duty than a joy; when God seldom places on your heart people who need prayer; when you seldom truly sense God's nearness when you pray.

When Should You Pray for Group Revival?

How do you know when you need to be deeply and prayerfully concerned for fresh revival in your local church or any group of which you are a participating member?

a. When your group prayer is lifeless; when people do not seem eager to lead in prayer; when there are few and only half-hearted praises to God for what He is doing.
b. When church or group services are seldom marked by a sense of God being present and speaking personally to people; when worship seems to lack spontaneity, joy, and overflowing thanksgiving; when there is an aging congregation with an obvious lack of young married couples and youth.
c. When members seem apathetic about the seriousness of sin or fail to demonstrate a strong sense of ethical and moral responsibility; when the church lacks vision and deep concern for bringing their community and new people to Christ.
d. When people are seldom led by God's Spirit to witness to others, assist people in need, or bring encouragement to others; when giving for God's cause is joyless, reluctant, and inadequate; when people lack vision for what God desires to do through them as a group.
e. When there is interpersonal tension, party spirit, or unforgiveness in the church or group.

Your Prayer Prepares the Way for Revival

You can help prepare the way for new spiritual awakening, for a real visitation of God's Holy Spirit upon God's people, and the moral and spiritual renewal that true revival brings. These simple suggestions and thrilling illustrations may guide you.

1. Ask the Holy Spirit to deepen your hunger. God's initial preparation for revival always begins in the heart of one or more people as they hunger for God's renewed presence and power. Someone has said, when God plans blessing for His people, He calls the church to prayer. If you have hunger to see God work among His people, that holy desire comes from the Holy Spirit. Ask God to deepen your hunger for His divine working in your own life, in your church or group, or wherever in the world you are led to focus your prayer.

2. Ask God to give you His prayer burden for revival. A prayer burden is a precious gift of God entrusted to you for the fulfilling of His purpose. Whether for revival in your own heart or church or on some mission field, God delights in assigning special spiritual responsibility to His intercessors.

A godly Christian brother in Britain many decades ago was one of God's hidden intercessors (Isa. 62:6–7). He prayed constantly for the work of one of the great missionary societies working in China. After his death, someone found in his diary more than twenty listings of the name of one of the mission stations in China, with notes indicating that God had enabled him to pray the prayer of faith for revival in that place. Upon investigation they found that, indeed, God had sent spiritual awakening to each of these places over a period of years, in the exact order in which His hidden intercessor had indicated God had helped him claim by faith the mighty working of God's Spirit! No one knew of this prayer warrior until after his death; but God kept the record. What rewards and holy surprises heaven will disclose when God's children who travailed in prayer receive their special rewards!

3. Ask God to give you some promise to claim by faith. God keeps His covenants; His promises are true. Ask God to impress upon your heart some promise on which to stand by faith as you pray for revival. A promise which has been used again and again is found in 2 Chronicles 7:14. But there are many other wonderful promises in God's Word. The Holy Spirit may impress any one of these on your heart.

4. Humble your heart before God in prayer. Tell God how unworthy you are to intercede for this need. God gives great grace and revival to those humbling themselves before God's throne (Isa. 57:15).

5. Ask God to lead you to a prayer partner. Then agree in prayer. As your concern deepens, God may lead you to someone who already shares your vision and burden, or who will quickly become one in spirit with you. As His children agree in prayer (Matt. 18:19), God's answers are speeded (see chapter 34).

The full history of how God uses the prayers of His children to prepare for revival is seldom known in this world. My dear friend Rev. Duncan Campbell, minister of the Church of Scotland and for many years the principal of the Faith Mission Training Home and Bible College in Edinburgh, shared with me some of the beginnings of the amazing Hebrides revival, known as "The Lewis Awakening."

Two elderly women in the village of Barvas on the island of Lewis began nightly prayer times when they agreed together to pray for God to send revival to their community. Night after night they interceded before God. After some months, unknown to them, several godly young men began to meet nightly on the other edge of the village to pray for revival. As the ladies prayed on, God revealed to them that the well-known Rev. Duncan Campbell would come to Barvas to lead them. When they wrote to him, he regretfully declined the invitation, saying his schedule was too crowded. They replied, "You may say you will not come, but God says you are coming!"

Some time later the pastor of the local Presbyterian church, Rev. James M. MacKay, attended one of the British Isles conventions. While there, Dr. T. Fitch suggested that he invite Mr. Campbell for special meetings.

In December 1949 Duncan Campbell finally reached the Hebrides to begin a series of meetings. After several nights God's awesome presence fell upon the village, bringing deep conviction of sin. From there, the revival spread from village to village in a series of waves, continuing from 1949 through 1953, until the life of whole communities was transformed. Many people, suddenly convicted by the Holy Spirit as they sat in their homes, fell on their faces before God and were powerfully converted. Others were seized by the Spirit as they walked down the street and dropped to their knees to pray. One night alone so many people were praying outside the police station that the officers had to send for the minister and Duncan Campbell.

Drinking houses were closed for lack of business. Buses came from across the island, bringing crowds to the meetings. Services lasted at times till two and three in the morning. Churches which had had an attendance of only four or five on Sunday mornings were now crowded week after week. Prayer meetings became the center of village life in many communities. The revival came from God, but as far as it can be humanly known, it began as God led two elderly ladies to agree together in prayer.

6. *Invite others to join in special prayer meetings for revival.* Local meetings can be called for the purpose of seeking God's face. Letters may be sent to people even in distant places to join in intercession until God answers. Revival came to the OMS work in Peking, China, after the missionaries prayed and fasted each noon for six weeks. Some of the national pastors asked to join the group. Revival fell, spreading first to our city churches in Peking and then out to the village churches.

The great revival that swept America in 1857–58 was known as "The Revival of the United Prayer Meeting." It began when one man invited some others to pray with him at noon on September 23, 1857, in the Dutch Reformed North Church in New York City. Gradually the crowds increased. As news of the prayer meeting reached outlying cities, other prayer groups sprang up.

After six months, ten thousand businessmen were meeting daily at noon in New York City alone. By May, fifty thousand had been converted in that city. United prayer meetings began to spread across New England, down the Ohio Valley to Texas, and across to the West Coast. Much of the United States and Canada was covered by this spirit of intercession fostered in the united prayer meetings.

Methodists reported eight thousand conversions in their churches in one week. Baptists reported seventeen thousand conversions over a three-week period. For two years there was an average increase of ten thousand weekly in the membership of churches across America. It is conservatively estimated that, of the total U.S. population of thirty million at that time, at least one million came to Christ in two years' time. That is nationwide revival. That is the sovereign working of God calling people to prayer and mightily answering that prayer. From the human standpoint, it began with one man in one city starting one prayer meeting for revival.

7. *Do not grow weary of holding on in prayer.* Prayer for local or national revival may continue for months or even several years before the full answer comes. Don't give up. In God's time revival will come if you persevere in prayer (Gal. 6:9).

Remember, you cannot choose the way God will work in revival. You cannot choose the people God will use in helping to bring revival. God has ordained to work through human instrumentality. You may never know all the people God was using in preparing the way for revival. But of this you can be sure, it is always God's will to convict people of sin and bring them to repentance. It is always His will to visit His people anew with spiritual blessing and revival. Are you willing to be one of God's channels for revival? Whatever He says to you, do it, and He will bless.

24

Let Jesus and Paul
Guide Your Prayer

If Jesus has one concern for our world today, it is the same concern He had when He was on earth—that the harvest be reaped. Jesus realized that His disciples had not yet caught the harvest vision; they were often more concerned about themselves than about reaching the unreached. Therefore, they failed to see from Christ's perspective the people they met.

Jesus saw people as they were, and loved them. His love was a reaching love that demonstrated His whole redemptive mission to earth. Moved by the needs of hurting people, Jesus reached out to them. Look at Jesus and learn how He desires for your love to reach out to others.

When Jesus saw Peter's mother-in-law ill in bed, He went to her, touched her hand, and healed her. When the leper fell at Jesus' feet, He reached out His hand and touched him. When two blind men came asking for mercy, Jesus touched their eyes, and they could see. He touched the ears and tongue of the deaf and dumb man, and he began to hear and to speak. "He went up and touched the coffin" of the widow's dead son and restored the boy to life. Jesus touched the ear of the high priest's servant and healed it after Peter had cut it off with a sword.

From other instances we know that all Jesus needed to do was to speak, and healing and life would have been granted. But He demonstrated His love by reaching out and touching. When He took the little children in His arms, He was demonstrating the love of God, the love which the Holy Spirit wants to channel through our lives to others (John 7:38).

Nor did Jesus use His God-given powers for personal gain. When the Samaritans refused Jesus the hospitality of their village, James and John were insulted and wanted to call down fire from heaven in retaliation (Luke 9:54). Jesus viewed the Samaritans as beloved of His Father, some of the sinful ones for whom He was going to die. He saw them as the harvest He had come to reap.

Jesus Wants You to Have Harvest Vision

Barbers and hairdressers are hair-conscious. As they look at people, the first thing they notice is the hair. Dentists are tooth-conscious. The moment they see a person, they focus on the teeth. Christians should be people-conscious, need-conscious, harvest-conscious. Jesus was. When a young man approached Him, He loved him and considered the vast potential of his life if he would only follow Jesus. Observing a fisherman, He recognized that he could become a fisher of souls. A sinful woman was viewed through His eyes as the pure child of God she could become when her sins were forgiven.

Jesus' disciples saw harvest in the future, but they did not see people as harvest. Jesus disagreed; He said harvest is now. Harvest is always here with us if we have eyes to see. Jesus pointed to the Samaritan people walking toward them and said, "I tell you, open your eyes and look at the fields! They are ripe for harvest" (John 4:35). The Samaritans were just one of earth's harvest fields. Jesus was pleading, "See people as harvest! Become harvest-conscious. Focus your interest on the spiritual harvest potential of all earth's peoples."

Jesus said three things to us about harvest:

Catch the vision of people as harvest. As you go through life each day, go with your eyes open. See people; see their needs. See them as harvest.

The Samaritan people whom Jesus pointed out to the disciples were unknown to them. The disciples did not know their names or anything much about them. But Jesus said, "Look! Those people are part of the harvest."

As you see people who need Jesus, see them as they can be in Christ; see what they could mean to the cause of Christ. See them as people Christ loved so much He was willing to die for them. Then love them and pray for them (John 4:35).

Pray for the harvest. Pray for everyone you see, meet, or have any contact with. Pray for those who serve you in business, everyday living, or travel. Pray for children at play, for the drivers of cars that pause beside you at traffic lights, for those waiting with you in checkout lines.

The harvest immediately before you should always remind you of the harvest beyond your sight. A foreign-made object you purchase or use calls you to pray for the people of that land. A telecast reporting strife in a foreign nation, a picture of a starving child, a news item from any place in the world is a call to prayer for those people and their needs. Be harvest-conscious.

Be a world Christian. Have a world vision. Be a world intercessor. Let your love be as extensive as God's. He loves the world; will you love that world for God today? Let the Holy Spirit pour God's love through you as you pray for all people. Don't just love the world theoretically; love the people actually. Don't just repeat, "Bless the whole world," and think your prayer responsibility for the world is fulfilled for the day. Love the persons, the peoples, the nations.

Even a two-word prayer, such as "Bless India," "Bless Brazil," "Bless China," "Bless Russia," "Bless Egypt," can be not only valid prayer but powerful prayer if it arises from a loving heart that longs to express Christ's love.

Pray that others will catch the harvest vision. "Jesus went through all the towns and villages . . . he saw the crowds, he had compassion on them, because they were harassed and helpless, like sheep without a shepherd. Then he said to his disciples, 'The harvest is plentiful but the workers are few. Ask the Lord of the harvest, therefore, to send out workers into his harvest field'" (Matt. 9:35–38).

Though you might expect that He would have done so, Jesus did not tell His disciples to look at the harvest and then get busy. He told them to pray. In a few short months after Pentecost, reaping the harvest would be the full-time assignment of the apostles. But before the reaping would come the preparation of prayer.

Jesus knew that as His disciples prayed, their harvest vision would ignite their souls and they would be moved with compassion to do something. It is a rare person who has a real harvest vision and prayer burden who does not become involved in additional ways as God opens doors. Real vision, which leads to real intercession, deepens the love and concern for a person or place and causes us to desire to help in any way possible—giving, going, serving. The danger is that we are so busy working we do not pray enough.

The only prayer request Jesus gave His church was to pray for harvest. Praise God when ninety-nine sheep are in the fold, but as long as one remains outside, do not rest until that one is found and gathered safely inside. Minister where you are, but never forget those who are yet unreached.

"Let us go somewhere else—to the nearby villages—so I can preach there also. That is why I have come" (Mark 1:38). So Jesus went throughout Galilee and the surrounding areas, from village to village, always reaching out. "I have other sheep that are not of this sheep pen. I must bring them also. They too will listen to my voice" (John 10:16).

Once you see the world through Jesus' eyes, prayer for world harvest will be one of the main priorities of your intercession.

Paul Also Calls You to Help by Prayer

In his letters to the churches he had founded, as well as to those he had only heard about (Rome, Colossae), Paul had one constant prayer request. He repeated it many times; and though the words varied, the message was always the same: "Help us by your prayers. Then many will give thanks on our behalf for the gracious favor granted us in answer to the prayers of many" (2 Cor. 1:11).

Paul desired that every Christian would pray for his ministry. The larger the number of Christians praying and the greater the volume of prayer, then the more people would be blessed and would rejoice and praise God when their prayers were answered.

Paul had never seen the Romans when he wrote to them, but he called God as his witness "how constantly I remember you in my prayers at all times" (Rom. 1:9–10). He begged them, "I urge you, brothers, by our Lord Jesus Christ and by the love of the Spirit, to join me in my struggle by praying to God for me" (15:30). To the Corinthians he wrote that he always thanked God for them and was praying for their perfection (1 Cor. 1:4; 2 Cor. 13:9). He asked them to help him by their prayers (2 Cor. 1:11).

He wrote the Ephesians that, from the time he heard about their Christian faith, he had never stopped thanking God for them and remembering them in his prayers (Eph. 1:15–16). He asked them to pray for him (6:19–20), giving them several specific prayer requests. To the Philippians he wrote that every time he remembered them he thanked God (1:3–4), and that he depended on their prayer (1:19). To the Colossians, whom he had never seen, he wrote that from the day he heard of them he had not stopped praying for them (1:9) and that he wrestled in prayer for them and the people of Laodicea (2:1). He requested their prayers, too (4:3).

As Paul wrote the Thessalonians about his prayer for them, he used such words as *always*, *continually* (1 Thess. 1:2–3), and *constantly* (2 Thess 1:11). In both letters he requested their prayer support (1 Thess. 5:25; 2 Thess. 3:1). He wrote Timothy, "Night and day I constantly remember you in my prayers" (2 Tim. 1:3), and told him how people ought to pray (1 Tim. 2:1–3, 8). In his letter to Philemon, Paul mentioned that he remembered him in prayer (vv. 4, 6) and was depending on his prayers (v. 22).

Paul was the greatest missionary of all time. What,

then, was the secret of God's blessing on his ministry? It was the prayer of God's children. To Paul this intercessory prayer was absolutely essential. He knew that the only way to plant New Testament churches was by prayer and fasting on his part, and the prayer of fellow Christians saturating his work.

There is no other way to harvest. If Paul could visit our churches today, I am sure he would say: Pray for harvest. Pray for the harvest workers. Pray for the new believers. By your prayer, you can become involved in world harvest.

25

Your Prayer Can Reap World Harvest

There is no more urgent concern in heaven today than for the church to complete its task of world evangelization. God wants a full house for the wedding supper of His Son to His bride, the church (Matt. 22:1–10; Luke 14:16–23). Christ's return will be delayed until all people everywhere have heard the Good News, but the inadequacy of our witness and harvesting can delay His coming (Matt. 24:14).

The task of world evangelization is primarily dependent on witness and prayer. Prayer must prepare the way for evangelization. Prayer must saturate and cover the work of evangelization. Prayer must follow up and conserve the fruit of evangelization. Only as the church prays will there be sufficient harvesters giving themselves to world evangelization and world harvest (Matt. 9:38).

There is tremendous waste in gospel efforts concerning harvest: (a) Only a small part of God's people are involved in seed-sowing. (b) Only a small part of the seed sown germinates. (c) Only a small part of the seed that germinates continues to grow until it produces harvest. (d) Only a small part of the actual harvest is fully utilized.

The purpose of this chapter is to point out some of the strategic ways in which your prayer can play a vital role in this task:

1. Through prayer you can join any team God is using.
2. Your prayer can water the harvest.
3. Your prayer can cultivate the harvest.

4. Your prayer can change the attitude of rulers. Their attitude is at times crucial to many aspects of Christian ministry and the Christian church.

You Can Be Involved in Harvest

You can have a thrilling role in reaping God's harvest. Only a small percentage of God's people are actually involved in seed-sowing, watering, cultivating, and preparing more harvesters, yet all of us could participate on a deeper level than we have ever dreamed.

If you are willing, prayer offers you a way to be significantly involved in world harvest. Prayer does not cancel your duty to witness, give, and help, but it provides an opportunity for you to exert a world-wide influence.

Through prayer you can join any team. Which team would you like to join? The Billy Graham team? The teams broadcasting over the superpower radio stations now sending God's truth into Russia, China, and Muslim lands, or teams on telecasts right here in our country? Your circumstances, your own talents, and other reasons may prevent you from doing all you would like to do. Even if you were a member of one of these teams, you could be in only one place at a time.

I have tremendous news for you! Through prayer you can join any or all of these teams! You can stand beside Billy Graham each time he steps before the microphone to face a waiting crowd. For years I have prayed for him daily, and at times feel I am standing right beside him as he preaches the gospel. I urge you to do the same. He may never be aware that you are part of his team. You can tell him about it when you get to heaven. But Billy Graham knows very well that there are thousands on his prayer team. If that number were doubled, think of the multiplied results!

While I was ministering in Palmerston North, New Zealand, some years ago, a lady came to me at the close of the service and told me that she had been on her knees each morning at four o'clock, praying for me! I was so deeply moved. She had driven some miles alone on a wintry night to tell me.

A few weeks later, at the close of a rural service in Australia, a dear lady and her husband, both in their eighties, spoke to me. "Brother Duewel, we've been praying for you every day at four in the morning. And for years we have been asking Him to send you to Australia, and to this church!" I felt so unworthy. Who was I to be the recipient of such prayer blessings? Then I understood why the new pastor of a city church, without informing us, had abruptly canceled the meeting for that night in his city church and booked me in this rural church. He knew nothing about the prayers of this couple. But God knew. They were on my team. They were retired missionaries to the aborigines of Australia, but they were also on my team in India.

Through prayer you can preach through any evangelist, broadcast a radio message in any country, write a Christian book or hymn, or work side by side with any missionary or national co-worker. As you pray, you become partners with all of these. You are not confined by time, distance, or space. Ask God to guide you to the ministry and person or persons He wants you to support in prayer.

Through prayer you can water the harvest. Perhaps the greatest need between seedtime and harvest is rain. Spiritually, the seed is the Word (Luke 8:11). It may be sown through a testimony given, a gospel tract distributed, a portion of the Bible read, or a radio broadcast heard. Often there is a long period of time—days, months, or even years—when the seed seems to lie dormant before it begins to grow.

Then, in some miraculous way, the Holy Spirit brings some of the seed to life. The catalyst may be the example of a godly life, or circumstances in the experience of the person who received the seed, or perhaps another contact with the Word. Not all seed sown bears fruit.

Jesus taught that the difference in the soil receiving the seed made a great difference in the harvest. In some people and in some parts of the world, the ground seems much more rocky and unproductive. Many hearts are so hardened by life and prejudice that they are like the seed sown by the roadside where the ground is almost impervious to penetration. There are also places where the new growth from the good seed is choked by weeds sown by the enemy, the Devil (Matt. 13:24–28).

Much soil is comparatively barren because of lack of moisture. If irrigation is introduced, the harvest will be abundant. The big difference between barrenness and harvest in most places is obtaining sufficient water.

Spiritually speaking, enough seed has been sown to bring millions to Christ. God's Word is true and effective. There is no fault with the seed. The problem is water! Prayer is your way, often the only way, to water the harvest. By prayer you can bring the Holy Spirit's blessing on any gospel effort anywhere in the world.

The Bible uses water as a symbol of the Holy Spirit. Rivers of living water are to stream out of your life as a believer (John 7:38). How? Probably in many ways— through your godly influence, the fruit of the Spirit produced in your life, your witness. But surely one of the main ways is through your prayer.

Prayer is God's ordained means to prepare God's highway through spiritually dry and arid places, and prayer is God's ordained way to bring the refreshing water of God's Spirit to barren lives. The more you pray, the more the water of the Spirit flows. The more you pray, the more the seed sown is watered. The prayer you pray has the potential to turn any heart or desert area into a garden of the Lord.

How can we reap a harvest from gospel radio broadcasts? By channeling constant streams of prayer to the broadcasts. The extent of the harvest will depend upon the amount of prayer that waters the seed.

How can we multiply the fruitfulness and lasting effectiveness of an evangelistic crusade? By adequate prayer saturation before, during, and after the meetings. So often prayer for a particular area rapidly diminishes after the close of the crusade when the team moves on to the next assignment, and the seed planted in many lives waits for the life-producing rains. This is the time to water the seed through prayer.

Christian literature organizations produce tons and tons of good evangelistic literature. Millions of Scripture portions are distributed world-wide each year. If one-tenth of the seed sown produced a harvest, what a harvest we would see! There is one thing lacking—adequate prayer to water the harvest. You can do something about this, if you will.

Through prayer you can cultivate the crop. The seed is sown and watered, and the tiny seedlings begin to spring up. This is another critical time, when cultivation depends upon follow-up prayer. Jesus warned that trouble, persecution, the worries of this life, and the deceitfulness of wealth would cause some to drop by the wayside and become unfruitful (Matt. 13:20–22).

As we have mentioned earlier, pressure from nonbelieving family and friends hinders many others. In some parts of the world, where families are close-knit and traditions are sacred, those who profess belief in Christ risk severe persecution. In addition to being cast out of their homes, young believers realize that educational opportunities may be lost; others may lose their customers or their jobs; some may have clothing and other possessions confiscated or destroyed. In certain Muslim and communist environments the risk includes imprisonment or even loss of life for those who are known followers of Christ.

There is something you can do to help them—something extremely powerful. You can pray daily. Help in any other way you can, but above all, pray earnestly for God to protect the young believers. Your prayer can encourage, strengthen, and protect during this crucial period of new life.

Through prayer you can influence world leaders. Government decisions and decrees are constantly taking away liberty of evangelism and liberty of worship and permitting or directing the persecution of Christians. No outside government can do much to help change this picture, but we are not completely impotent. Through prayer you can become a hidden counselor of these government leaders and authorities without their awareness. How? "The king's heart is in the hand of the Lord; he directs it like a watercourse wherever he pleases" (Prov. 21:1).

It was the Lord who moved the heart of Cyrus, king of Persia, to issue the edict to permit the Jews living in captivity to return freely to Jerusalem (Ezra 1:1). When, for sixteen years or longer, the leaders of surrounding nations prevented the building of the temple, Ezra records that it was the Lord who changed the attitude of the emperor Darius (Ezra 6:22) and caused him to order the temple to be rebuilt and the surrounding nations to cease interfering.

It was as Nehemiah prayed and fasted that God prepared the heart of King Artaxerxes, who had already ruled Persia for twenty years. He then authorized Nehemiah, his official, to take a leave of absence and go to Jerusalem to rebuild its walls (Neh. 1:4, 6).

When Queen Esther, Mordecai, and the hundreds of Jews in Susa spent three days in prayer and fasting, God would not let King Xerxes (Ahasuerus) sleep (Esth. 6:1), and so began the series of actions which preserved the Jewish nation.

We can be sure that it was while Daniel was praying that God delivered the three young Hebrew men and changed King Nebuchadnezzar from persecutor to protector (Dan. 3).

Today, as in the past, rulers of nations plot against Christians and against the Christian church. Laws are promulgated repeatedly to restrict missionary work, Christian witness, the baptism of believers, the assembly of believers in public services, the erection of new church buildings. In some lands Christians are repeatedly imprisoned, severely mistreated, and tortured. Thank God, persecution cannot destroy the church (Matt. 16:18)!

Seldom does the church adequately exercise its prayer privilege and prayer authority to change the attitude of political rulers and the treatment of suffering Christians. While again and again God does intervene to protect or help His own, who knows what changes might occur if the church would only unite to focus earnest, daily, prevailing prayer for authorities in Russia, China, Iran, Ethiopia, or any of the other nations where there is active opposition to Christianity.

It is not always God's will that His children avoid all suffering, or that all the missionary visas applied for be granted. But until God checks our prayer, why not unite in prayer agreement and prayer warfare? Why not use the command of faith in a united effort to change the attitudes of earthly rulers? Satan does not want you to contemplate the miracles that can be wrought through your prayer. Rise up in holy determination to oppose him and bring about God's harvest!

26

You Need to Prevail in Prayer

To be a Christian is to be a praying person; certainly all Christians pray at times. Such ordinary praying is a joyous blessing, but there are times when extraordinary praying is called for. And even more mature Christians often do surprisingly little of this kind of praying. It is the person who practices prevailing prayer, however, who wields power with God and with men.

There is an essential interrelatedness between prevailing prayer, prayer warfare, the binding of Satan in prayer, and using the command of faith to move mountains for God. All may be involved in a given situation. All are related to Christ's victory at Calvary and to the power of the Holy Spirit. In some situations the Holy Spirit guides into one level of prayer and then may deepen and intensify the praying as one moves from level to level. Paul, in his challenge to spiritual warfare, urges believers to "pray in the Spirit on all occasions with all kinds of prayers and requests" (Eph. 6:18). Christ would teach you each of these divine strategies to use at His direction.

Why is prevailing prayer necessary? What experience have you had with prevailing prayer? When have you prevailed in prayer? How much do you desire to learn how to prevail in prayer? These are very important questions. Your success in prayer will be determined by the depth of your desire to practice prevailing prayer.

Why Is Prevailing Prayer Necessary?

To prevail is "to be successful in the face of difficulty, to completely dominate, to overcome and triumph."

Prevailing prayer is prayer that pushes right through all difficulties and obstacles, drives back all the opposing forces of Satan, and secures the will of God. Its purpose is to accomplish God's will on earth. Prevailing prayer is prayer that not only takes the initiative but continues on the offensive for God until spiritual victory is won.

In many situations, before prayer is answered, people must take certain actions. Whether they are saved or unsaved people, human beings cannot control others' wills because God has given us freedom to choose. In addition to human influence, the Holy Spirit and Satan are influencing the thought life of human beings.

The Holy Spirit speaks directly through God's Word, through other people's words, and often through angels who suggest thoughts without the person being aware of the source. He may prepare circumstances that exert pressure or make certain actions possible. Similarly, Satan, the master of deception, tries to influence the thought life of people, whether through the actions or words of others or through demonic suggestion.

Prevailing prayer is necessary in the following situations:

To oppose Satan in his battle for souls. When you pray for an unsaved person to yield to Christ, you are praying in harmony with God's will, with the ministry of the Holy Spirit, and with the assistance of God's angels. But you are also praying in direct opposition to Satan and against the actions of all his evil spirits.

Even when we are sure we are praying in accordance with the will of God, we are often met with surprising resistance. God never overpowers the human will. He speaks to conscience, but a person's conscience may be deadened. Satan's prime battleground is the human mind, and his demons must be resisted and driven away.

In the case of a sinner, it is comparatively easy for Satan to get a hearing for his suggestions. Serious prayer is necessary to offset his diabolical schemes.

To overcome the satanic seduction of Christians. Even strong believers are subject to demonic suggestion. On one occasion Satan succeeded in persuading David to

194

take a wrong action by "inciting" his mind (1 Chron. 21:1). He guided Peter's thought processes in an encounter with Jesus, and Jesus instantly realized that Peter was unconsciously voicing Satan's suggestion (Matt. 16:23). Satan also injected evil thoughts into the minds of James and John (Luke 9:55–56).

Sometimes even the most spiritual may temporarily lapse into uncharacteristic displays of weakness. The critical word spoken in a committee meeting, the malicious gossip whispered in conversation, the lack of faith evidenced in decision-making may actually have originated as a suggestion from one of Satan's demons.

If Satan could penetrate even the mind of Christ, tempting Him for forty days and forty nights (Matt. 4:1–11), then we should not be surprised that we need to prevail in prayer.

To protect yourself or others from direct satanic attack. Job was not the only one who was attacked physically by Satan. One wonders, however, if Job's trials might have been lifted much sooner if his three "friends" had been praying Christians! The thorn in Paul's flesh was a messenger of Satan (2 Cor. 12:7). Luke 13:10–17 tells of a woman crippled for eighteen years by Satan. In Mark 9:17–20 a demon spirit robbed a boy of speech and caused convulsions.

Near-fatal accidents have often convinced Christian workers that Satan was trying to destroy them. In the mountains of India, while en route to ministry, our Christian co-workers have suddenly been confronted by wild animals. A new group of believers was frightened one New Year's Eve by a trumpeting herd of elephants, who had demolished their simple church structure on three previous occasions.

Over Whom Do You Prevail in Prayer?

You must prevail over yourself. Prevailing prayer can be exhausting work. Many Christians are so spiritually frail, sickly, and lacking in spiritual vitality that they cannot stick to prayer for more than a few minutes at a time. Such people are too spiritually weak to know how to pray with real soul travail.

Others are so carnal that not only does their physical nature shrink from prayer, but their carnal nature fears prayer involvement, holds back from prolonged praying, and finds a multitude of excuses for not prevailing in prayer. A Spirit-filled person is hungry to pray, rejoices in extra time for prayer, and is eager to sacrifice other things in order to pray more.

Many people need to confess their prayerlessness and ask God to deliver them. I urge you to claim God's victory by faith over your prayer defeats, inner hesitations, and prayerlessness.

You must prevail over Satan. Satan and his demons do not want you to learn the secrets of prayer. They fear your prayer more than your witness and your work. They would rather have you to be busy for God all day than to pray for one hour.

Spiritual victories are normally won in spiritual warfare. We see so few great spiritual victories because we fight so few prayer battles. We are powerless and fruitless because we engage in prayer so casually. We have never learned prayer warfare. If you are unwilling to fight, don't expect great victories (Eph. 2:2; 6:11–12; John 14:30; 1 John 4:4; 5:19).

Daniel's prayer was granted, but for twenty-one days his answers were delayed by demon powers (10:12–13). If Daniel had not fasted and fought the prayer battle the full three weeks, if he had stopped one day short of victory, we would not have the great tenth chapter of Daniel. If you ask for something in God's will and do not persevere in prayer, you may never receive God's answer.

You must prevail before God. Not only must you prevail over yourself and over the powers of darkness, but God will also test your earnestness and depth of desire.

Jesus tested the Greek woman whose daughter was suffering from demon-possession (Matt. 15:21–28). At first Jesus kept silent, and the disciples said, "Send her away, for she keeps crying out after us" (v. 23). But she pressed her case before Jesus until she prevailed and received total deliverance for her little girl.

In Gethsemane, Jesus prayed three hours until He prevailed. His prayer agony was so great that God sent an angel to strengthen Him.

You will learn many spiritual lessons because of God's delayed answers to prayer. Perhaps these delays are for the purpose of teaching you how to prevail in prayer.

27

How You Can Prevail in Prayer

There may be times when prevailing prayer is a fierce but brief battle. Normally, however, prevailing prayer is characterized by these elements.

You Must Be Willing to Take Time

There are few instant answers in matters of spiritual importance. God has performed miracles in response to urgent, on-the-spot pleas, of course, but many spiritual battles take much time. You cannot earn God's blessing by virtue of the amount of time you pray. Yet no one ever became mighty in prayer without spending much time praying.

Listen to Isaiah's testimony: "For Zion's sake I will not keep silent, for Jerusalem's sake I will not remain quiet, till her righteousness shines out like the dawn, her salvation like a blazing torch. . . . I have posted watchmen on your walls, O Jerusalem; they will never be silent day or night. You who call on the Lord, give yourselves no rest, and give him no rest till he establishes Jerusalem and makes her the praise of the earth" (Isa. 62:1, 6–7).

Nehemiah prevailed day and night in prayer: "Let your ear be attentive and your eyes open to hear the prayer your servant is praying before you day and night for your servants, the people of Israel" (Neh. 1:6).

Daniel prayed regularly at stated times, but spent as much as three weeks in prevailing at a time of special need (Dan. 10:2).

Paul prayed night and day, prevailing for his converts and his new churches (1 Thess. 3:10). We will do no less when we learn how to prevail.

Jesus often prayed all night. "One of those days Jesus went out to a mountainside to pray, and spent the night praying to God" (Luke 6:12). "Will not God bring about justice for his chosen ones, who cry out to him day and night? Will he keep putting them off? I tell you, he will see that they get justice, and quickly. However, when the Son of Man comes, will he find faith on the earth?" (18:7–8).

You learn to pray by praying. The singer spends hours in vocal practice and rehearsal. The athlete trains to perfect his skills and strengthen his muscles. The army that does not toughen its soldiers with constant drilling wins few victories. There is only one way to learn to pray. It is not by reading books on prayer, not by singing about prayer, not by hearing sermons on prayer, but by praying more and more and more.

By the very nature of things, prayer victories often take time. Prayer seeks to dislodge long-entrenched foes. Prayer seeks to change the wills of people. You may have to environ them for days with prayer before they understand or become willing to obey God. Prayer answers often require complex coordinating and timing of events and lives by God.

Prayer force can be built up to an almost irresistible level. You cannot store up grace, but you can store up prayer. Mounting flood waters can sweep away any obstruction and burst any dam. In the same way the accumulated power of prevailing prayer can move immovable obstacles. The foundation is praying without ceasing. This is more than an activity; it must become an attitude of life.

You Must Pray in the Spirit

Over the centuries, the history of God's people proves the relationship of the Holy Spirit and prayer. Spurgeon said, "Prayer is an art which only the Holy Ghost can teach us. He is the giver of all prayer." E. M. Bounds believed, "The secret of feeble praying everywhere is the lack of God's Spirit in His mightiness."

You must be filled with the Spirit and live in the Spirit if you would really prevail in the Spirit as you intercede. Feeble praying is caused by a shallow experience of the Holy Spirit. To be filled with the Spirit is to be controlled by the Spirit, and only He can qualify you for an effective prayer life.

"And pray in the Spirit on all occasions with all kinds of prayers and requests. With this in mind, be alert and always keep on praying" (Eph. 6:18). "Pray in the Holy Spirit" (Jude 20). "In the same way, the Spirit helps us in our weakness. We do not know what we ought to pray, but the Spirit himself intercedes for us with groans that words cannot express. And he who searches our hearts knows the mind of the Spirit, because the Spirit intercedes for the saints in accordance with God's will" (Rom. 8:26–27). "We . . . have access to the Father by one Spirit" (Eph. 2:18).

The Holy Spirit is the great Enabler of this His dispensation. A major role of His ministry in the Christian is to enable him to pray as he ought. Praying thus becomes a real partnership with the Holy Spirit. To watch and pray requires that you be very sensitive to the Holy Spirit—to His checks, His promptings, His moods. Keeping spiritually awake and alert helps you live in the Spirit, walk in the Spirit, and pray in the Spirit. You thus come to experience His mind and His desires.

You Must Pray with Urgent Persistence

Importunity is shameless persistence in asking; it indicates an urgency of spirit so great that it cannot be deterred from pressing its requests. The Bible repeatedly shows the importance of holding on in urgent prayer and not fainting or giving up.

Jesus told His disciples a parable to illustrate this truth. There was an unjust judge whose heart was hardened to God and man, yet because of the shameless persistence of a needy widow, he acted in her behalf (Luke 18:1–8). How much more surely, Jesus promised, will God answer the persistent prayer of His children.

Jesus taught that urgent persistent asking will bring results from a friend who would not help for the sake of mere friendship. He concludes, "I tell you, though he will not get up and give him the bread because he is his friend, yet because of the man's persistence he will get up and give him as much as he needs." Then Jesus immediately gave His great prayer command and promise, indicating increasing degrees of importunity: "So I say to you: Ask and it will be given to you; seek and you will find; knock and the door will be opened to you. For everyone who asks receives; he who seeks finds; and to him who knocks, the door will be opened" (Luke 11:5–10)

Judson said, "God loves importunate prayer so much that He will not give us much blessing without it." Urgent persistent prayer trains you in the life of prayer. Bounds wrote, "Few things give such quickened and permanent vigor to the soul as a long, exhaustive season of importunate prayer." Such seasons of prayer are times of tremendous growth in grace and spiritual maturity.

Urgent persistent prayer involves your whole soul and being. It is a mighty movement of your whole soul toward God. "You will call upon me and come and pray to me, and I will listen to you. You will seek me and find me when you seek me with all your heart. I will be found by you" (Jer. 29:12–14).

Bounds said, "Heaven is too busy to listen to half-hearted prayers." God cannot tolerate lukewarmness. Prayer feeds on flame. It is the fiery intercessors who conquer. Such burning desire makes intercession invincible. Importunity is prayer on fire. Desire is the flame within; intercession is the flame leaping out to God.

White-hot prayer burns its way through obstacles to the throne of God. A burning heart is your best preparation for prayer. Fiery prayer is the intensity born of the Holy Spirit. The fire of the Spirit baptizes your heart as a prayer warrior and empowers your praying. If your prayers are not touched with holy fire, you have not yet felt the heartbeat of God. To be absorbed in God's will, God's purpose, God's zeal, and God's glory will set your heart and prayer aflame.

You cannot manufacture this fire of the Spirit, but you can prepare for it, welcome it, pray until you receive it, and refuel it to keep it from dying out. Such flaming prayer at times causes sleep to vanish and makes the heart hungry to fast. Worked-up emotion is cheap; human zeal is sometimes offensive. But Holy Spirit-empowered prayer brings fire from heaven, fire in the soul, and exhilaration of spirit.

Bounds wrote, "Fire is the life of prayer; heaven is reached by flaming importunity rising in an ascending scale." Heaven pays little attention to casual requests. God is not moved by feeble desires, listless prayers, and spiritual laziness. God rejoices to see a soul on fire with holy passion as the heart reaches out to Him.

Both heaven and hell respect earnest, bold, insistent prayer. There is no place for timidity in intercession. We are to come boldly to the throne of grace (Heb. 4:16). God has no time to waste on so-called prayers which are only passing fancies of some lukewarm soul. Isaiah lamented, "No one calls on thy name or bestirs himself" (Isa. 64:7 BERKELEY; "arouses himself," NASB).

Importunate praying is so absorbed in the need and God's answer to the need that all else is disregarded. This is the secret of effective prayer. Jesus' illustration of the importunate widow was given after the disciples had asked Jesus, "Lord, teach us to pray."

Urgent prayer increases in intensity until the answer comes. Prayer can be an ever more intensive sequence of ask, seek, knock, and fast. The man caught up in such praying cannot stop because he knows the will of God and must see the glory of God.

Even after God has given you His promise in some special quickening of your heart, you must press on in active faith. Elijah knew God had promised to send rain, but Elijah persevered seven times in continued prayer, with his face between his knees (1 Kings 18:41–46). Daniel knew God's promise to deliver the Jews, but Daniel interceded until God sent His archangel to deliver the answer and tell Daniel how greatly beloved he was (Dan. 10:10–11, 19). God was working in power, but Paul kept pressing the prayer battle day and night for all his converts and churches.

Urgent prayer can be agonizing. Prayer is hard work and more. There are wonderful times of refreshing in prayer, but there are also times of hard, unglamorous, unspectacular labor in intercession. Prayer is realism. Mountains are to be moved; demons are to be routed. The superficial Christian resents prayer that is work, wrestling, warfare. Then suddenly there is a tragic accident, terminal illness, or imminent death. Then the superficial Christian pleads for the prayer of those who know how to prevail. Suddenly he wants nothing less than importunate praying.

Prayer is wrestling, like Jacob at Jabbok. The wrestling may be quietly wrought, but it will be in an agony of earnestness. The word in Colossians 4:12 concerning Epaphras was that he was agonizing in prayer: "He is always wrestling [literally, "agonizing"] in prayer for you, that you may stand firm in all the will of God, mature and fully assured." Is that an accurate description of your prayer for your friends, for your church, for your nation? Paul pleaded for this kind of agonizing importunity on his own behalf: "I urge you, brothers, by our Lord Jesus Christ and by the love of the Spirit, to join me in my struggle by praying to God for me" [literally, "to agonize with me in prayer"] (Rom. 15:30).

When Moses stood in the gap for Israel, he engaged in agonizing importunity. It was agonizing importunity when Paul prayed for the unsaved Jews: "I speak the truth in Christ—I am not lying, my conscience confirms it in the Holy Spirit—I have great sorrow and unceasing anguish in my heart. For I could wish that I myself were cursed and cut off from Christ for the sake of my brothers, those of my own race" (Rom. 9:1–3). It was such agonizing importunity in Gethsemane when Christ's prayer perspiration turned to great clots of blood, falling down on the ground (Luke 22:44 WEYMOUTH).

You can learn to prevail in prayer. You can learn to prevail over yourself and over Satan until God sees and sends His angels to hasten the answer. It will often take time. It will usually grow out of your ever-deepening life of intercession. You must learn to persist until the answer comes. You must learn to be so Spirit-controlled in your praying that He leads you step by step until you prevail. Only He can give you the urgency until your whole being cries out to God and refuses to be stopped by Satan or discouraged by delay. You will not pray thus for every need nor will you pray this way each day. But as God directs, the Spirit will place that urgency in your soul.

Your urgent prevailing prayer may increase in intensity until you are truly wrestling in prayer. This is soul wrestling, not a physical wrestling. This is the prayer that prevails over all the power Satan hurls against God's will. This is the prayer that brings God's miracle power to bear on man's need. Oh, my beloved brethren, let us prevail in prayer!

28

You Can Be
a Prayer Warrior

Effective intercessors who are greatly used by God in prayer are at times referred to as "prayer warriors." It is correct to use the term in this way, for great prayer demands doing battle with the forces of evil. God wants all His children to be prayer warriors. Have you ever doubted that you yourself could ever become mighty in prayer? Do you feel you know your own prayer weakness too well to expect that you might become one of God's prayer warriors? Be encouraged. You can develop your own prayer life until God will surely count you as one of His real prayer warriors.

God is constantly at war with the power of Satan. From the time of Adam and Eve till the present day, Satan has been trying to delay or defeat God's eternal plan for our earth and mankind. He will never abandon that purpose. In the Book of Revelation we glimpse the new heaven, the new earth, and the New Jerusalem which will fulfill God's original purpose for which He created the world. Satan knows he cannot defeat that plan, but from Eden till now he has used every possible tactic to stall its completion. He was defeated at Calvary, but he is determined to fight on until his final prophesied defeat at the battle of Gog and Magog (20:7–10).

God also has a personalized plan for every one of His children, coordinated to harmonize with His supreme overall plan. Satan attacks God today chiefly by attacking and hindering God's children and by seeking to deceive, harm, and damn all of unsaved humanity. Satan's efforts can be defeated only by engaging him in spiritual warfare on two levels—angelic warfare and our prayer warfare.

God's children are to be warriors, advancing for God and defeating Satan again and again through prayer and obedience. Prayer alone will not be sufficient to do the job, but prayer is the basis for all obedience and the indispensable human element in the effectiveness of our obedience. While we may be limited in the areas where our obedience can be used, every Christian can be effective in prayer warfare anywhere in the world.

God desires that you maintain a militant spirit, ever ready to take the initiative for God and against sin and Satan. God wants you to be always on spiritual alert, on call, ready at a moment's notice for special assignment. This means you must be vigilant and knowledgeable of the methods of prayer warfare.

Satan will oppose every effort to wage prayer warfare. He is counting on the reluctance of many Christians to enter into this kind of sacrificial prayer. Many are comfortable praying along with two or three other more spiritual Christians, but like Peter, James, and John in the Garden of Gethsemane, they do not know how to spend an hour in prayer. Many have almost never had a prayer burden, or do not know how to respond to prayer burden. God wants you to have great liberty in prayer and deep experience in all forms of prayer.

While all prayer is important, prayer warfare—the highest level of prayer—is heavily dependent upon prayer warriors. This level of prayer goes even beyond prevailing prayer. We seem to have ten thousand prayer amateurs for one true prayer warrior. This need not be. Will you be willing for God to train and use you as one of His alert and available prayer warriors? World evangelization involves heavy spiritual warfare since all spiritual advance is contended by Satan. Spiritual conquest depends on constant prevailing prayer and repeated prayer warfare. Don't be one of those Christians who would rather work than pray.

You Are Equipped to Be a Prayer Warrior

God has prepared spiritual armor for His children. "Finally, be strong in the Lord and in his mighty power. Put on the full armor of God" (Eph. 6:10–11, 13). This armor consists of (a) the belt of truth, (b) the breastplate of righteousness, (c) the shoes of the readiness of the gospel of peace, (d) the shield of faith, (e) the helmet of salvation, and (f) the sword of the Spirit, the Word of God (vv. 14–17).

Why have we been given this armor? Because we are engaged in a battle to dislodge and defeat Satan. "Put on the full armor of God so that you can take your stand against the devil's schemes. For our struggle is not against flesh and blood, but against the rulers, against the authorities, against the powers of this dark world and against the spiritual forces of evil in the heavenly realms" (Eph. 6:11–12). Six times Paul uses the word *against*. We are against Satan as much as he is against us!

With all this equipment, how do we fight? The answer is found in verse 18: "Pray in the Spirit on all occasions with all kinds of prayer and requests. With this in mind, be alert and always keep on praying for all the saints." So the great Bible passage on spiritual warfare says the most effective way to engage in war with Satan is to pray. And you can pray! You don't have to travel to the other side of the earth. The front line in this warfare is right where you are. You can win victories on the other side of the earth, but you can win them from the place where you are.

Because of the nature of prayer warfare, you never know how many people the Holy Spirit has alerted to pray at a given moment or for a specific situation. Some prayer needs are sudden emergencies for which there has been no prior warning. You may be the only one the Spirit assigns to pray for the person or for a particular aspect of the need. Or, because of the severity of the need, you may be one of several the Spirit assigns to the battle. In some cases, however, you may be His key prayer partner because of your knowledge of or special relationship with the person needing prayer.

Other prayer needs are of long standing. Satan may be

deeply entrenched, his forces amassed against a person or group of people. It may take prolonged prayer warfare on the part of many people to bring God's victory.

Whether you stand alone in the prayer battle or whether you are one of many, your prayer is always strategically important to God's plan.

How You Can Win Prayer Victories

Prayer warfare is not your begging God to help you do His will, or trying to convince God of the magnitude of a need. Prayer warfare is joining Christ in driving out and defeating Satan and in setting his captives free. It is advancing against Satan's strongholds and dislodging and expelling his demon forces. Satan is a pretender, with no right to dominate and enslave the lives of those for whom Christ died. He has no right to harass and oppress people, to dupe and frighten them into submitting to him. Satan has been totally defeated at Calvary (see chapter 14). As compared with God's hosts, His evil spirits are fewer in number and greatly inferior in power. Prayer warfare is enforcing the victory of Calvary against Satan's deceptive schemes and defeated spirit-helpers.

1. Take the offensive in prayer. God called Moses to lead Israel out of Egypt, not to defend them in Egypt; to attack and defeat the enemy nations, not to protect Israel from them. God sent Joshua to invade and conquer Canaan, not to negotiate detente. The Holy Spirit was given at Pentecost, not to keep the church blessed and comfortable, but to make the church invincible.

The weapons of your spiritual warfare, says Paul, are not defensive weapons, but weapons of attack. "The weapons we fight with are not the weapons of the world. On the contrary, they have divine power to demolish strongholds. We demolish arguments [from Satan] and every pretension [literally, "lofty thing"] that sets itself up against the knowledge of God, and we take captive every thought to make it obedient to Christ" (2 Cor. 10:4–5). We are not to build a bypass when Satan throws up a mountain of resistance against us; we are to challenge Satan and hurl his mountain into the sea (Matt.

17:20). We are not to "hold the fort" until Jesus comes and rescues us; we are to storm the gates of Hades (16:18).

Ask God to give you a militant spirit. Ask Him to point out to you the specific needs for which to pray. Ask Him to show you the blindness, the slavery, and the lostness of the unsaved. Ask God to help you feel His longing love for the sinner, His hatred for the sin which is destroying the sinner, and His passion for the church, the kingdom, and the waiting harvest.

Ask God to give you a new joy and expectancy in prayer, a holy boldness to see Christ triumph and Satan defeated. Ask God to give you increased faith to see God's promise fulfilled and Satan put to shame. Ask God to light a holy fire in your soul by the power of the Holy Spirit, to transform your praying from weakness to prevailing power and an urgent insistence to see God's will be done on earth as it is in heaven. Insist on this prayerfully for the specific situations God puts upon your heart. Ask Him to clothe your praying with the authority of Calvary, the power of Pentecost, and the almightiness of His name.

This is your hour to see God's miracle power revealed, God's purposes fulfilled, and God's enemies routed. This is your hour to triumph on your knees with Christ. The victory was won and assured at Calvary. Satan and every demon from Hades knows their battle is already lost. In the name of Jesus, call their bluff!

2. *Do all in the power of the Holy Spirit.* The Holy Spirit has come to represent Christ and to deliver the victory Christ won at Calvary. He has come to drive out Satan before you. Resist the Devil; he will run from you because the mighty Holy Spirit will back up your faith and your Christ-given authority (James 4:7). "When the enemy comes in like a flood, the Spirit of the Lord will put him to flight" (Isa. 59:19 NIV alt.).

If the Spirit is filling you and leading you in your praying and you are invading Satan's territory to deliver Satan's captives, the Holy Spirit is right there with you to clothe your words with Christ's authority. In prayer warfare you do not fight alone. The Holy Spirit will be upon you and pray through you. "Pray in the Spirit on all occasions" (Eph. 6:18).

3. *In holy faith resist, bind, and rout Satan.* Let me give you a word of caution—don't become Devil-conscious. Don't be absorbed by your enemy. Don't keep talking about him. Resist him when you need to; command him to go. But focus your eyes on Jesus seated on the throne of heaven. Remember, through prayer you are hastening the day when all things shall be put under Jesus' feet.

Resist every sign of Satan's working, every attack he makes upon a child of God. In the name of Jesus, rebuke Satan. Tell him to get behind you and Jesus. Call on Jesus Himself to rebuke him (Zech. 3:1–2). The Lord came to destroy the Devil's work (1 John 3:8). In the name of Jesus, bind Satan's dark power by the almighty power of God. Whatever you bind on earth will be ratified, enforced, and bound by heaven (Matt. 16:19). Don't worry about how it will be done. All Christ needs to do is to speak the word. Just believe it and bind the strong man from Hades (Luke 11:21). God has myriads of mighty angels ready to assist in enforcing your command of faith.

There are situations in which Satan is now dominating that will not change until you take the offensive and drive him out. There are people enslaved by Satan who are unable to free themselves. They will remain in Satan's bondage until you, or others of God's children, drive back the darkness, bind the demonic powers, and force Satan to release his captives.

Don't tremble before Satan; challenge his authority. Don't cower when he roars like a lion. Take the authority of the name of Jesus and the old lion will slink away with his tail between his legs; he will slither off like the old serpent he is (Rev. 12:9).

4. *Saturate your soul with the Word of God.* Since you never know when the Holy Spirit may alert you to special prayer or prayer warfare, it is important to maintain your spiritual strength at all times by feeding on God's Word.

No one can stay spiritually fit by reading only a few Bible verses a day. Even one chapter a day provides a very inadequate spiritual diet. Nothing can substitute for God's Word; no devotional book can replace the reading of the Scriptures.

At the beginning of any extended prayer time or prayer battle, feed deeply on the Word of God. "Faith comes through hearing the message, and the message is heard through the word of Christ" (Rom. 10:17). Saturate yourself with God's Word. (For more extended discussion, see chapter 19.)

During your prayer warfare quote or read the promises of God. If possible, use one or two special promises that you can claim for the victory you seek. If God so leads, read the promises aloud in the Devil's hearing. Remember, the mightiest name in the Bible is "Jesus." Again and again Satan, his demons, or demon-motivated enemies have been routed by the use of the name of Jesus. Millions of times demons have been cast out by the authority of the name of Jesus.

I know of no better exhortation in a prayer battle than Ephesians 6:17: "Take the sword of the Spirit." The Holy Spirit will endorse and empower your use of the Word in prayer. As I mentioned earlier, you may even feel led to hold your Bible to your heart, or in your hand, or to place your hand upon a promise you are claiming. This but symbolizes what you are doing in the spiritual realm as you defeat Satan by the Word. As Jesus made a whip and drove the merchants out of the temple, take the Word and expel every demon who blocks God's will and fights a rearguard action against God's people.

5. *Rout the Devil by praise.* Just as in human warfare soldiers use any weapon which will help them attain victory, so in spiritual warfare the Holy Spirit may lead you to change your prayer approach from time to time. He will lead you to such faith that your mouth becomes filled with praise to God. Satan is frustrated by praise, for he fears the name of Jesus. Praise the Lord!

"Let the saints rejoice in this honor and sing for joy on their beds. May the praise of God be in their mouths and a double-edged sword in their hands . . . to bind their kings with fetters, their nobles with shackles of iron, to carry out the sentence written against them. This is the glory of all his saints. Praise the Lord" (Ps. 149:5–6, 8–9)!

With God's Word, your double-edged sword (Heb. 4:12), in your hand and God's praise on your lips, all the demons of hell will flee before you. Just as the Lord set ambushes (probably by angels) when the Israelites praised Him, so, as you praise the Lord, He may ambush Satan.

6. *Enlist the prayer of others.* There are spiritual situations of such difficulty that the prayer of many of God's prayer warriors is demanded. This is why the Lord gave the special promise to those who agree in prayer (Matt. 18:19). There is added spiritual power in united prayer. It was after ten days of united praying by the one hundred twenty believers that Pentecost came, and three thousand were saved in one day (Acts 1:14). It was after united prayer by hundreds that the place where they were praying was shaken and God gave great grace, great power, and great harvest (Acts 4:23–33; 5:12–16). It was while the Jerusalem church was earnestly praying that Peter was delivered from prison by an angel and "the word of God continued to increase and spread" (Acts 12:24).

OMS International began its work in India in 1941. The first twenty-five years of hard labor, sweat, tears, prayer, and fasting saw an average of one to two new local churches per year. As I flew across the Pacific to furlough in 1964, I was praying about what more we could do to see India's harvest reaped. God led me to ask for at least one thousand prayer partners to spend fifteen minutes a day in prayer for India and our work.

A few years ago I was back in Allahabad, India, with our senior leaders during a day of prayer and report. One by one they told how mightily God was working. One of them turned to me and said, "Duewel Sahib, all of us . . . all of us are seeing results beyond anything we have known."

"Praise the Lord!" I said.

He continued, "Duewel Sahib, are you surprised?"

"Yes, praise the Lord!" I replied.

"You ought not to be!" he immediately responded. "Did you not go to America and get one thousand people to pray fifteen minutes a day for us?"

"More than that."

"Then why are you surprised?"

"Thank you, George. I needed that reminder," I said. "Why should we be surprised when God answers prayer!"

Now our churches number about three hundred with some twenty-five thousand believers, and with twenty-five or more new churches established every year. One thousand prayer warriors united in praying for harvest was the secret!

The greater the spiritual resistance, the more difficult is your task of moving the mountain before you. The more entrenched Satan is, the greater the need of enlisting the support of more and more prayer warriors to drive him out. It may take multiplied prayer times and longer hours than you had anticipated, but as sure as God is in heaven, in due season you will reap if you do not give up (Gal. 6:9).

7. *Pray on till Satan is defeated.* How long should you continue the prayer battle? Until the victory comes. If God gave you the initial prayer burden, the battle is not yours, but His. If the battle continues over a period of days or months, you will not always have the same prayer burden or the same amount of time to devote to it. But you can maintain your prayer commitment. You can keep standing on God's promises, praising Him for the answer that is coming.

Keep the prayer pressure on Satan. Take your place of authority with Christ. Stand firm in the authority of Christ's name. Continue repeated longer prayer times as the Holy Spirit leads and enables you.

This was Isaiah's determination: "For Zion's sake I will not keep silent, for Jerusalem's sake I will not remain quiet, *till* her righteousness shines out like the dawn, her salvation like a blazing torch" (Isa. 62:1, italics added). What instruction of Christ kept the disciples praying in the Upper Room? "Stay in the city *until* you have been clothed with power from on high" (Luke 24:49, italics added). How long must you pray? *Until.*

When God gives you a prayer assignment, consider that your sacred responsibility *until* (1) the answer comes, (2) the situation or person is removed, or (3) God lifts the prayer concern from your heart. When you know you have been praying in the will of God, you can be sure that Christ continues to intercede also. Don't break your prayer partnership with Him *until* the need is past.

How long should you ask? *Until* the answer is given to you. How long should you seek? *Until* you find. How long should you keep knocking on heaven's door? *Until* the door is opened. May I repeat, as surely as God is on His throne, in due season you will reap if you do not give up (Gal. 6:9). Heaven and earth may pass away, but His Word will never pass away or fail.

29

Your Prayer Can Be
an Eternal Investment

Prayer is not only a way to commune with God and to receive help from God, it is an eternal investment! Heaven's records are adequately kept by the angels. Our God is not so unjust as to forget your work and the love you show Him by helping others (Heb. 6:10). Neither is He likely to forget your holy longings, your intercession, and your tears. Self-centered prayers will be lost, but such is not true prayer. Nor do prayers prayed from the wrong motivation have any validity before God (James 4:3).

Intercession for the salvation of others, for the building of Christ's church, for revival among God's people, and for the evangelization of the world all partake of the quality of the eternal. God's holy will is eternal and such prayers are prayed in harmony with that will, commended by our great High Priest who is the Amen of our prayers (Rev. 3:14), and energized by the hunger, power, and intercession of the Holy Spirit. Such prayers cannot die until they are fulfilled to the measure of God's holy will. All such prayers are eternal investments.

Prayer Is an Intensely Personal Investment
of Love

Through prayer you can give your love, your very self to any person, group of people, or nation. Prayer is the only expression of love which cannot be stopped or rejected. Through prayer you can convey love to those who love you as well as to those who do not even know you. Through prayer you can even surround with love the lives of those who reject you. They may not accept it, but they cannot destroy it. It is all stored up in the treasure house of heaven and in the memory of God.

I cannot prove this by Scripture, but I believe that prayer for a person who rejects all of God's goodness and grace until death remains as a potential heritage for others of his family, area, or nation. For example, prayer for a communist leader may be rejected and the leader may eventually die an atheist. But he has not been totally untouched by your prayer or God's grace. God has done His part, and you have done yours. Since the leader represented his nation, in a sense your love for him was a love for the nation. You will have your reward because you loved him as God loved him. You were Christlike in your intercession. It may be that one day that prayer will be answered in a way that will glorify God far beyond your expectations—perhaps in some national awakening. It is stored in God's reservoir of unanswered prayer for that nation. It is not lost. The next chapter describes this more fully.

My parents were invited to a country schoolhouse to hold weekly Bible study/prayer meetings. Often they spoke to me of the unusual sense of God's presence and blessing they always experienced there. One day they mentioned this at the schoolhouse. Immediately the people said, "Oh, did you not know that years ago on this very spot there was an old Baptist church?" Is it not possible that after all those years prayer was still being answered for that community?

Prayer Can Build Up an Endowment of Blessing

Praying parents can intercede for their children and grandchildren until, long after the death of the parents, those prayers still convey wonderful blessings. The godly intercessions of church and mission founders and leaders are answered over the decades. Every true intercessor prays many prayers which will not have their full answer before the prayer warrior joins the church in heaven.

Prayers prayed in the Spirit never die until they accomplish God's intended purpose. His answer may not be what we expected, or when we expected it, but God often provides much more abundantly than we could think or ask. He interprets our intent and either answers or stores up our prayers (Rev. 8:2–5). Sincere prayers are never lost. Energy, time, love, and longing can be endowments that will never be wasted or go unrewarded.

Jesus Christ continues to endow the church with His intercession. Paul endowed the church with prayer. So did innumerable Old and New Testament saints and leaders. The mighty outpourings of God's Spirit in the Millennium and in the new heaven and the new earth will surely be built upon all those holy intercessions which were not fully answered before.

Do not be discouraged when prayers are not immediately answered. You can endow with God's mercies, with the Holy Spirit's ministries, and with angelic assistance and protection. Pray on and on; prayer is never, never in vain.

Prayer Is Not Limited by Length

Every holy desire that arises in your heart as you pray for others while you go about your normal routine can multiply your prayer investments. Over and over throughout the day, call out to God in a sentence or two of intercession. Every such prayer counts before God. Throughout each day there are small segments of time that you can use for prayer. Don't waste these precious minutes.

> Don't despise a single minute—
> Each has sixty seconds in it.
> If you seize it, you can use it.
> Do not waste it or abuse it.
> If you pray, your little minute
> Has eternal value in it.

Don't treat your prayer responsibility as legalistic bondage and feel you can never take time to relax, chat with others, enjoy God's nature, beautiful music, or time

217

with family and friends. However, countless minutes are wasted by the average person each day—minutes which could all be invested in prayer.

If you have a praying heart, there are multiplied opportunities to make brief prayer investments. If you listen to the radio every time you are in the car alone, if you turn on the television the instant you sit down at home, if you crowd every moment with trivial pursuits, your priorities are clearly not characterized by concern for eternal values. You can spend those minutes carelessly, and they are gone forever; or you can seize them for brief, loving intercession, and they will be eternally blessed. The choice is yours.

But, oh, how wonderful when you deliberately plan for longer times in prayer! Block out a half-hour, an hour, or longer for prayer, then shut your door at the time of your appointment with God. If you cannot arrange for a special place in your home for your prayer time, work within your circumstances. If you are a truck driver, use the driving time during long hauls for prayer. If you are an invalid lying in bed day after day, make the time fly on wings of prayer. If you are a farmer plowing the fields, plant priceless seeds of prayer.

One of the greatest blessings of retirement, for example, is the possibility of large blocks of time for extended prayer. In Upper Hutt, just outside of Wellington, New Zealand, one such brother showed me his prayer room and explained with great joy: "You see, I am now retired and can spend my whole day in prayer. I wash and shave, have my breakfast, and then spend my hours in this room. Would you like to see my prayer book?" I was happy to do so. He showed me a large loose-leaf notebook filled with pictures of OMS missionaries, national co-workers, maps of various nations, and similar items. "You see, every day I go around the world in prayer," he said. What a reward has now accrued for him in heaven! He will eternally collect dividends on his investment in prayer.

You Can Diversify Your Prayer Investment World-wide

One can support financially only a certain number of ministries, organizations, or individuals. Through prayer, however, there is no limit to the scope of investment possible to you. (See chapter 33 for suggestions as to how to prepare prayer lists.) Perhaps there are children or young people in whose lives you want to make prayer investments. You may have a major interest in an unsaved family, in one or more missionary societies. Certainly you will want to invest prayer in the ministry of your own church. If God has placed one or more nations on your heart, you can invest in prayer for them. You can invest in people and nations that you may never see in person.

While traveling on a bus in Northern Ireland years ago, I was praying for my meeting to be held that night in a rural town. As I hungered to enlist more prayer support for India, I was inspired to write a poem. I became so absorbed with my writing that I was unaware of the passing scenery or my traveling companions. Suddenly I was startled to hear my name called. Looking up, I found a woman standing in the aisle. "I just happened to notice you sitting here," she said. "I recognized you from a picture in your missionary paper, and just wanted to tell you that, for the past eighteen years, I have been praying for you every day, and especially for your wife Betty." Tears sprang to my eyes as I realized that God had graciously allowed me to meet one who had invested in prayer for me and my family.

On another occasion, I was driving alone in my car on the West Virginia turnpike when I became so sleepy I feared it would be dangerous to continue my trip. I asked the Lord to keep me alert until I could find a place to get a snack and some coffee. A little farther on, I noticed a sign indicating an all-night diner at the next exit. Pulling up in front of the diner, I entered and took the only empty stool at the counter. The man seated to my right initiated a conversation. "I stopped here because they don't sell liquor," he ventured. I turned to him in surprise. "I share your sentiments," I commented. "I'm a missionary." "A missionary!" he exclaimed. "Come with me." He got up from his seat, and I followed him, a bit puzzled. Stopping behind a man seated at the far end of the counter, he tapped the diner on the shoulder. As the man turned around, he looked me full in the face. "I pray for you every day!" he said, as recognition lighted his eyes. We had each traveled hundreds of miles that day, with different destinations. In God's providential timing, however, our paths crossed, and I was allowed to encounter yet another prayer investor who gave me an encouraging word.

What joys heaven will afford as we meet and fellowship with those who have blessed our earthly lives and supported our ministry through investment of prayer! I wonder if the angels will join in those conversations and tell how they alerted someone to pray for you at critical moments in your life?

Even if we pray for people who never yielded to Christ during their lifetime, we will not regret having done our part. One day, as I shook hands with Prime Minister Nehru of India, I wondered what word I could say in the brief moment I would have with him. How glad I was that I could tell him I had been praying for him each day.

If you love someone, invest prayer in that person. If you love your church and pastor, pray sacrificially for them. If you love your nation, be sure you spend more time in prayer than in criticism. You have no right to criticize your leaders if you are not praying for them. Love the world through prayer. Spread your prayer investments all over the world, and expect rich dividends!

Prayer Can Be the Best Investment You Will Ever Make

God's special blessings are reserved for those who work discreetly for Him, desiring to please only Him and not people. So often financial gifts become public knowledge that part of one's reward is realized here on earth as others become aware of the service and praise it. We are encouraged in God's Word to be faithful and obedient servants, and He will reward us openly. We pray not for the sake of reward, however, but because He has asked us to do so.

We have no way of estimating how great heaven's rewards and prayer dividends will be, though God does give us some thrilling suggestions. For one thing, God's ways are so much higher than our ways—as much higher as the heavens are above the earth (Isa. 55:9); surely that includes His ways of rewarding. Likewise, Jesus emphasized that God knows infinitely better than any human father how to give good things to His children (Matt. 7:11).

The rewards of prayer are indescribably greater than any dividends paid by an earthly investment. The Bible teaches that a sinner who denies God is of all men a fool. I sometimes wonder if some Christians also should not be classified as fools. A Christian whose prayers are almost always self-centered "give me" prayers, who can spend an hour a day reading the newspaper and not even five minutes reading God's Word, who averages more than two hours a day watching television and cannot even give one hour to prayer—surely he or she is, of all people, most foolish!

That person knows the power of God, the glory of heaven, the length of eternity, the certainty of God's rewards for all we do for Him, yet places most of the emphasis of life on that which will have no value at all in eternity. That person wastes earthly time and loses eternal rewards. Much of the life investment of such a Christian will be burned up in a flash at the fiery judgment seat of Christ before which we all shall stand (Rom. 14:10–12; 2 Cor. 5:9–10). This Christian, though saved, is building on Christ with materials of wood, hay, and straw (1 Cor. 3:11–15). Paul says that individual will "suffer loss."

Prayer is your opportunity to transmute minutes and hours into eternal reward, earthly time into eternal blessings. Prayer is one of the most godly activities anyone on earth can engage in, perhaps the most godly of all. It is the constant activity of God the Son and God the Spirit. Surely time invested in partnership with Jesus and the Holy Spirit is the wisest use of time you can ever make.

"Be very careful, then, how you live—not as unwise, but as wise, making the most of every opportunity. . . . Therefore do not be foolish, but understand what the Lord's will is" (Eph. 5:15–17).

30

Prayers That Can Never Be Lost

Prayers prayed in accordance with the will of God are never lost. God preserves them in His own records, and one day they will be answered. He will reward fully all those whose prayer helped win the spiritual battle and opened the door for God's great work in the world.

A dramatic prophecy of how all such unanswered prayer will one day be answered is presented symbolically in Revelation 8:1–5. There is silence in heaven for about half an hour, as if all heaven is waiting in breathless anticipation of what is about to happen. An angel approaches with a golden censer—a container in which incense is burned. "He was given much incense to offer, with the prayers of all the saints, on the golden altar before the throne. The smoke of the incense, together with the prayers of the saints, went up before God from the angel's hand. Then the angel took the censer, filled it with fire from the altar, and hurled it on the earth; and there came peals of thunder, rumblings, flashes of lightning and an earthquake" (Rev. 8:3–5).

Do you understand this picture? The fragrant incense probably typifies the intercessions of Christ who is seated at the right hand of the Father, where He constantly intercedes (Rom. 8:34). His fragrant intercession is added to the prayers of God's children for God's kingdom to come and His will to be done on earth. Fire from the altar, symbolic of the mighty power of the Holy Spirit, is added to the combined prayers of Jesus and His saints, and all is poured down upon the earth.

Immediately there follow the seven trumpets as outlined in the subsequent chapters of Revelation. These awesome demonstrations of God's power work dramatically to speed the accomplishment of God's will on earth and the total defeat of Satan. What prayers were these preserved in heaven? The prayers which can never be lost. Many saints have much prayer of that kind stored in the treasuries of heaven. Have you?

When we know we are praying according to God's will, our faith is greatly strengthened. Daniel reported that when he learned the length of time Israel would be in captivity, and realized that the time for the return of the Jews to Jerusalem was nearing, he sought God's face with tremendous urgency: "So I turned to the Lord God and pleaded with him in prayer and petition, in fasting, and in sackcloth and ashes" (Dan. 9:3).

Daniel then outlined for us his intercessory identification with his people. (Read Dan. 9:4–23.) So powerful was this prayer that God sent the archangel Gabriel to deliver His answer in person. Though Daniel did not live to see his request granted, it was fully granted shortly after his death. Daniel's prayer did not die; it could not be lost, for it was prayed in accordance with the will of God.

"Always" Prayers

There are some prayers that we may be sure are always in the will of God. One of the most powerful prayers to pray is the one Jesus taught us: *"Your will be done."* It is always appropriate to pray those words, even though we often do not know how to pray specifically about a given situation. I have found in militant prayer warfare that these words are a powerful weapon in defeating Satan.

"Bless." While this is a very general prayer, it can be both deep and emphatic. It expresses the heart of God who longs to bless everyone. Needs may vary, but some form of blessing is the answer to every need.

Rev. Harry Woods, OMS China director, stayed in Peking for some time after the communist takeover in order to identify with the Chinese church. The time came, however, when he felt his presence was becoming an embarrassment to them. When he asked for an exit permit, he was interrogated by the Chinese police who seemed reluctant to let him go. Rev. Woods said, "I love China. I pray for China every day. I pray for Chairman Mao every day." "What do you pray?" they shot back. "I pray God to bless him, and to give him wisdom to rule this great nation," replied the minister. Rev. Woods was permitted to leave.

There are other "always" prayers, such as: "Lord, undertake." "Lord, reveal Yourself to them." "Lord, may Your Spirit be outpoured." "Come quickly, Lord Jesus." According to the Scriptures, a number of prayers are always in God's will.

Prayer for the building of Christ's church. Jesus said, "I will build my church" (Matt. 16:18). It may not always be God's time to establish a local congregation in a particular town or section of a town, but it is always God's desire to build His church. Sample "always" aspects include the planting of new congregations of believers, the growth of existing congregations, God's blessing on ministry to special groups (children, youth, families, the unchurched, the poor, and so on), the unity of the church, increased vision and zeal to witness and win souls, sacrificial giving and tithing, discipling of believers, increased spirit of prayer, and establishing in sound doctrine.

Prayer for revival in the church. "Will you not revive us again, that your people may rejoice in you?" (Ps. 85:6). "For this is what the high and lofty One says—he who lives forever, whose name is holy: 'I live in a high and holy place, but also with him who is contrite and lowly in spirit, to revive the spirit of the lowly and to revive the heart of the contrite' " (Isa. 57:15). "For Zion's sake I will not keep silent, for Jerusalem's sake I will not remain quiet, till her righteousness shines out like the dawn, her salvation like a blazing torch" (Isa. 62:1). "You who call on the Lord, give yourselves no rest, and give him no rest till he establishes Jerusalem and makes her the praise of the earth" (Isa. 62:6–7). Sample "always" aspects include a new awareness of God and reverence for God, a hunger among God's people to see God work in power, new richness (life, anointing, blessing, and power) in congregational services, new evidence of repentance (humbling of self before God, asking forgiveness, and making restitution), and revival (local, regional, or national).

Prayer for laborers in God's harvest. "Ask the Lord of the harvest, therefore, to send out workers into his harvest field" (Matt. 9:38). Sample "always" aspects include God's clear call to young people and others, the training of Christian workers called by God, and God's guidance to His workers concerning the place of ministry.

Prayer for harvest. "I tell you, open your eyes and look at the fields! They are ripe for harvest" (John 4:35). Sample "always" aspects include Bible distribution, literature evangelism, radio and TV evangelism, evangelism of specific groups (youth, students, prisoners, military people, religious groups such as Jews, Muslims, and Hindus), evangelism teams, evangelism by lay believers, follow-up of evangelism, sinners being convicted of their sins, and new people being able to fully understand the gospel.

Prayer for the salvation of an individual. You are always in God's will when you pray for the salvation of any unsaved person. Jesus gave Himself a ransom for all (1 Tim. 2:5–6). Anyone who thirsts may come (John 7:37). Anyone who will may come (Rev. 22:17). Sample "always" aspects include the Holy Spirit's conviction of sin, the Spirit's enlightenment so the person understands the gospel, God's revelation of His love, His release of people from Satan's bonds, God's gift of yielding grace, and His bestowment of the assurance of salvation.

Prayer for God's blessing on a nation. "Ask of me, and I will make the nations your inheritance" (Ps. 2:8). Ask God to give you some special nation as your prayer assignment. How well I remember my mother's weeping every time she mentioned China in her daily prayers. I believe the recent harvest in China is in part an answer to her prayer and similar prayer burdens by a host of others. Sample "always" aspects include blessing on the nation, blessing on the leaders of the nation (wisdom and integrity for them), adequate food and housing for the people, God's anointing and fruitfulness for gospel workers, strengthening of and blessing on the church, advance of the gospel, and greater freedom for the gospel.

Prayer for the restraint and defeat of Satan. "Resist him" (1 Peter 5:9). "Our struggle is ... against the rulers, against the authorities, against the powers of this dark world and against the spiritual forces of evil in the heavenly realms. ... Pray in the Spirit on all occasions with all kinds of prayers and requests" (Eph. 6:12, 18). We should pray always for Satan's plans to be defeated, Satan to be rebuked, Satan's darkness to be lifted, Satan's chains of sin and evil habits to be broken, doors closed by Satan to be opened, demonic spirits to be driven away, Satan's slaves to be set free.

Prayers That Depend Upon God's Will

Some categories of prayer may or may not be in God's will. You are totally dependent upon the guidance of the Spirit when you pray for these things, and you should always word your petitions "if it be Your will." You have every right to be bold in your requests, to be persistent in prayer, and to claim God's promises again and again. Pray on until you get God's answer unless He guides you to discontinue your specific petition. He may do this by taking away your interest or desire, or by giving you an inner restraint that suggests this is not His will. However, until He does so, press on in faith.

Prayer for material benefits. "If you then, though you are evil, know how to give good gifts to your children, how much more will your Father in heaven give good gifts to those who ask him!" (Matt. 7:11). God loves mankind so completely that He delights in helping them. The only times God is not willing to grant material blessings are when He must punish because of sin, when He must discipline His children, or when, in God's infinite wisdom, such blessings are not best at the time.

227

Sometimes the specific blessing you are asking God to bestow might tend to make the recipient spiritually careless or self-sufficient, feeling able to get along without God. Again, God may have something far better in mind for that individual, or a better timing for the particular blessing. God's highest love may be revealed by not granting your request in exactly the way you have asked, since His ways are far beyond yours.

Prayer for removal of trials, problems, and difficulties. Trials can be a source of great spiritual blessing to you and can lead to great eternal reward (1 Peter 1:6–7). Present sufferings can prepare for eternal glory (2 Cor. 4:17). "I consider that our present sufferings are not worth comparing with the glory that will be revealed" in heaven (Rom. 8:18).

Just as hard work is good for the physical health of a normal person, so pressures, problems, and trials can increase your spiritual muscle, your spiritual vitality, your faith, patience, and other spiritual virtues. "We know that suffering produces perseverance; perseverance, character; and character, hope. And hope does not disappoint us" (Rom. 5:3–5). "You know that the testing of your faith develops perseverance. Perseverance must finish its work so that you may be mature and complete, not lacking anything" (James 1:3–4). God does not willingly bring affliction and grief to mankind (Lam. 3:32–33). It pains Him to see anyone suffer. But He works for our eternal good. Hence the psalmist could say: "Before I was afflicted I went astray, but now I obey your word. . . . It was good for me to be afflicted so that I might learn your decrees" (Ps. 119:67, 71).

Prayer for physical healing. God's general will for mankind is physical and mental health, but it is not always God's will to heal in a specific situation. God's grace is built even into our genes and chromosomes. God does not delight in any suffering, whether it be physical illness, cruelty, persecution, or deprivation. He is pleased when mankind seeks to discover the medical and surgical procedures that benefit life. We should use great boldness in prayer for the physical, emotional, and mental healing of ourselves and others. We have every right to plead God's promises in holy persistence until God checks us or suggests that healing is not His will. Undoubtedly it would please God if our faith for healing were much stronger.

Divine healing for physical and mental affliction is common on the mission fields. Christ must prove that He is the living, prayer-answering God in contrast to the impotent false gods and religions of pagan nations. It glorifies Christ to answer prayer. Perhaps we who have shared such full gospel light do not need so many evidences of the supernatural. On the other hand, God is just the same today as He has been in the past or will be in the future (Heb. 13:8). This means He is the same in wisdom, compassion, love, power, and readiness to answer prayer.

There are occasions when suffering can bring blessing to the person who suffers and to others who observe the grace God gives to the sufferer. Sickness is sometimes permitted by God because, through it, He will gain the glory (John 11:4).

Most commentators believe that Paul's thorn in the flesh (2 Cor. 12:7–10) was physical illness of some kind, probably eye trouble. Interestingly enough, it was because of illness that Paul was able to found the church in Galatia (Gal. 4:13). The Galatian Christians loved Paul so much they would gladly have plucked out their own eyes and given them to him if that had been possible (4:14–15). Paul asked for healing, not just once, but three times. It was right for him to ask until God healed him or else refused his request. This request was eventually refused as explained in 2 Corinthians 12:8–10.

Prayer for the extension of life. Sometimes God does grant our request, even if it is not His perfect will, to teach us a valuable lesson. For example, Hezekiah may have been too insistent in his prayer for deliverance from death (Isa. 38:1–6). "Hezekiah became ill and was at the point of death. He prayed to the Lord, who answered him and gave him a miraculous sign. But Hezekiah's heart was proud and he did not respond to the kindness shown him; therefore the Lord's wrath was on him and on Judah and Jerusalem" (2 Chron. 32:24–25). God extended his life fifteen years. During those added years his son Manasseh was born.

When Manasseh succeeded his father Hezekiah as king, he was the complete opposite of his father. He cursed the nation by introducing idolatry wholesale and became known for his cruelty and bloodshed. Judah was destroyed as a nation under his rule. "Surely these things happened to Judah according to the Lord's command, in order to remove them from his presence because of the sins of Manasseh and all he had done" (2 Kings 24:3). How much better, it would seem, if Hezekiah had not been so insistent on living longer.

Naturally we would all like to postpone death for as long as possible. Too, there are certain situations in which it would appear that God's will would be to prolong life (for example, the parents of young children, Christians in critical places of leadership, and so on). Unless God checks us, we should feel free to ask Him to extend the life of His servants. But let us always pray for His will above all else.

31

How to Hold
a Personal Prayer Retreat

A personal prayer retreat involving most of a day, a weekend, or a period of several days affords an extended period of time with God. I can echo the testimony of thousands who can testify that their spiritual lives would be far less effective had they not repeatedly set apart such times. God has revealed His will to me in ways and concerning matters that I had not even thought about prior to extended time alone with Him. I would not want to have missed those experiences for anything in the world, for they had a tremendous effect upon all my later service for the Lord.

Such prolonged time with Jesus can bring personal revival, renewed peace and soul-poise in the midst of pressure, and a clear understanding of God's guidance and will in planning your life or in facing crucial decisions. It is usually most unwise to make a major decision until you have had such a personal prayer retreat. Special prayer retreat time can also have a very important role in preparing the way of the Lord (see chapters 21 and 22).

Charles G. Finney, the Congregational evangelist so greatly used of God in the 1850s, is considered by some to be the greatest evangelist since the apostle Paul. Over half a million people were converted to Christ in the mighty revival that began in his meetings. It is estimated that in 1857–58 alone, over a hundred thousand people found Christ directly or indirectly through his ministry and that eighty-five percent of those converted in

Finney's meetings remained true to their original commitment and followed through in church membership and spiritual growth. Yet today, if six percent of the people making professions of faith in crusades later join a church, we are satisfied!

What is the difference? Finney wrote how God gave him mighty infillings of the Holy Spirit "that went through me, as it seemed, body and soul. I immediately found myself endued with such power from on high that a few words dropped here and there to individuals were the means of their immediate conversion. My words seemed to fasten like barbed arrows in the souls of men. They cut like a sword. They broke the heart like a hammer. Multitudes can attest to this. . . . Sometimes I would find myself in a great measure empty of this power. I would go and visit, and find that I made no saving impression. I would exhort and pray with the same results. I would then set apart a day for private fasting and prayer . . . after humbling myself and crying out for help, the power would return upon me with all its freshness. This has been the experience of my life."

John N. Hyde, Presbyterian missionary to India, was one of the founders of the great Sialkot Convention in India in 1904, about the time of the great revival in Wales. To this day the Sialkot Convention has continued as a great source of blessing to Christ's church. Before one of the first conventions, Hyde and R. M'Cheyne Paterson waited before God for thirty days. A little over a week later George Turner joined them. For twenty-one more days and nights these three men prayed and praised God for a mighty outpouring of His power. Was it worth it? Literally thousands over the years came into the kingdom through the prayers of those men.

Personal prayer retreats have a definite biblical basis. It is quite possible that, before his translation, Enoch had such retreats with the Lord. Enoch "walked with God 300 years . . . then he was no more, because God took him away" (Gen. 5:22–24). Moses spent two periods of forty days each on Mount Sinai alone with the Lord. During that time God revealed Himself more fully to

Moses than He has to any other human being either before or since. Much of Elijah's time by the brook Kerith (1 Kings 17:2–7) was undoubtedly spent in prayer for Israel and Judah.

Jesus had personal periods of prayer retreat. He began His ministry with forty days of prayer and fasting. At times He spent the whole night in prayer (Luke 6:12). It seems that often He used the Mount of Olives as a place for prolonged personal prayer (Mark 11:19; Luke 21:37).

Many Korean Christian leaders understand this concept. They have made it a practice of spending time alone with the Lord in order to seek His face and learn His will. On the seventy-fifth anniversary of the OMS work in Korea, we held a series of seminars on the life of the Korean church that grew out of our ministry there—the Korea Evangelical Church. A panel of ministers answered our questions. When the subject of fasting was mentioned, they reported that their records showed more than twenty thousand Korean Christians had spent forty days in fasting and prayer.

You will probably not be led by the Holy Spirit to spend forty days in a prayer retreat, or to fast for a prolonged time. If He does lead in this area, you will learn how to care for your body and how to break the fast. But the results are clear: Those who seek God's face in personal prayer retreats receive tremendous blessing.

The Purpose of a Prayer Retreat

The purpose of your personal prayer retreat may be to draw near to God. "Come near to God and he will come near to you" (James 4:8). "But as for me, it is good to be near God" (Ps. 73:28). Oh, what a privilege to spend time close to the heart of Jesus!

You may desire time alone with God because you need to discover His will in some matter of great importance. Don't be embarrassed. He wants you to understand His will. He has a "good, pleasing, and perfect will" for you (Rom. 12:2). He wants "to fill you with the knowledge of his will through all spiritual wisdom and understanding" (Col. 1:9). He may reveal some new direction to you during your prayer retreat. He has done this for me. Or He may begin a process which will lead to your full understanding at a later time. He loves you so much He wants you to know and do His will.

You may desire this extended time alone with God out of concern for an important or urgent need. The need may be for some aspect of God's cause, for your nation or community, for some friend or loved one, or for yourself. Do not hesitate to pray for personal needs.

How to Plan for a Prayer Retreat

1. Plan for a place for prayer where you will be undisturbed. On several occasions in India, when privacy was at a premium, I took a train to the next stop and spent the day in the railway waiting room, reading and praying. Though the conditions were not ideal, for there were people all around me, I was relatively undisturbed.

A number of our OMS-related churches in Korea have in their church building several prayer rooms just large enough for one person. Any member can come at any time, leave his or her shoes outside the little door to show the room is occupied, and spend hours or even a day or two praying there. Other churches have a special prayer house in the mountains, available to any member of the church.

When my wife and I were serving as missionaries in India, we went to Landour, Mussoorie, in the Himalayas for several weeks in the summer to escape the oppressive heat. I found some ideal spots on the mountainsides for my prayer retreats—one, only nine miles beyond Landour. Several times during each hot season, I would slip out at daybreak, walk the nine miles to the spot, and spend the day alone with the Lord. Oh, what blessed times!

In the city of Allahabad, I had an arrangement with friends to use an empty storage room in a kind of outbuilding as a place of retreat. There was no phone there or people who could interrupt my time alone with God. At other times I have used an empty room of a church building.

If you sincerely desire to seek Him in prolonged fellowship, He will lead you to the place.

2. *Schedule a time when you can be free from pressures and interruptions.* For some people Sunday afternoon is a good time for a shorter prayer retreat. Consider spending part of your vacation, or choose some office holiday for a longer retreat. Perhaps a half-night of prayer could be planned, beginning at suppertime. You might want to skip your evening meal and strengthen your prayer time with a brief fast.

3. *Collect all the supplies you will need.* A list of items to take along on your prayer retreat might include (a) Bible, (b) hymnbook, (c) notebook and pen, (d) concordance (if your Bible does not include one), (e) one or two other translations of the Bible or of the New Testament alone, (f) devotional book or a book on revival, prayer, or the Holy Spirit, (g) flashlight (if necessary), (h) cushion or something to kneel on, (i) watch or alarm clock (especially if you are planning several days of prayer), (j) adequate wraps, and (k) your prayer diary.

4. *Inform someone where you may be reached in case of emergency.* Though you will not publicize this sacred time alone with God, you will want to notify some member of your church or family where you will be spending these hours or days. After the retreat you may need to refer to it, especially if someone tried to contact you in your absence, but this should be done matter-of-factly. There is a place for testimony, but be careful to give all the glory to God and not attract attention to yourself.

5. *Begin the retreat as rested as possible.* If you plan a prayer retreat of several days' duration, you will need to be properly refreshed for your time with the Lord. It is perfectly spiritual to sleep when your body demands it. At some point during your retreat, you may want to take a brief nap before resuming your prayer and meditation. Here, your alarm clock will come in handy.

How to Invest Your Prayer Time

God may direct you to vary your methods of prayer from time to time. Trust the Holy Spirit to guide you. However, the following suggestions may be helpful.

1. Begin your prayer time with joyful worship. Psalm 100:4 exhorts us to enter God's presence with thanksgiving and praise. Take time to thank God for who He is, for His love and other attributes, for His leaving heaven to come to earth, for His loving deeds, for His death and resurrection, for His goodness to you, for His beautiful creation, for your Christian friends, and for church.

The word pictures in the Book of Revelation suggest that the angels, other heavenly beings, and God's saints sing also (Rev. 4:8–11; 5:6–14; 7:9–12; 14:2–3; 15:2–4; 19:1–7). God loves singing. There were singing and rejoicing in heaven before there was a human being on earth (Job 38:7). God Himself is pictured as singing with joy over us or perhaps with us (Zeph. 3:17). God created birds, men, and angels to sing. You give joy to the heart of God when you sing His praises, whether audibly or in your heart.

Some of the great hymns of the church are hymns of praise. You will want to memorize some of the verses and choruses to use from time to time in your daily prayer times.

I have found that my heart begins to thrill with joy as I near the place and time for special prayer. I am going to be alone with Jesus! How sacred! How wonderful! How blessed!

2. Begin to feed upon God's Word. Normally it is important to listen to God first. Listening is as important as speaking; feasting on the Word is as important as interceding. You can often hear His voice through the reading of His Word.

Take all the time you need to saturate your heart with the Word. You may at times want to read some portions of Scripture on your knees. It is often wise to continue your systematic reading of the Bible rather than to skip around. On the other hand, you may feel led to begin by reading a portion of the Psalms—perhaps as many as twenty-five or more—or to read through one of the Gospels or the Epistles. Freely follow the suggestion made by the Holy Spirit to your heart.

Read to be blessed. Don't prepare formal Bible studies or read analytically, unless the Lord directs you to do so. Just feast on God's Word and God's goodness. You are preparing your heart to commune with Him, to worship at His feet, to intercede for others, and to win prayer battles. In all of these, the Word of God lays an enduring foundation.

3. *Focus your prayer on God's interests.* In the prayer Jesus taught His disciples to pray, His priorities were (a) the hallowing of the name of God the Father (His reverence, honor, and glory), (b) the coming of God's kingdom (the total fulfillment of God's plan for the church and the world, the advance of His rule over and among men, and the final return of Jesus), and (c) the fulfilling of God's will on earth here and now. These elements should be a part of your daily prayer concern, but particularly of extended prayer periods.

Pray for revival among the people of God. Pray that the church as a whole may exhibit holiness of life, separation from the attitudes and actions of the world, and an overflowing love toward all people, especially toward one another. Then the unsaved will say again today what they said in the first century of the church: "Behold how these Christians love one another!"

Pray for the salvation of multitudes of the unsaved. God is glorified when the gospel is proclaimed to the unreached, when a harvest of new believers is reaped here and around the world. This is the great purpose of God, the Great Commission of the church. Intercession for the lost should be a part of every believer's prayer time.

Beware of becoming so absorbed in your own needs and interests that you neglect to pray for others. If self-centered prayer becomes characteristic of your prayer life, your prayers may remain unanswered. Make it a habit to pray more for others than you pray for yourself and your own loved ones. When you follow the order of priority that Jesus taught us, it will take less praying to get your own needs met! "Seek first his kingdom and his righteousness, and all these things will be given to you as well" (Matt. 6:33). This is His promise.

4. Humble yourself before the Lord. Humility before God prepares the way for petition for personal needs. Confess your need for Him. Acknowledge His sovereignty. Bow in humble submission before Him. Lift your eyes to Him as you rejoice and thank Him; then bow in lowliness of heart as you begin your intercession.

There are times when we are driven to our knees by a sense of personal, group, or national sin. In such instances confession of sin and total humbling of the self before God may well precede almost all other aspects of prayer. This is the pattern of Psalm 51 in which David approached God under deep conviction of personal sin.

If you are cherishing sin in your heart, the Lord will not hear your prayer (Ps. 66:18). At Kadesh-Barnea God did not hear the prayers of Israel when they wept tears of self-pity (Deut. 1:45). Nor will He honor the prayers of the unrepentant (Job 35:13). Forgiveness for personal sin and reconciliation with Christian brothers and sisters you may have wronged must precede your prayer retreat (Matt. 5:23–24; Rom. 12:18).

When a Spirit-filled believer walking in God's light comes into God's presence, it is appropriate to come with joy, not with head drooped and downcast eyes like the publican (Luke 18:13). Rather, like Jesus, one should lift one's eyes to heaven and first praise the Lord and rejoice in His love. Then, having followed with intercession for kingdom interests, the Spirit-filled believer naturally comes to his own personal needs.

With gratitude to God for His goodness and mercy, but with true humility, tell God how unworthy you are of all His goodness, how far short of His glory you so often come (Rom. 3:23). Then as you look into your own heart in the light of God's holiness, you may recall hasty words you have spoken, unwise steps you have taken, and instances in which you have grieved the Holy Spirit. Then is the time to pray, "Forgive me my debts as I forgive my debtors" (Matt. 6:12).

God "gives grace to the humble. Humble yourselves, therefore, under God's mighty hand, that he may lift you up in due time" (1 Peter 5:5–6). In such humility you can then cast all your care on the Lord (v. 7). God will revive the spirit of the lowly and contrite (Isa. 57:15). When God's people humble themselves and confess their sin and the sins of their land, God always forgives and heals (2 Chron. 7:14).

5. *Present your personal petitions to the Lord.* Because you are God's child, everything which concerns you is important to God. Nothing is too great or too small to share with your heavenly Father. You pray, not to inform Jesus of what He does not know, but to share your heart's desire, your problems, and your needs. You come to talk it over with your beloved Lord. He will hear you, for He has been waiting for you to present your personal petitions.

As you looked forward to your prayer retreat, you probably made a list of persons and needs. Now is the time to consult the list. As additional items occur to you, jot them down. Present your petitions, one by one. The time to ask Him for all you need is when you are in God's presence (1 John 5:14–15; Phil. 4:19).

Just as Hezekiah, upon receiving a threatening letter from Sennacherib, went to the temple and spread out the letter before the Lord (2 Kings 19:14–20), so you can open your heart and share freely with Him. Then, just as the Lord replied to Hezekiah, so He will say to you, "I have heard your prayer."

6. *Plan for some variety or change during your prayer retreat.* Prayer can be exhausting as you continue hour after hour. You may need to change your posture. Get up and walk around a bit, sing a song quietly, alternate audible prayer with silent prayer, or, in some other way, introduce a change of pace. If you are not fasting, a small snack may refresh you. God is your Father; He understands your physical need. Be free and relaxed in His presence.

7. *Lay hold of God's promise.* Earlier, when you laid the foundation of your prayer time by first saturating your

soul with God's Word and feasting on the Scriptures, God may have impressed on you some special promise. Use it now. Or, as you sense the nearness of God's presence, and as you intercede for others and pray for your own needs, God may bring to your memory other special promises. If not, perhaps He will guide you now to turn again to His Word and will bless to your heart a promise which you have not noticed for a long time, or it may be one you have used in prayer repeatedly. There are no promises more filled with blessing than the ones you have used again and again. Now He may apply it in a new, fresh way to your need.

When Jacob returned to Canaan and spent all night in prayer, he reminded God of His promise (Gen. 32:9). When Moses interceded with God, he reminded God of His Word (Exod. 32:13). The psalmist prayed, "Remember your word to your servant, for you have given me hope" (Ps. 119:49). Peter urged his hearers at Pentecost to claim what God had promised (Acts 2:39). Like Abraham, we must not waver through unbelief regarding His promise but, strengthened in faith by the promise, give praise and glory to God (Rom. 4:20). Why? Because we are "fully persuaded" that God has power to do what He promises (v. 21).

With your Bible in your hand and your finger on His promise, come boldly, confidently, and joyfully to His throne of grace. "In him and through faith in him we may approach God with freedom and confidence" (Eph. 3:12). "Therefore, brothers, since we have confidence to enter the Most Holy Place by the blood of Jesus, by a new and living way opened for us through the curtain, that is, his body, and since we have a great priest over the house of God, let us draw near to God with a sincere heart in full assurance of faith" (Heb. 10:19–22).

8. *Be sure to close your prayer retreat with another time of praise, worship, and thanksgiving.* When you have come to the conclusion of your prayer time, God will probably give you a blessed peace of heart, a renewed, confident assurance, and a deep joy of soul. Now is the time for the doxology. Now is the time once more to love the Lord, adore Him, and praise Him.

Even if you cannot yet see God's full answer or be sure just how He will work, return to your duties with a singing heart, strengthened in faith. In the words of a classic hymn, "In the Secret of His Presence," written by Miss Ellen Lakshmi Goreh of Allahabad, India:

And whenever you leave the silence
Of that happy meeting place,
You will surely bear the image
Of the Master in your face.

32

How to Pray
for a Person

God will place on your heart many people for whom you will want to pray daily. For these, you can intercede briefly as you hold them before the Lord in loving petition that God will meet their needs. Blessed is the person who blesses many others through regular and systematic prayer.

When God desires to transform the spiritual condition of a person from sin to salvation, or from self-centered living to obedient living, however, He may call on you to carry a special prayer burden which may require more intensive prayer. This person may be someone close to you—a relative or friend—or some national or world leader or government figure. The subject of this prayer assignment may be influential in the field of education, business, sports, the judiciary, the news media, or the military. Those who serve as role models need to be undergirded by prayer as well as those who move in less public circles.

How should you pray for such individuals? The following are suggestions which may be used for prolonged prayer or adapted to periods of shorter intercession:

1. Again, begin by focusing on God Himself. (a) Thank God for His good will toward all people; His love for the world. (b) Thank God for His intensely personal love for this person. (c) Thank God for His plan for the life of this person. (d) Thank God that Jesus' death on the cross was intended for this person, too. (e) Thank God for the Holy

Spirit's presence and activities for this one: His eyes constantly beholding him, his work, and his needs (Gen. 16:13; 2 Chron. 16:9; Zech. 4:10; Rev. 5:6); His providence coordinating all that touches the person's life; His instant availability. (f) Visualize Jesus standing by the person with His arms outstretched in love and saying, "Here am I! Here am I!" (Isa. 65:1–2). (g) Visualize Jesus' tears of loving longing for the person (Matt. 23:37). (h) Thank God for the availability of God's messenger angels to help bring answers to your prayer (Heb. 1:14).

2. *Thank God for this person.* Begin praying for the person by thanking God for him. Never yield to the temptation of criticizing the object of your concern. Don't point out how difficult, how stubborn, how wayward the person is. It is Satan's role to accuse. He not only accuses our brothers in Christ (Job 1:6–11; 2:1–5; Zech. 3:1; Rev. 12:10), he injects his accusations to intensify interpersonal friction.

Satan will do anything to discourage our prayers for others. If he cannot stop us, he will try to short-circuit our prayer by making us petulant, critical, and negative. Such a spirit hinders our love, destroys our faith, and cancels our spirit of praise. Don't expect answers to prayers prayed in a spirit of negative criticism. (a) Thank God for this person's potential, abilities, and skills. (b) Thank God for the good qualities that you can recall. (c) Thank God that you know the Holy Spirit is already at work even though His work may not yet be visible to the eye. (d) Thank God for the answer you believe will come in God's own timing.

3. *Intercede for the person.* (a) Ask God to guide you in praying for this person and to increase your concern. (b) Ask God to block and frustrate Satan's plans against the person. (c) Ask God to bless the person and to manifest His goodness in such ways that there can be no doubt that it is God's goodness and not coincidence or chance. (d) Ask God to strengthen every good personality trait, every good desire, and every right decision of the person. (e) Ask God to make the person open and receptive to God's voice and sensitive to his own

personal sin and need. (f) Ask God to release the person from any prejudice, to break any chain of sin, evil habit, or satanic power with which Satan may have bound him. (g) Ask God to surround the person with His holy presence, to remind him of God's many past mercies, to prove His merciful intervention in new and powerful ways, and to melt away all hesitation with His great love. (h) Ask God to use any means He deems best to dissolve any resistance to His Spirit. Ask Him to use any of God's children, any circumstance in life, or any ministry of His holy angels.

4. *Claim God's promise for salvation or need.* (a) Plant your faith firmly on the promises of God which apply to the person for whom you are praying. (b) Keep alert to any other promise which may apply as new situations develop. (c) Ask God to make some special promise come alive to you for this person. While you are reading the Scriptures, the Holy Spirit may grip your heart by impressing upon you a particular verse or passage. Hold on in prayer and plead that Scripture again and again.

5. *Persevere in prayer.* (a) Remind God that you love the person and know that His divine love will never cease reaching out. (b) Recognize that some of God's greatest answers to prayer do not come instantly. The seeming silence of God does not imply that God is inactive. Often it takes time to disentangle a person's thinking from error, prejudice, or willfulness. He may not be able to recognize God's voice or fully understand what God is trying to say. Be willing to be as patient as the Holy Spirit. (c) Remember that no prayer you pray is ever lost. Perhaps every time you pray, the Holy Spirit speaks in some new way to the person. (d) Recognize that God's purposes are usually accomplished within a person's mind and heart. God may choose to use overt means of intervention—such as blocking a trip, causing cancellation of plans, permitting illness. But whether or not you can discern God's activity in the life of the person for whom you are praying, you can be sure God is at work. (e) Remember that outward appearances are often the exact opposite of what is happening within. God may be

knocking the most loudly at the very time the person puts on a brazen exterior and seems totally unresponsive. God reminded Saul that it was painful to kick against the promptings of the Holy Spirit. Thus Saul, the persecutor, seemed most violently opposed to Christ at the very time the Holy Spirit was goading his conscience with the memory of the radiant face and forgiving prayer of Stephen (Acts 26:14). (f) Believe God in the face of discouraging symptoms and hostile reactions. It is not God's will that anyone should perish, but that all should come to repentance (2 Peter 3:9). (g) God may lead you to enlist the prayer of others. This must always be done with the assurance of God's guidance and with subtlety and discretion. You want to unite in prayer to bring power and blessing, not to offend. (h) God may lead you to tell the person that you are remembering him or her in loving prayer. Even if that person does not show appreciation at the time, God may bring to his memory your patient and persistent intercession. This can be a particularly powerful witness when you pray for a person whom you have no hope of contacting personally. (i) When God has confirmed to your heart a specific prayer assignment, expect God's answer at any time. When a person has been covered and saturated with much prayer for a protracted period of time, it may be that the final yielding to the Lord will come quite suddenly. God does not call you to pray in vain. Pray, believe, and praise till the answer comes.

Sometimes those for whom we pray may appear to be spiritually unresponsive for years after we have made them an object of our prayers. At such times it is natural to wonder why our praying seems so ineffective. Do not be discouraged. God may be accomplishing far more than you realize.

33

How to Prepare
Prayer Lists

All Christians who take their call to intercession seriously pray with some agenda in mind. But intercession can be greatly enhanced through the use of written prayer lists. God will lead you in the names to be included.

Some intercessors have several such lists—one basic list which is used daily, and others which may be rotated on different days of the week. Some have a longer list for Sunday or other days when they can spend more time in prayer.

The following suggested categories will guide you in preparing your own personal prayer lists:

Government leaders. Christians are commanded to intercede for the leaders of our government (1 Tim. 2:1–4). Such leaders include the president, governors, and mayors. You will probably want to mention also the two senators from your state, your representative to Congress, and perhaps each of the Supreme Court justices. Be sure to pray for other officials, especially those whom you know to be Christians serving in frontline positions, or others who play a strategic role in policy making.

Church leaders. Praying daily for all the leaders of your local church—pastor, Sunday school teachers, elders and deacons, and others—is your spiritual responsibility (1 Thess. 5:12–13).

Other Christian leaders. Pray for other influential Christian leaders. You may want to pray for one or more evangelists, Bible teachers, editors and writers, gospel singers, youth leaders, and children's workers.

Missions. Since world evangelization is the priority Jesus gave to His church until He comes again, and since so much of the world is largely unreached, God obviously expects every Christian to pray for missions (Matt. 24:14; 28:18–20; John 20:21; Acts 1:8). In your prayer for missions, include the following specific areas:

- *Missionaries.* As God leads, select one or more missionaries with whom to be in daily prayer partnership.
- *Nations.* Ask God to lay on your heart one or more nations as your special inheritance by prayer (Ps. 2:8).
- *Missionary Organizations.* Pray generally for all such organizations; focus on one or more as special needs arise.
- *National Christians.* Pray for one or more national pastors or lay workers in other countries.

Other Christian ministries. Radio and TV ministries, evangelistic teams, prison ministries, youth ministries, city missions, Christian publishing houses—all are targets for Satan's attack, hence, essential areas for intercession.

Your loved ones. Include both saved and unsaved family members for whom you feel personal responsibility.

Unsaved people. Ask God to assign some unsaved person as your personal prayer responsibility. Pray daily until that person comes to Christ. God will likely also provide opportunities for you to show Christian interest or love, or an opportunity to witness. You may also be led to pray for some to whom you will never be able to give a word of testimony.

Special needs. The Holy Spirit will suggest urgent needs for immediate intercessory prayer. This list will change from time to time. You may be impressed to pray as you read the newspaper, or listen to television newscasts reporting tragedy, famine, special international conferences, court cases, people injured in acci-

247

dents, people seriously ill, problems of domestic unity among people you know, special church meetings.

How to Use Prayer Lists

1. Record prayer lists in a small diary or notebook. A portable list can be kept in a man's shirt or vest pocket or a woman's handbag. A small ribbon or piece of paper may serve as a marker. Seize spare moments during the day for prayerful meditation, using the names and items on this list.

During my college days I prayed for several hundred missionaries and Christian leaders each day. To my surprise I discovered numerous times when I could use my lists—in the cafeteria line, at the post office, before class.

Brief prayers can be much used by the Holy Spirit. These instant expressions of your Christian love, concern, and desire have been called "telegraphic prayers," "lightning prayers," or "moment prayers." You could call them "God bless" prayers. They are always heard by God. All praying people use this method of letting Him know of immediate concerns. There are many people whom you simply want to mention, asking God to bless them, guide them, heal them, or surround them with His love. Occasionally God may impress you to pray for a longer period of time for someone on your "God bless" list, because of some special need you could not know. Rely on the guidance of the Spirit.

2. Keep prayer lists handy. Keep a short list by the kitchen sink where you can refer to it while washing dishes or preparing meals. Place another near your dinner table for use at mealtime. Post a short list on your bathroom mirror for reference while shaving or grooming. Use your basic list as a Bible marker for your time of daily devotions.

3. Use the incidents of the day as an unwritten prayer list. Passing a church, you can pray for the pastor or people who worship there. Passing a school, you can pray for the students and staff. Pray for the clerk as he rings up your purchases at the store, for the waiter who serves you in a restaurant. When you hang up the telephone, pray for a few moments for the one to whom you were speaking. When you seal a letter, pray for the person who will receive it. When your pastor preaches, ask God to anoint and use him. When a singer sings in a church service, ask God to bless the singer and song. When you note a newspaper headline, pray a "God bless" prayer for the person needing prayer.

Praying through your day in this way is a beautiful way to pray without ceasing (1 Thess. 5:17).

34

How to
Agree in Prayer

Jesus promised special blessing to those who meet in His name and agree in prayer (Matt. 18:19–20). It is fully possible to agree with others in prayer even though you are miles apart and your only communication is by correspondence or telephone. You are more likely, however, to agree with one or more people as you meet together to pray.

Prayer partners, as they habitually pray together, develop the ability to agree in prayer more easily than people not so closely related in prayer. Dr. R. Stanley Tam, president of the United States Plastics Corporation of Lima, Ohio, and vice-chairman of the Board of Trustees of OMS International, has for twenty-three years maintained a regular time of prayer with Art, another Lima businessman. The two men meet at the city park or sit together in a parked car for their weekly prayer times. They have seen remarkable answers to prayer as they have agreed together concerning prayer topics.

Blessings from Agreement in Prayer

Agreement in prayer increases awareness of God's presence. Theologically we know that God is always with us, for He is omnipresent. We know Christ is always with us when we meet together in His name (Matt. 18:20). But as you agree in prayer with another, there is often a special awareness of God's presence. "And if we know that he hears us—whatever we ask—we know that we have what we asked of him" (1 John 5:15).

Agreement in prayer helps clarify the will of God.
God may give special inner assurance of His will to one
of the group agreeing in prayer and, through that person,
to the others. As the group again unites in intercession,
someone else may sense God's will in another aspect of
the prayer need. As the group prays on, the Holy Spirit
can unite all in a deep consensus of God's purpose and
desire. This unified assurance brings special encouragement and conviction of God's will—an assurance that
may transcend that which is possible when one person
prays alone.

*Agreement in prayer helps deepen the concern of each
member of the prayer group.* In close prayer communion, when hearts are blended in intercessory agreement,
God uses the depth of desire in one heart to deepen the
hunger in the others. They, in turn, may be moved to
express their deepening desire in words or tears by
which God then blesses the whole. True heart hunger
gives tremendous power to intercession before God.

Agreement in prayer helps purify our praying. It is
possible when praying to be unconsciously motivated by
self-interest or other less desirable reasons. As several
agree in their praying, God refines, guides, and purifies
the motives of all.

*Agreement in prayer increases faith and confidence
before God.* God wants us to pray with deep confidence
and holy boldness. "Let us then approach the throne of
grace with confidence, so that we may receive mercy and
find grace to help us in our time of need" (Heb. 4:16). As
one prevails with holy insistence in prayer, others join in
with increasing urgency of intercession. This bold
confidence is highly valued by God (Eph. 3:12; Heb.
10:19).

*Agreement in prayer strengthens persistence in
prayer.* Those situations in which prayer agreement is
necessary tend to be situations in which persistence in
prayer is essential before the full answer comes. Jesus
was deeply concerned that His followers learn to persist
in prayer (Luke 18:1). When several agree in prayer, each
is an encouragement to the other.

Agreement in prayer brings spiritual blessing to all concerned. Spiritual agreement in intercession deepens the mutual understanding, empathy, and fellowship of all in the group. It is effective, also, in strengthening unity in the Spirit (Eph. 4:3, 13). The followers of Christ persisted in prayer for ten days before the Holy Spirit was poured out at Pentecost. Could this delay have been necessary for the disciples to dissolve their petty jealousies and self-centered ambitions before God could send His Spirit? Disunity is a major hindrance to much prayer, and the history of revival in the church proves that deep, pervading unity in the Spirit can lead to spiritual refreshing and blessing.

How to Agree in Prayer

As you begin to agree in prayer with one or more believers, you may initially find yourselves agreeing on one specific aspect of the need. As you seek God's face, however, you will find your hearts moving toward a more complete harmony. The following steps are suggested:

1. Agree that God has given you a need for which to pray.
2. Agree to present this need to God in mutual concern and faith.
3. Agree that your supreme motivation in prayer is the glory of God.
4. Agree that, though the request is worded differently by various members of the group, the "Amen" will be unanimous.
5. Agree to claim one or more of God's promises relating to this need.
6. Agree together in faith that God will meet the need. Agree that God has already been working and is even now working through the Holy Spirit to answer your prayer.
7. Agree to persist until the answer comes.
8. Agree to pray together at a set time each day, even though you may not always meet together physically.
9. Agree to resist Satan in his opposition to God's

answer to your prayer. Stand firm in faith against him, agreeing that, as you resist him, he must flee (James 4:7).

10. Agree, as God leads, to bind Satan regarding this situation (Matt. 12:29; 18:18–20).

11. Agree to give God all the glory when the answer comes.

My Prayer of Commitment to Intercession

Lord Jesus, I thank You that You have revealed in Your Word that God is my Father, that I am a child of God by faith in You, and that there is always a welcome for me at the Father's throne.

I thank You for the life of prayer You lived when You were on earth, for teaching us to pray, and for Your victorious prayer agony in Gethsemane.

I thank You for going to Calvary for me, for dying in my place, and for defeating Satan forever through Your death on the cross.

I thank You that You rose from the dead, ascended to heaven, and now sit enthroned at the right hand of the Father, ever living to intercede for me and all Your church, and for the world for which You died.

Lord Jesus, I want to worship You, adore You, and love You more each day. I want, like Mary, to choose the better part and sit at Your feet. Teach me to worship You more, teach me to feast on Your Word. Teach me how to live a life of uninterrupted communion with You.

Thank You for teaching me through Your Word that I am to be an intercessor-priest of God. Thank You for giving me permanent access to You at any time through prayer, and for calling me now to be a prayer warrior for You in Your army of intercessors.

Lord, who am I that You should desire me to join You and the blessed Holy Spirit in interceding for the needs of Your church and for the world still unreached, yet so constantly loved by You? I am unworthy of Your love. I know not how to pray as I ought. But I want to touch the world through prayer. Let the power of Your Spirit anoint me to touch and bless Your world and its people. Lord, teach me to pray.

Teach me, Lord, to see the world through Your eyes, to love the world with Your love, to weep with You over the sorrows and sins of the world. I am unworthy to carry prayer burdens, but I am willing to share them with You. I know not how to prevail in prayer. Teach me, Lord, to prevail.

Teach me how to discipline my life so that I take time to intercede. Teach me to have a listening ear so I can discern Your prayer assignments for me. Let my heart share something of Your longings and tears as I intercede. Empower me by Your Holy Spirit to believe and stand on Your promises. Empower me to be strong in prayer warfare, to withstand the powers of darkness and to drive them back by the authority of Your name.

Lord Jesus, I do not ask for worldly success or acclaim; I ask for a praying heart. I do not ask for a leadership role; I ask for the power to prevail in intercession. I do not ask anything but Your will, Your glory, and Your triumph. Make me a person after Your own heart. Make me Your partner in intercession.

May my worship, my love in prayer, my hidden intercession bring joy to Your heart, victories in Your cause according to Your will, and glory to Your name. I love You more than my tongue can ever express. I am Yours eternally, my Savior and my Lord.

By Your grace I live; in Your love I rejoice; and in Your name I pray, Jesus, my wonderful Lord, Amen.

If God has made this book a blessing to you and you wish to share a testimony, or if you wish the author to remember you in a moment of prayer, feel free to write:

Dr. Wesley L. Duewel
P.O. Box A
Greenwood, IN 46142-6599